Native American Astronomy

native
american
astronomy

Edited by Anthony F. Aveni

University of Texas Press / Austin and London

Library of Congress Cataloging in Publication Data
Main entry under title:

Native American astronomy.
Edited versions of papers presented at a symposium held at Colgate University,
23–26 September 1975.
      Bibliography: p.
      Includes index.
      1. Indians—Astronomy—Congresses. 2. Indians—Antiquities—
Congresses. 3. America—Antiquities—Congresses. 4. Mayas—Astronomy—
Congresses.
I. Aveni, Anthony F.
E59.A8N37 520′.972 78–53569
ISBN 0-292-75511-2

Second Printing, 1979

This text is dedicated to the memory of Sir Eric Thompson (1898–1975), whose studies of the Maya calendar helped make the world aware of a supreme intellect residing within the Americas

Contents

Foreword

This volume and its predecessor (*Archaeoastronomy in Pre-Columbian America*) are ample witness that there are some new winds blowing in New World archaeology. It takes little imagination to see that there is much in this subject which has not been, and cannot be, explained from a purely materialistic point of view: for instance, the astonishing markings in the desert pampa of southern Peru, or the strange Building J at Monte Alban in Mexico, or the crescent moons and stars in the rock art of the American Southwest. It is clear that there were powerful currents of thought at work among the early inhabitants of the New World which went far beyond economic, political, and social needs.

Unfortunately, this inability, or refusal, by archaeologists both "new" and "old" to deal with American Indian mental systems—as found in religion, cosmologies, and mythology—has left the field open to the wildest speculation. The public on both sides of the Atlantic has been led to believe in the existence of voyagers from outer space, in sunken continents, in white "culture gods," and in heaven knows what else, a state of affairs heavily exploited by book publishers and television producers.

It is thus a welcome development that professional astronomers, archaeologists, and architects represented by Anthony Aveni and his colleagues have joined in tackling the problem of ancient astronomy and cosmology. They have revived a forgotten tradition of scholarship, for in the last century some outstanding Americanists like Daniel G. Brinton and Zelia Nuttall were interested in like matters.

The importance of this research is twofold. Not only are we beginning to discover why certain buildings, sites, and even whole cities are placed as they are, but it seems that we also are on the verge of seeing the first steps taken by American Indians toward true science. Otto Neugebauer, in his magnificent book *The Exact Sciences in Antiquity*, was able to show that the observations of the starry heavens by Near Eastern priests, night after night through many centuries, eventually led them to scientific thought. Might not the same process have taken place in our hemisphere, if only these brilliant cultures had not been so brutally extinguished by European arms and technology?

Michael D. Coe

Introduction

"Maya astronomy is too important to be left to the astronomers." Sir Eric Thompson frequently exhibited the enviable ability to sum up a situation in few words. His statement, in its broadest application, might well serve as the theme of this collection of essays. When Thompson wrote it he was criticizing those astronomers who would attempt to prove a theory by juggling the numbers in the inscriptions without referring to the context in which they were written.

In defense of my own profession, I must reveal some of the outrageous astronomical statements uttered by trained anthropologists. For example, one scholar suggested that the stars of the Little Dipper might have been hundreds of times brighter a few centuries ago, while another dismissed the sidereal revolution periods of the planets as determinable "quite simply by observation." An understanding of basic elementary astronomy could have gone a long way in the hands of those individuals, both of whom were well versed in native folkways.

A search of the old literature reveals that most Americanists seem to have been aware that astronomy was important in pre-Columbian society. The strong bond between astronomical interests and other aspects of native American culture, particularly religion, has been duly noted. But much of the early literature relating to astronomical knowledge and methods is woven with speculation. As a result of our inability to deal with the facts of the issue we have come to know relatively little about actual astronomical practice among these people.

The decade of the 1970's has witnessed the development of an interdisciplinary approach to ancient astronomical studies. In some quarters it is called "archaeoastronomy," in others "astroarchaeology." It appears in both hyphenated and unhyphenated form. What matters is that, to practice it, the serious scholar must become acquainted with certain segments of established fields of inquiry which border upon one another.

More than most disciplines, the lateral field of archaeoastronomy is a social enterprise. It demands that scholars share knowledge and expertise with colleagues in traditionally remote fields. For the initiate this can seem strained, difficult, and uncomfortable. The interaction is complicated by the existence of jargon and terminology often not mutually shared. Worse still is the natural conviction we all possess, at least to some degree, that our approach is the correct one and that of another is not worth bothering with. C. P. Snow warned of a gulf of mutual incomprehension between the disciplines two decades ago. It stems from an intellectual stubbornness—the unwillingness to understand a different point of view.

The participants at the first organized gathering of archaeoastronomers transcended most of these difficulties. The joint meeting of the American Association for the Advancement of Science and the Consejo Nacional Ciencia y Tecnologia held at Mexico City in June 1973 was an unusual convocation of individuals representing a wide range of disciplines: astronomers, anthropologists, archaeologists, and historians presented papers on the correlation of the Mesoamerican and Christian calendars, astronomical motifs in Mexican and southwestern U.S. art and sculpture, and the astronomical orientation of ancient Mesoamerican buildings and ceremonial centers. The conference proceedings were published under the title *Archaeoastronomy in Pre-Columbian America*, hereinafter referred to as the "first volume," a text which has been well received by the broad academic community toward which it was directed.

Many of the conferees who had been examining their subject matter from one angle benefited by seeing their problems viewed with fresh eyes. To no surprise, two years after the meeting several participants expressed an interest in reconvening for a few days in order to read papers outlining the progress of their studies. It was decided that at the second conference the broader theme of native American astronomy would set the principal guideline for acceptable papers. Thus for the first time some of the recent astronomical studies taking place in North and South America could be contrasted with the Mesoamerican work on calendar and building orientations, which had made considerable progress since the 1973 meeting.

With the generous support of the Tinker Foundation a four-day symposium entitled "Native American Astronomy" was held at Colgate University, 23–26 September 1975. Eight representative scholars working in the fields of North, Meso-, and South American archaeoastronomy were invited to present review papers centering on their particular area of interest. The meeting was then opened for additional short reports, and a total of twenty-six papers was read over the four-day span. This text contains edited versions of the eight review papers and a selection of short reports.

In order to lend a dimension of coherence to the volume, we group the papers by geographic region rather than order of presentation at the meeting. We begin with Mesoamerica in general (Aveni, Gibbs, and Hartung [astronomical signs]), move to the Maya area (Schele, Kelley, Remington, Closs, Carlson, and Hartung [architecture]) and the southwestern United States and Great Plains (Wedel, Eddy, Brandt and Williamson, Mayer, and Williamson), and close with the single South American contribution, by Zuidema.

With the publication of this volume we hope to begin to synthesize some of the common elements regarding the development of science among the civilizations of the pre-Columbian New World. We also expect to sort out and reflect upon the many dissimilarities in astronomical practice between north and south.

We know that early in the development of Mesoamerican civilization astronomer-priests named the fixed stars and followed the courses of the planets moving among them. They recognized the emerging morning star Venus as the same object which disappeared as evening star several nights before. Most of their calendric cycles were derived from astronomical observations. But how did the derivation proceed? Which specific observations were made? And what was the modus operandi? When, if at all, did the astronomer-priest elevate his art to the state that his astronomical cycles achieved predictability? And, finally, was he ever capable of formulating world models which could be altered by comparing observation with prediction—true scientific astronomy? These are some of the questions addressed in this volume.

There is little doubt that astronomy was connected with site planning in Mesoamerica. While the pictures in the codices hint at it, Father Motolinia tells us directly that Moctezuma, king of the Aztecs, tore down and reconstructed at least one building so that its alignment would correspond with sunrise at the equinoxes.

The reader of this text who is familiar with the first volume will observe that the study of building orientations in Mexico has made considerable progress on two fronts. First, the interdisciplinary approach has opened our eyes to the multiplicity of factors which shaped the plan of the Mesoamerican ceremonial center. They range from functional astronomy to religious hierophany. Today the study of Mesoamerican building alignments is no longer an astronomical match game played with the modern electronic computer. Often many design schemes are found blended together in one site giving a clue to the complexity of the Mesoamerican mind which conceived it. Second, masses of accurate data, once an unknown commodity, have been collected at the sites. In my essay, I discuss new information I have accumulated regarding the orientation of buildings and the axes of ceremonial centers in Mexico, Guatemala, and Honduras. My efforts have been duplicated in North America by Eddy, who reports on his study of the medicine wheels. Here a number of significant alignments are turned up but, curiously, the east-of-north trend exhibited by so many of the Mesoamerican structures does not appear. To this we add Wedel's work on solstice registers at Great Plains sites and Williamson's studies among the Anasazi and Pueblo sites. Zuidema discusses his inquiry into the relation between the astronomical calendar and the *ceque* system, which incorporated astronomical sight lines at Cuzco, the Inca capital. Though the South American studies currently lack the data base which can be employed to test astronomical orientation theories, Zuidema's examination of the historical record, calendric intervals, and complex interrelations among the Inca social, political, and religious systems suggests that much information about their astronomical system may be retrievable with further study. This is a landmark paper, the first thorough inquiry into Inca astronomy in modern times. All these efforts have done much to clarify some of the myths regarding astronomical observatories which have been propagated through the literature. But as Carlson's paper demonstrates, some of the old legends persist and many tasks still lie ahead of us on this front.

   Given their preoccupation with color-coded cardinal directions, it should come
as no surprise that a common characteristic shared by the New World civilizations
was a horizon-based system of astronomy. Such a system is shown in these articles to be capable of delineating a period in the calendar with remarkable accuracy. This celestial arrangement provides a marked contrast to the pole-oriented
Chinese astronomy or the ecliptic (zodiac)-based Babylonian system. The best
evidence for the existence of a Mesoamerican zodiac still comes from the animal
signs suspended from sky bands in the codices, though some of the recent suggestions (see, e.g., Kelley) that planetary sidereal periods may be recorded in the
inscriptions would tend to support the use of a zodiacal system. This issue aside,
it has become increasingly difficult to find similarities between the basic astronomical systems of the New World and the Old World.
   For a long time we have pondered the question of how the accuracy in the
Venus tables in the Dresden Codex was attainable. The answer may lie in the
architecture. In the Caracol of Chichen Itza we find a building incorporating precisely those horizon-based Venus alignments which could have served to reckon
its 584-day period and 8-year cycle exactly as depicted in the Dresden. The association of the round shape of the building with the Venus god Quetzalcoatl-Kukul-
can and a building period and province common with the Dresden support this
view. Horizon-based observations are strongly supported by evidence gleaned
from the codices, as Hartung reports in "Astronomical Signs in the Codices Bodley
and Selden." He discusses the occurrence and possible meaning of the eye-and-
crossed-stick symbolism, revising and extending Zelia Nuttall's long-forgotten
study in the Franz Boas anniversary volume.
   Orientation studies suggest that there were many different ways of executing
long-distance astronomical baselines—between cairns on the spokes of a medicine wheel, between cross petroglyphs at Teotihuacan, between vertical columns
atop mountains on opposite sides of the Valley of Cuzco, or among stelae around
the Valley of Copan. Baselines between cities have been reported. They may reflect a tendency toward geographic-cosmological planning on a large scale, a concept which the inscriptions support.
   The principal objects which figured in all the early astronomies were the sun
(sunrise and sunset at the equinoxes, solstices, and zenith passage dates were
marked for use in determining dates and periods of civic, religious, or agricultural
significance within the tropical year), the moon (usually a lunar count was kept by
recording phases rather than horizon positions as at the megalithic sites), and the
brighter planets and stars. It is interesting to find some of the same stars fitting
Mesoamerican and North American horizon alignments, for example, Sirius and
Aldebaran. This could have resulted from the special relation each star bore to a
solar, lunar, or planetary position; both these stars functioned as markers for determining lunar month intervals at the latitude of the Big Horn Medicine Wheel.
In Mesoamerica, Aldebaran transited the zenith, while the first and last appearance of Sirius could be used as an approximate divider of the tropical year into
seasons. Thus, the bond between calendar and positional astronomy has been
strengthened by some of our recent inquiries.
   Following Coe's fervent plea at the end of his paper on ethnoastronomy in the

first volume, current ethnographic studies relating to the astronomy in the written and archaeological records now appear to have begun. Though she did not interview the most remote Maya people, Remington illustrates in her paper, "Current Astronomical Practices among the Maya," how westernized the Cakchiquel have become—they call the Great Bear a "car with a tail"! Yet the rudiments of the pre-Hispanic calendar and astronomy persist—observations of Venus as morning star, the 260-day count, and some interesting constellations hitherto unrecorded. Her discovery that these people utilized a coordinate system skewed from the cardinal directions may tie in with the asymmetric axiality of 90 percent of the Mesoamerican ceremonial centers. Clearly we need more of the kind of work she has initiated. Remington's paper, and to some extent Zuidema's, are among the few which attempt to tap the ethnographic reservoir. Their work, like that of Haile among the Navaho and Lincoln among the Ixil, attempts to search out the dying pulse of an ancient civilization that once thrived all over the Americas. We still have much to learn from the study of linguistics, the old dictionaries, and the postconquest documents of Sahagun, Cobo, Molina, Motolinia, Duran, and others who touched upon astronomical matters as they interacted with the civilization while it was still alive. But our interpretation of the record must be tempered by an awareness of the peculiar relationship between interrogator and informant which existed in sixteenth-century America.

Hartung's studies of Mesoamerican building orientations stress the importance of geometrical as well as astronomical relations. In a paper appearing in the first volume he laid down guidelines for examining the relationships between structures—an architect's attempt to examine various elements of design. In this volume he looks at the architecture of Tikal within the context of these guidelines. Resolving a disputed issue, he presents results which make it clear that the Maya were quite capable of executing accurate right angles in their architecture. In many cases the asymmetries exhibited in Maya architecture seem to have been deliberate, as for example in the Caracol of Chichen Itza.

Two subtle considerations regarding building orientations emerge for the first time in this volume: the role of light and shadow and hierophanies (manifestations of the sacred in the worldly domain). Hartung, briefly, and Schele, in some detail, dwell upon these ideas. It is suggested that at Palenque the architectural hierophanies associating the winter solstice sun with the death of Shield Pacal and the accession of Chan Bahlum dictated the placement of some of the principal buildings of that ceremonial center. The event of winter solstice sunset, intended to reproduce events portrayed symbolically in the Palenque inscriptions, is seen as more experimental than astronomically functional.

The fusion of astronomical concepts with Palenque rulership also carries over into Maya calendrics. The trend toward a purely historical interpretation of the Maya hieroglyphs had given an archaic appearance to any attempt to interpret them astronomically, an overworked habit around the turn of the century. In this text we see a fresh approach fusing dynastic history with astronomy. Kelley shows that Maya rulers seem to have directly attached the important events of their lives to astronomical phenomena, particularly eclipses and planetary conjunctions. His evidence bridging the Palenque inscriptions with the Venus and lunar tables in the

Dresden Codex is compelling. Floyd Lounsbury's recent work on the use of combinations of prime numbers in producing Long Count dates further demonstrates the multifaceted nature of Maya numerics.

The theories on the actual structure and operation of the Venus tables expressed in the papers of Gibbs and Closs imply that, while the calendric system served a divinatory purpose, the foundation of this complex time machine was built out of real astronomical observations. We must never lose sight of the fact that, in order to perform his augury, the priest required certain devices by which he could reach the dates of future astronomical events. The long time span encountered in the astronomical almanacs and correction tables suggests that the priests performed laborious calculations. The knowledge of the existence of the lunar nodes, though taking a different form from the traditional western idea of intersecting orbits, affords the possibility that the Maya could have used their long-distance warning tables to predict eclipses which occurred outside their territory.

By contrast, Mayer's and Brandt and Williamson's papers indicate that the written record of the native people to the north of Mesoamerica took the form of a less abstract picture writing. Papers in the first and present volumes suggest that the astronomical content of the iconography of the southwestern United States may be considerable. Is the Crab Nebula supernova event of A.D. 1054 recorded among the petroglyphs? The controversy debated in the first volume continues, with evidence being presented on both sides. We might wonder how the neighboring astronomers to the south would have recorded this dazzling phenomenon. Surely such avid sky watchers could not have overlooked it. The answer may lie hidden among the dates in their inscriptions or in the alignments of their buildings.

Perhaps the readers of this collection of essays can best reckon the progress in recent archaeoastronomical studies by frequently reflecting back to the treatment of the subject matter in the first volume. It is expected that in the present volume they will generally perceive a refined quality and greater unity along the lines suggested in this introduction. Some of the research fronts discussed in E. C. Baity's checklist summarizing the first volume have clearly advanced. But many of the grandiose questions she phrased still go unanswered. We have yet to see the full impact of our studies upon certain basic chronological questions. When and where did the elements of the complex Mesoamerican calendar originate? To what state did the art of eclipse prediction elevate itself? Can building orientations be used as a date-reaching mechanism? What further possibilities are offered for comparison with Old World systems? This is the work of the future.

Sir Eric Thompson, taunted by innumerable speculators who theorized about the nature of Maya astronomy, developed an intolerance toward those who would play with numbers. Yet through it all he managed to leave with us some of the deepest insights into the nature of Maya astronomy. We would do well to follow the path he mapped out for us in pursuing our future studies of native American astronomy. His advice is simple: we must immerse ourselves in the knowledge of the culture and history of these people. Together with an understanding of astronomy, we must also pay close attention to the findings of archaeology, and, finally, we must try not to look at their astronomy through European eyes. Only then can we begin to "get inside the skin" of the priest-astronomer.

Acknowledgments

I gratefully acknowledge the Tinker Foundation and Colgate University for generously and enthusiastically supporting the Conference on Native American Astronomy from which this collection of essays emanates. I thank the anonymous referees who consulted with the University of Texas Press for valuable suggestions pertaining to individual papers; and Laura Hagopian, Beth Collea, Shelly Orenstein, Mary Gow, Susan Grimwood, and Helen Payne for an excellent job of proofreading and typing.

Anthony F. Aveni

Native American Astronomy

1

Concepts of Positional Astronomy Employed in Ancient Mesoamerican Architecture

Anthony F. Aveni

The Mesoamerican written record strongly suggests that the positions and periods of fundamental celestial bodies were noted with precision for the purpose of setting dates in the civil, agricultural, and ritualistic calendars (Coe 1975b; Nuttall 1906). In certain cases the plans of ceremonial centers as well as peculiarly oriented individual buildings may have been adjusted in order to face a particular direction of astronomical significance (Aveni 1975; Fuson 1969; Hartung 1971; Maudslay 1912).

In this report we summarize the results, much of which has been published piecemeal elsewhere (Aveni 1975; Aveni and Gibbs 1976; Aveni, Gibbs, and Hartung 1975; Aveni and Linsley 1972), of six years of field investigation relating to building orientation at sixty Mesoamerican sites. The aim of the program has been to determine with accuracy the extent to which building orientation might relate to concepts of positional astronomy in use in the New World.

One of the undeniable oddities about building orientation in Mesoamerica results from an examination of the distribution of the principal axes of Mesoamerican ceremonial centers relative to true north. Plotted on a polar diagram, the axial directions of the sixty sites we have measured center on the direction 17° east of north with only a few sites oriented west of north (fig. 1.1).

Teotihuacan, largest and most influential of all the early cities of ancient America, may be the origin of this peculiar trend. Built about the beginning of the Christian era in a valley which does not conform to the grid plan (even the course of a river was diverted to fit the preordained pattern), the city possesses a major axis (the Street of the Dead) skewed 15°28′ to the east of north. Careful studies by workers of the Teotihuacan Mapping Project (Dow 1967, p. 327; Millon 1973, p.29) reveal at least two other axes lying nearly perpendicular to this direction (16°30′ south of east and 16°55′ south of east). Project workers noted the existence of a long-distance baseline which may be related to the plan of the city. A design consisting of a pair of concentric rings and a cross was laid in the stucco floor of one

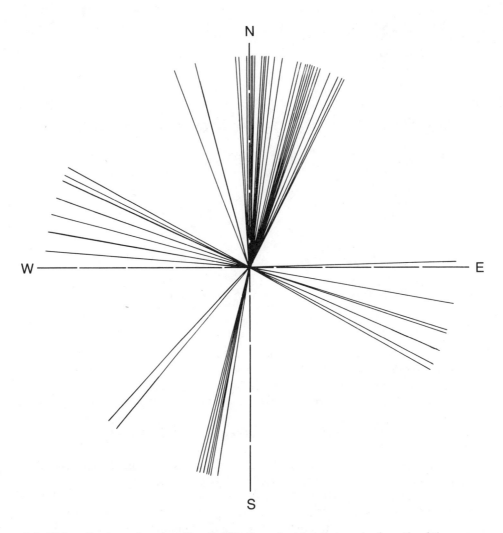

1.1. *Polar diagram showing the distribution about astronomical north of the axes of ceremonial centers in Mesoamerica.*

of the buildings near the Viking Group adjacent to the Pyramid of the Sun. About ⅔ meter in diameter, it consists of holes spaced a few centimeters apart. Three kilometers to the west on the slope of Cerro Colorado lies a cross of similar size and shape for which we measured a bearing of 15°21′ north of west (within 7′ of the direction obtained by the mapping project) as viewed from the cross near the Viking Group. Therefore, the east-west baseline is almost exactly perpendicular to the Street of the Dead. The Teotihuacanos could have employed the baseline to determine the principal axis of the site. According to Dow they may have constructed a very accurate right angle to lay out the Street of the Dead. Alternatively, the baseline may have served to transfer the basic axis of the ceremonial center, established earlier, to the outlying section of the city.

We tested the baseline for astronomical orientation by determining, for the latitude, building time, and horizon elevations at Teotihuacan, which astronomical bodies could have been viewed along either direction. While Sirius rose along the baseline viewed west to east, we found a more likely astronomical possibility in the Pleiades (both had been mentioned by Dow). Not only did this conspicuous star group set within 1° of the baseline between the crosses, but it also functioned in a most unusual way in the space-time location of Teotihuacan. The Pleiades underwent heliacal rising on the same day as the first of the two annual passages of the sun across the zenith, a day of great importance in demarcating the seasons. The appearance of the Pleiades may have served to announce the beginning of this important day, when the sun at high noon cast no shadows. In view of the coincidence of astronomical events and the central importance of the Pleiades in Mesoamerican star lore, they must remain the prime candidate for an astronomical motivation in the orientation of Teotihuacan.

A third Teotihuacan cross was located on Cerro Gordo 7 km to the north of the Pyramid of the Sun. It has a bearing of 16°30' east of north as viewed from the Viking cross. This baseline forms a nearly perfect right angle with one of the east-west Teotihuacan axes, as fig. 1.2 illustrates. No astronomical explanation is offered for this direction although the bright star Dubhe has been suggested as a stellar reference (Dow 1967, p. 330). Other petroglyphs have been noted at Teotihuacan (Gaitan et al. 1974) though their connection with building orientations has not been studied in detail.

Pecked-cross petroglyphs have been reported elsewhere in Mesoamerica. One design having the same number of holes on its axes as that in the center of Teotihuacan appears at Uaxactun (see Hartung 1971, fig. 8), and two similar cross petroglyphs recently have been reported by J. C. Kelley at Alta Vista, Zacatecas (private communication). The latter site is situated within 2 km of the Tropic of Cancer, where the sun would reach the zenith at noon on but one day of the year. Two pecked crosses appear at Tepeapulco, northeast of Teotihuacan. Further investigations on the cross symbolism and its relation to Mesoamerican architecture and building orientation now seem warranted.

Among the nonastronomical hypotheses for the orientation of Teotihuacan, that of Heyden (1975) must be given serious consideration. She suggests that the Pyramid of the Sun may have been deliberately placed above the location of a multichambered cave. Furthermore, a line from the center to the mouth of the cave nearly coincides with the direction of the Teotihuacan east-west axis. A number of historical references allude to cave deities in Central Mexico. As Heyden has pointed out, even in the consideration of alternate hypotheses we still should not overlook the astronomical possibilities, as the cave may possess a symbolic significance which relates to astronomy.

Ceremonial centers built in the vicinity of Teotihuacan as much as fifteen centuries later reflect a similar orientation which cannot be coincidental. These include the pyramid of Tenayuca 30 km to the southwest (16°27' east of north and 17°42' east of north according to measurements made on opposite sides), the Casa de Tepozteco 100 km to the south (18°00' east of north), both built immediately before the conquest, and Tula (17°10' east of north), the Toltec capital 70 km to the northwest. All fourteen of the Central Mexican sites we have measured to

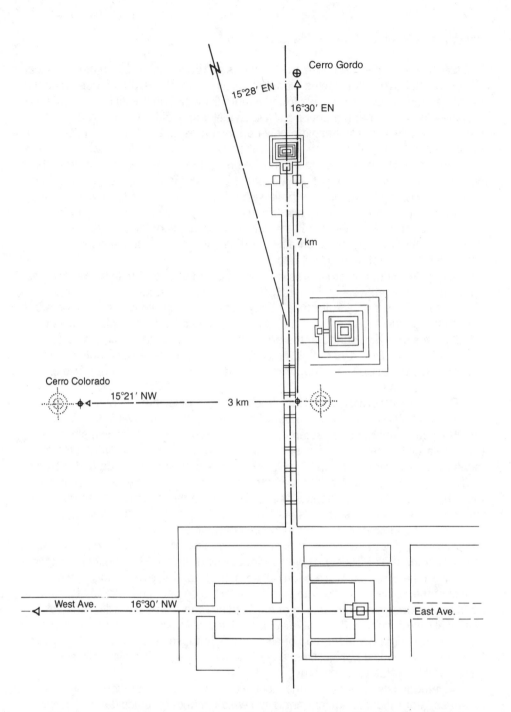

1.2. *Baselines between pecked-cross petroglyphs which may be associated with building orientations at Teotihuacan. The 15°21' N-of-W orientation is perpendicular to the principal axis of the ceremonial center and the 16°30' E-of-N orientation is perpendicular to the East-West Avenue.*

date are situated within 100 km of Teotihuacan and in every case the orientation is east of north.

The architects of Tenayuca, Tepozteco, and Tula simply may have copied the Teotihuacan tradition, though they could not have oriented their buildings on the Pleiades. Because of a slow shift due to precession of the equinoxes, by the time these centers were erected the Pleiades no longer set along the Teotihuacan east-west axis, nor did they announce the zenith passage of the sun by the tenth century, a time when the great civilizations of Mesoamerica were already on the decline. The priest-rulers of these new centers probably looked upon Teotihuacan as a holy city in ruins. In reverence of the past, they may have planned their centers of worship with the same directional axes. The old alignment could have been transferred astronomically, simply by sighting a substitute star which had replaced the Pleiades; by this time they would have set well to the north of the Teotihuacan east-west axis. Thus, the axes of Tula and the other members of the 17° group can be viewed as nonfunctional imitations of Teotihuacan. By the Postclassic phase of civilization in Mexico, the original purpose of the orientation was probably completely lost.

At Tenochtitlan, the deliberate orientation of the Templo Mayor toward the equinoctial sunrise is documented in the literature: "The festival of Tlacaxipeualiztli took place when the sun was in the middle of Huicholobos which was at the equinox, and because it was a little out of the straight Montezuma wished to pull it down and set it right" (see translation of Motolinia in Maudslay 1912, p. 175).

The position of the circular Temple of Quetzalcoatl, west of the Templo Mayor along its extended axis, makes it a suitable spot from which to view the sun rising in the notch between the twin oratories at the top of the building, but because the baseline, determined from our measurements on the surviving SW corner of the Templo Mayor, is skewed 7°30′ south of true east, an observer at the base of the circular temple would not see the equinoctial sun appear along the horizontal axis between the two buildings until it had risen to an altitude of 22° above the astronomical horizon (see Aveni and Gibbs 1976 for details). From simple geometry it can be shown that if the twin towers lay 55 meters above ground level they would have framed the elevated sun perfectly for an observer situated 142 meters away at the Temple of Quetzalcoatl. If the observer were positioned at a higher level on the circular tower, the height of the Templo Mayor would be 55 meters plus the height of the observer. Height estimates for the building based upon archaeological and historical data are found to be consistent with this archaeoastronomical evidence. The method offered as a possible means of reconciling history and archaeology in the case of the Templo Mayor emphasizes the importance of considering dimensions and careful measurement in any study of astronomically related building orientations.

Figure 1.3 summarizes the orientation data for the Central Mexican sites. It is a time-direction diagram showing the Central Mexican building orientations and the astronomical events which may be offered as the most likely determinants for the measured directions. The diagram reveals no temporal dependence upon the orientations, but it does show the 17° family and the nearly perfect fit of Teotihuacan with the Pleiades setting position. It also demonstrates the importance of

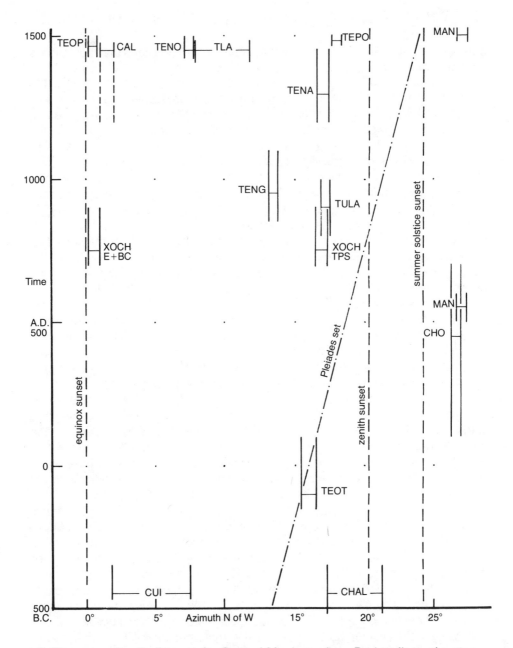

1.3. *Time* vs. *azimuth diagram for Central Mexican sites. Broken lines show occurrence of important astronomical horizon events. For each site the vertical limits illustrate uncertainties in building time, the extent of the horizontal line for each site indicating the most probable building time. Horizontal extremes include orientations of all buildings actually measured. Site abbreviations:*

considering elevation as a parameter in determining orientations. If fig. 1.3 alone were used to determine the orientation of Tenochtitlan, the equinoctial sunset would hardly be a candidate.

The measurements on the Templo Mayor suggest that, by varying the elevation of the observer relative to the sunrise event, the position of equinox sunrise can be shifted horizontally to match many of the measured east-of-north orientations (especially those in the range 0° to 10° E of N). For larger deviations from the cardinal points, other astronomical possibilities can be suggested. Alignments with a large skew could be related to a sunrise or sunset position on some significant agricultural, civil, or religious date of the year.

The recent work of Tichy (1974) suggests that many postconquest villages and towns in the region of Puebla align in the same direction as prehistoric sites in the vicinity. Three distinct families of axial directions appear in his data: a group near 7°, a group near 17°, and a group near 26° E of N. The existence of similarly oriented pre-Columbian buildings in the Mexican highlands led Tichy to postulate that the later structures preserve directions already important in antiquity. His studies add an interesting dimension to the work on pre-Columbian building orientations.

Multiple axes are found in the plans of a number of the ancient cities of Mesoamerica. Having determined the principal axes of buildings at Chichen Itza by transit measurements of original walls, we find that most of them are aligned in three distinctly separate directional categories: 10°–12° E of N (e.g., the Nunnery and the Red House, both of the Puuc style); 16°–18° E of N (e.g., the Great Ballcourt, the Tzompantli, the Platform of Venus, and the High Priest's Grave, all belonging to the later period of Toltec influence); and 21°–23° E of N (e.g., the Castillo, the Temple of the Warriors, and the Upper Platform of the Caracol, constructed during the earliest period of Toltec influence). The second direction closely matches the 17° family of Central Mexico.

At Copan we also find three sets of axes: (*i*) 6° W of N (the area from the Great Plaza to the Hieroglyphic Stairway); (*ii*) 1° E of N (Court of the Hieroglyphic Stairway); and (*iii*) 5°–9° E of N (Eastern and Western Courts). Since they have not been published elsewhere, the measurements are listed in table 1.1. Unfortunately, we know relatively little about the time spread in building periods among these areas.

The 7-km baseline (Morley 1925; Spinden 1913, table 1) between Stela 12 on

---

CAL = *Calixtlahuaca*
CHAL = *Chalcatzingo*
CHO = *Cholula*
CUI = *Cuicuilco*
MAN = *Manzanillo*
TENA = *Tenayuca*
TENG = *Tenango*
TENO = *Tenochtitlan*
TEOP = *Teopanzolco*

TEOT = *Teotihuacan*
TEPO = *Tepozteco*
TLA = *Tlatelolco*
TULA = *Tula*
XOCH (E+BC) = *Xochicalco Structure E and Ballcourt*
XOCH (TPS) = *Xochicalco Temple of Plumed Serpents*

Anthony F. Aveni

Table 1.1.
Building Orientations at Copan

Area i	Great Plaza, east side	5°51′ W of N
	Great Plaza, west side	6°47′ W of N
	Ballcourt Axis	6°31′ W of N
Area ii	Hieroglyphic Stairway, top	0°52′ E of N
	Hieroglyphic Stairway, base	1°15′ E of N
Area iii	Eastern Court, west side	8°42′ E of N
	Eastern Court, north side, perpendicular	8°02′ E of N
	Bldg. 22, base, perpendicular	7°40′ E of N
	Western Court, base, north side	{ 5°27′ E of N
		9°36′ E of N
Stela 12–10	Baseline	9°00′ N of W

1.4. *View along the Stela 12–Stela 10 baseline from east to west. The position of the western stela is circled. The ruins of Copan which lie among the trees at the center are cut by the baseline.*

the east side of the Copan Valley and Stela 10 on the west is directed 9°00′ N of W (cf. Morley's value of 8°51′) and passes over the archaeological site at the extreme southern end of the West Court where the buildings are oriented in approximately the same direction. The implied association between the building orientations in this part of Copan and the long-distance baseline parallels the case at Teotihuacan except that a pair of stelae replace cross petroglyphs as markers of an important astronomical direction. As viewed from Stela 12 the sun sets over Stela 10 on 12 April and 1 September. The view from east to west is shown in fig 1.4 (see Hartung's paper, this volume, fig. 9.5, for the view in the opposite direction). The first event has been connected with the initiation of the milpa agriculture which is still practiced at this time in the area (Morley 1925). The setting of the sun along the Stela 12–10 baseline announced the start of the rainy season, which must be immediately preceded by the clearing and burning of the bush. According to Morley (1925):

> It is the general custom in western Honduras at the present time to burn off the fields some time early in April to clear them for planting at the beginning of the rainy season, a month later. It is certain, that after burning had once been started, no sunset observation on Stela 10 would have been possible from Stela 12. Such was the hazy smoke-laden condition of the atmosphere from April 9 to 14 of the present year at Copan, that even with a high-powered telescope it was impossible to see Stela 10 from Stela 12 at sunset, and without any instrument of precision it would have been even more hopeless. Indeed, the only way it was possible to secure the azimuth of this line was by erecting behind Stela 10 an enormous pile of fat-pine faggots, 16 feet long and 10 feet high, and setting fire to it at night. This caused such an illuminated field behind Stela 10 that, even in spite of the heavy pall of smoke overhanging the valley, it was possible to see the monument outlined against this illumination and to secure the azimuth of the line.

The Long Count dates inscribed on the stelae (9.10.19.13.0 3 Ahau 8 Yaxkin for Stela 10; 9.10.15.0.0 6 Ahau 13 Mac and 9.11.0.0.0 12 Ahau 8 Ceh for Stela 12 according to Morley [1920], plates 15–17) appear to have no obvious astronomical significance, though the Spinden correlation gives a close match of the first date with the September sunset event.

As first pointed out by Merrill (1945), sunsets along the Stela 12–10 baseline occur midway in time (though not in direction along the horizon) between equinox and Copan zenith passage. The April event occurs 21 days after vernal equinox and 19 days before first zenith passage, while the September event takes place 19 days after second zenith passage and 21 days before autumnal equinox. The time diagram in fig. 1.5 illustrates the resulting division of the Copan tropical year. Note the inequality in the intervals between autumnal and vernal equinox (180 days) and between vernal and autumnal (185 days), a disparity which would be easily detectable by attentive Maya astronomers. These intervals become surprisingly

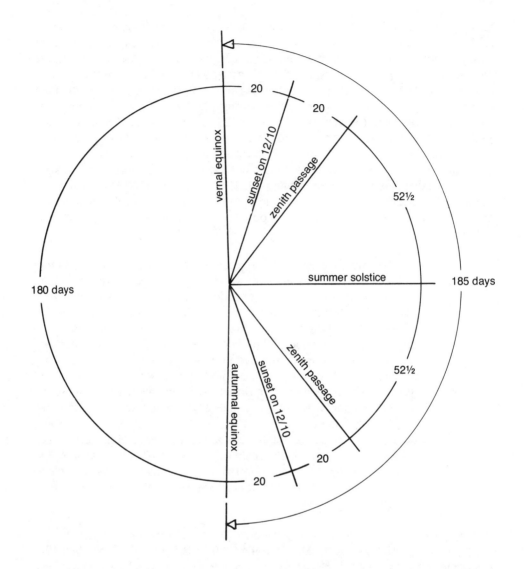

1.5. *Division of the year at Copan by alignments directed toward the solstice, equinox, solar zenith passage, and sunset along the Stela 12–Stela 10 baseline.*

consonant with the tropical year by utilizing the 12–10 baseline in Merrill's hypothetical calendar. Beginning the year with the second solar zenith passage we have the following intervals marked by significant sunset points along the western horizon:

Second zenith passage to sunset on 12–10	1 uinal
Sunset on 12–10 to autumnal equinox	1 uinal
Autumnal equinox to vernal equinox	9 uinal
Vernal equinox to sunset on 12–10	1 uinal
Sunset on 12–10 to first zenith passage	1 uinal
First zenith passage to second zenith passage	5 uinal plus 5 kin

Building 22 (the Temple of Venus) may be of particular interest in connection with the Copan baseline. Its western side possesses a single narrow recessed window, found intact by Trik (1939). This aperture, the only one appearing at Copan, bears a distinct resemblance to Windows 2 and 3 of the Caracol. Narrow and recessed, it looks out on the western horizon. The axis of the window and its diagonals were measured with the transit in January 1975 and possible astronomical events were sought for each spatial direction.

The most significant result of this inquiry is the discovery that the midline of the window faces the sunset position on precisely the same dates determined for the Stela 12–10 baseline. The absolute difference in the azimuth of the 12–10 baseline and the axis of the window (amounting to about one solar diameter) is due to the difference in elevation of the western horizon from the observation points (½° in the former and 2 ¾° in the latter). A sketch of the western horizon as seen from the window of the Venus Temple is shown in fig. 1.6. A heavy growth of vegetation along the line of sight prevents a direct view today.

The foregoing evidence suggests a connection between Copan acropolis architecture and the Stela 12–10 baseline straddling the site. The window may have been intended to provide the priests of the temple with a simultaneous sighting of the sunset at the start of the agricultural year, while other ritual ceremonies were being conducted at the base of Stela 12 on the slope of the hill to the east. The triad design of shell, flame, and crossbands which adorns Temple 22 has been thought to represent the act of firemaking. Kubler (Robicsek 1972, p. 123) has suggested that the temple may have been used to store the ritual paraphernalia used for the yearly burning of the cornfields.

Next, we turn our attention to the analysis of individual structures of peculiar shape or orientation relative to other buildings at a given site. The peculiar nature of such buildings suggests that they may have been distorted deliberately to emphasize an astronomical event of importance occurring along the horizon. Two unusual buildings in this class are the 5-sided arrow-shaped Building J at Monte Alban (Aveni and Linsley 1972) and Building O at Caballito Blanco (Aveni 1975), 40 km southeast of and contemporary with Building J. These buildings not only possess similar shapes but also exhibit similar orientations relative to other buildings at the respective sites; yet, their absolute orientations differ. The unusual form and orientation of Building J at Monte Alban is apparent in fig. 1.7.

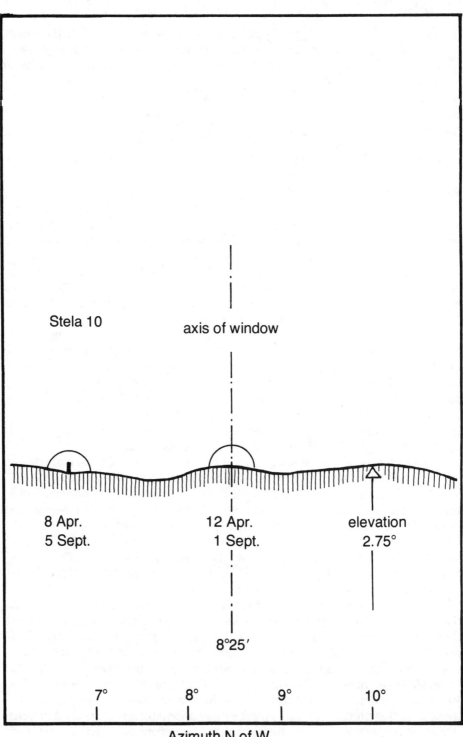

Stela 10　　　　　axis of window

8 Apr.　　　　12 Apr.　　　　elevation
5 Sept.　　　　1 Sept.　　　　2.75°

8°25′

7°　　　　8°　　　　9°　　　　10°

Azimuth N of W

1.7. *Aerial view of the plaza of Monte Alban, Oaxaca, from the west. Building J appears at right of center; Building P, with the entrance chamber to the zenith solar observatory visible in its stairway, is above center. (Courtesy Mexicana Aerofoto, S.A.)*

Significant astronomical phenomena match both the directions of the arrow points and the perpendiculars to the fronts of the buildings. In each case the astronomical events occurring along the horizon served a functional purpose; for example, at Monte Alban the perpendicular to the doorway is directed toward Capella, the heliacal rising of which announced the passage of the sun across the zenith. A more subtle architectural relation is indicated by the precise alignment of the doorway of Building P with the stairway of J. Building P contains a chamber housing a vertical shaft which gives access to a spot of blue sky overhead.

We will never know whether the shaft served as a sight tube for the purpose of observing the zenith passage of the sun, but if the deliberate disorientation of the front of Building J relative to neighboring buildings at Monte Alban was astronomically motivated, we must regard the phenomenon of the heliacal rising of Capella on the day of zenith passage as the most likely explanation. Capella, by

---

1.6. *View of the western horizon from the window of the Temple of Venus (Temple 22) at Copan.*

making its first annual appearance in the early morning sky, announced the day when the sun would cast no shadow at noon at Monte Alban. The priests could descend into the passage in Building P to confirm it. The importance of the zenith passage dates in Mesoamerica has received strong ethnographic documentation (e.g., Nuttall 1930). Evidently this cosmic event was so important to the Zapotecans that they endowed their earthly realm with an architectural symbolism of that event by skewing Building J to direct attention to the zenith tube in Building P.

The Caracol, a cylindrical tower at Chichen Itza, has also been studied in detail for astronomical alignments (Aveni, Gibbs, and Hartung 1975) with the result that twenty of twenty-nine significant architectural alignments taken along baselines and through the doorways and windows point to astronomical events. Those events most frequently occurring which also receive historic and ethnographic documentation are as follows:

Venus
> Perpendicular to base of Lower Platform
> Perpendicular to base of Stylobate
> Inside left to outside right diagonal of Window 1
> Inside left to outside right diagonal of Window 2

Sun
> Solstice
>> Perpendicular to base of Lower Platform
>> SW–NE diagonals of Lower and Upper platforms
> Equinox
>> Inside right to outside left diagonal of Window 1
> Zenith passage
>> Perpendicular to base of Upper Platform

The discovery of Venus alignments in the Caracol tower is especially significant when we consider the importance of that planet in Maya folklore and religion. The Venus tables in the Dresden Codex were composed in the vicinity of Chichen Itza during the Mexican period. These people must have followed the motions of the planet, for we know they were particularly concerned about its heliacal rising and setting. The first appearance of Venus in the east before dawn was considered an unlucky omen by Mexican worshippers of Quetzalcoatl, who no doubt carried this belief with them to the Yucatan. They had good reason for watching the movements of Venus on the western horizon, for its last appearance there was the best warning that a heliacal rising would soon occur. By the official calculations represented in the Dresden Codex, heliacal rise followed heliacal set by 8 days; however, its appearance could be hastened or delayed depending on the declination of Venus at the time it disappeared. In turn its declination was reflected in its setting position. When Venus disappears near the west point of the horizon, the duration of its disappearance in front of the sun can vary from 5 to 9 days depending on the time of year. Native astronomers may well have contrasted this variation with the relative constancy of the interval of disappearance noted for Venus at its setting extremes. Having observed Venus disappear in the west at one of the extremes, an experienced astronomer could predict the date of its reappearance in the east with confidence. The provisions for correction of the formal Venus tables suggest that observations of Venus were indeed made. We may suppose that the Caracol windows were placed to aid such observations and, specifically, to preserve the direction of the most predictable disappearances of Venus before helical rise.

Other circular towers exist in the area of Chichen Itza (e.g., at Puerto Rico, Campeche; Paalmul, Quintana Roo; San Gervasio, Quintana Roo; and Mayapan, Yucatan), some possessing shafts and small chambers. The historical and archaeological records suggest that the Paalmul and Mayapan towers may have been patterned after the Caracol. From careful measurement one should be able to determine whether these structures might also have served an astronomical purpose.

The Maya expression of an astronomical interest in the planet Venus appears to be quite different in the architecture at Uxmal (Aveni 1975). Here, most of the structures are oriented 9° east of north but a notable deviation occurs in the arrangement of the Palace of the Governor. This building is erected on an elevated artificial platform skewed 20° clockwise from the common axis. From its central doorway precisely along a perpendicular to the façade, we were able to view the ceremonial center of Nohpat, 6 km distant. A perpendicular line extended from the central doorway of the Governor's Palace also pointed exactly to the southerly extreme rising position of Venus during the Uxmal building period.

Flannery (1972) and Marcus (1973) have suggested that some Maya centers appear to display a simple geometric relationship to others nearby. Secondary centers are nearly equally spaced in a latticelike arrangement around a primary center. They suggest a structural plan on a grand scale, with four regional capitals symbolic of the Maya four-directional view of the universe. Each city is the geometric center of a cluster of secondary centers. Thus, cosmology may have played a major role in the large-scale territorial organization of the Maya. A. G. Miller (1974) gives a similar argument for the relative locations of Palenque and Tulum. We do not know whether the placement of other centers was determined astronomically, but the planned location of Nohpat relative to buildings at Uxmal now seems well established.

Any discussion of special assemblages of buildings in Mesoamerica should include the Group E structures at Uaxactun. An astronomical function for this grouping was first suggested by Frans Blom (1924). Standing on Building E-VII, a pyramidal structure, one looks out toward the east over an open plaza. In the foreground are the remains of three small buildings constructed on a single platform, the outside ones equidistant to the north and south of a west-east line from the central buildings; the central building is situated due east of the observer. Over the buildings the observer sees the sun rise above the northeastern mound on the summer solstice, over the southeastern mound on the winter solstice, and over the central mound at the equinoxes.

The arrangement may be considered as an astronomical solar observatory since the eastern buildings at Uaxactun line up extremely well with key solar positions as the plan of Uaxactun shows. Ricketson (1928a) noted that if the observer's viewpoint be shifted from the top of the pyramid to a position on its stairway 15 feet above the level of the plaza, the lowest point from which the horizon could be viewed over the eastern buildings, the bearing of the northwestern corner of the central building coincides with the sunrise on the same dates indicated by the Copan baseline. As Hartung (1971, fig. 5) has pointed out, this observing position would correspond to standing on the top of an earlier building, E-VII sub, lying beneath E-VII.

The Group E assemblage seems to have been copied at a dozen more sites within a 100-km radius of Uaxactun, though none of the other sites has been measured and carefully studied for solar orientation. Included in the group are Nakum, Yaxha, Uxul, Benque Viejo, Ixkun, and Rio Bec. Apparently the form of the Group E assemblage was of great importance in the Peten.

A preliminary examination of the Group E–type structures at the outlying sites by Ruppert (1940) led to the conclusion that most of the arrangements were nonfunctional copies of the working-model solar observatory at Uaxactun. In many instances (e.g., Naachtun) the buildings were thrown out of symmetry with respect to the cardinal points. Often more than three structures were built on the eastern platform, though the three primary buildings were easily distinguishable since they were higher than the others. At Cahal Pichik the assemblage is so distorted that a derivative from the Group E arrangement at Uaxactun is debatable. When the long axis of the east mounds deviates from the north-south line, it is always (with one exception) to the east of north. Builders of the other sites may have paid more attention to the associated ritual and less to the actual astronomical observations.

Outside the Peten region we find a possible Group E arrangement at Dzibilchaltun, a site which is relatively distant both culturally and geographically from Uaxactun. In this case, however, the structures are reversed, with the observer standing in the doorway of a building on the east side of the plaza and looking over three buildings to the west. At this site the north-south axis of the three buildings is rotated 3° east of north. The Dzibilchaltun "solar observatory" is not functional in the exact sense, but the form of the arrangement and the east-of-north deviation seem too similar to that of the Peten Group E structures to be coincidental.

In this brief review of the role of astronomical considerations in New World architecture, we have tried to apply a systematic quantitative approach, one which has been seriously lacking in Mesoamerican archaeoastronomy. Attempting to look at the logical possibilities, we have discovered that historically documented astronomical events of functional importance, such as those which would fix a date in the religious, agricultural, or civil calendar, often provide the best match for a given orientation.

The use of heliacal risings and announcer stars as well as pictures from the codices suggests that a horizon system of observations was employed throughout Mesoamerica. This is quite in contrast with Old World systems of astronomical observation and, if anything, militates against extended transoceanic contact.

One of the most puzzling facts about building orientations in Mesoamerica is the east-of-north skew of so many ceremonial centers, a phenomenon which occurs throughout Mesoamerica over a long time base. A single astronomical explanation is not possible for all that appears in the data.

The most likely buildings endowed with special astronomical consideration by the ancient architects are the abnormally shaped structures like Building J of Monte Alban and the Caracol of Chichen Itza. But the question of which astronomical objects actually served as orientation points can never be decided on an absolute basis and it would be inappropriate to apply statistical considerations to the argument. Venus and the Pleiades are frequently excellent matches for some of the alignments and both are mentioned in native American folklore and legend, but Sirius and Capella, which also fit some of the architectural alignments, are not recorded to our knowledge. While the surveyor's transit and the computer tell us that these stars could have served to mark special dates in the calendar, the ethnohistoric sources do not support their importance. Perhaps more attention should be paid to the study of the surviving traditions and current folk practices among the people of Mexico and Central America as Coe (1975*b*) has recently suggested and Remington (these proceedings) has now begun to carry out.

Solar horizon positions at the solstices and equinoxes as well as the zenith passage dates were evidently key references. It is surprising that no lunar alignments appear. On the other hand, the lunar observations used in the Supplementary Series of glyphs and the eclipse tables in the Dresden Codex can easily be derived from a phase count rather than by noting horizon positions of the moon.

Notably absent from this discussion are some of the more subtle environmental considerations which also must have played a decisive role in placing and orienting buildings, as other papers suggest (e.g., Hartung, this volume). The "hierophanies" associated with the Castillo at Chichen Itza (Rivard 1970) and the Temple of Inscriptions at Palenque (Schele, these proceedings) may have been of great significance in a ritualistic sense; nevertheless, investigators must pay more attention in an astronomical context to the role of light and shadow changes in the environment of the ceremonial center.

We have seen in these pages several cases suggesting that astronomical observations along the horizon were of great importance to the people of ancient Mesoamerica. In view of the deep devotion of these people to calendar keeping, an art which can readily develop from such observations, it seems logical that astronomical baselines would be incorporated into their architecture. Objective evidence based upon careful measurement at the archaeological sites lies at the foundation of any investigation of building orientations, but this evidence must be reflected against our knowledge of the cultural background of the architects who erected the buildings and worshipped in them. In this sense, all such studies, conducted properly, are interdisciplinary.

Acknowledgments

I am grateful to Horst Hartung for drawing figs. 1.2, 1.3, 1.5, and 1.6 and to the National Science Foundation (Grant No. OIP75-05196) for supporting this research.

2

Mesoamerican Calendrics as Evidence of Astronomical Activity

Sharon L. Gibbs

My purpose in initiating a discussion of Mesoamerican calendrics in the context of a seminar on native American astronomy is to consider the ways in which an understanding of the former can contribute information to a study of the latter. As anyone who is familiar with the topic has discovered, a considerable amount of evidence has been brought to bear on the question of the Mesoamerican calendar in the centuries since Diego de Landa first reported that "with all the months joined together they made a sort of calendar, by the aid of which they regulated not only their festivals but also their accounts, contracts and business" (Tozzer 1941, p. 149). My own contribution represents a historian of science's interpretation of some of these earlier results. It begins with a brief introduction to the mechanism of the calendar, an introduction which emphasizes certain implications for the study of astronomy in the New World. A major portion of the text, however, is devoted to a discussion of two very different ways in which Mesoamerican calendrics can be considered as evidence of astronomical activity.

Calendrics

For our knowledge of the Mesoamerican calendar we rely on three important sources of information: (1) ethnographic accounts which may be either (a) reports of ancient practices dating from the Spanish colonial period[1] or (b) reports of modern practices which appear to belong to ancient tradition;[2] (2) original Maya manuscripts, the Dresden, Madrid, and Paris codices,[3] which contain tables of calendric significance; and (3) monumental inscriptions of both Maya and Mexican origin which appear to place events of history in the context of chronology.[4] Evidence from all three sources suggests that Mesoamericans employed multiple interrelated time-keeping conventions which emphasize different fundamental units.

The Ritual Count

Because of its wider distribution and more complete absorption into the cultural life of the native of Central America, a cyclic count of 260 days was regarded by Thompson (1960, p. 150) as the earliest Mesoamerican calendric convention. The convention designates days by the numbers in order from 1 to 13, each designation being a reference to an associated celestial deity. At the same time, the convention assigns twenty ritual day names in order to the counted days (see table 2.1). In such a system a given combination of deified number and ritual day name recurs every 260 days ($13 \times 20 = 260$). Americanists remain divided on the significance of this number. Some, like Thompson (1960, p. 99), contend that it is merely the inevitable result of a combination of its more important components. Others, notably Nuttall (1928) and, more recently, Malmstrom (1973), postulate a relationship between this cyclic period and the interval separating dates of zenith passage in the southern Maya zone.

Speculations on its significance are not the only aspects of the 260-day ritual calendar which raise questions of interest to historians of astronomy. Of equal interest would be some knowledge of when the ritual day began. While it is apparent from various ethnographic sources that an astronomical event marked the beginning of the ritual day everywhere in Mesoamerica, no single event has yet been clearly defined as a common delimiter. On the basis of evidence in the Codex

Table 2.1.
Equivalent Yucatecan and Central Mexican Ritual Day Names

Imix	Cipactli
Ik	Ehecatl
Akbal	Calli
Kan	Cuetzpallin
Chicchan	Coatl
Cimi	Miquiztli
Manik	Mazatl
Lamat	Tochtli
Muluc	Atl
Oc	Itzcuintli
Chuen	Ozomatli
Eb	Malinalli
Ben	Acatl
Ix	Ocelotl
Men	Cuauhtli
Cib	Cozcacuauhtli
Caban	Ollin
Etz'nab	Tecpatl
Cauac	Quiahuitl
Ahau	Xochitl

Telleriano Remensis, Alphonso Caso (1967, p. 53) became convinced that the Aztec day began at noon. Caso did not suggest a possible association between his conviction and the supposition that the 260-day cycle first marked the interval between astronomical events occurring at noon (i.e., zenith passage). At least in the Valley of Mexico the interval between zenith passages is too large, about 290 days, to be considered the model for the ritual calendar. Other opinions as to the start of the Aztec day are based on certain passages in Sahagun which describe the new year ceremonies (book 7, chap. 11, and book 4, app.). The fact that these apparently began at midnight suggests a second viable starting point for the Aztec ritual day.

The question of when the Maya ritual day began has no direct answer in any of the early sources. By reading between the lines of the books of Chilam Balam of Chumayel (Roys 1967, pp. 38, 116) one can—as Thompson did (1960, p. 174)— come to the conclusion that "the count of the first day started in the east, and therefore in all probability . . . at sunrise." Complicating this seemingly convincing evidence are modern ethnographic accounts of calendric practices among the inhabitants of the Guatemalan highlands. They indicate that the Jacalteca (LaFarge and Byers 1931) and the Ixil (Lincoln 1942) currently begin ritual days at sunset.

Uncertainty over the beginning of the ritual day in Mesoamerica clearly creates problems for historians of astronomy. It complicates association between ritual calendar dates and specific astronomical events. A solar eclipse occurring on one ritual date in a Chumayel-like calendar would occur on the immediately preceding date in a calendar of the Ixil type. Furthermore, calendric practices supply confusing evidence concerning the nature of astronomical interests in Mesoamerica. Astronomical events relating to the Aztec calendar are meridian oriented; calendric delimiters occur near the horizon in the Maya area.

The Vague Year

A second calendric convention in use in Mesoamerica seems to have a history which is nearly as long as that of the ritual count. Evidence of its early existence can be found in both Central Mexico and the Maya area. The major divisions of the count are its 18 "months" of 20 numbered days (see table 2.2 for Maya month names). To this 360-day period is added a singularly significant 5-day interval, the complete convention allowing for effective designation of 365 days before repetition.

The resemblance between this 365-day count and the true length of the solar year suggests a relationship between the two cycles. However, the implication of the vagueness of the similarity is far from apparent. The question of whether the Maya knew the true length of the year has been discussed since Landa's claim (Tozzer 1941, p. 133) that "they [the Maya] had a year as perfect as ours, consisting of 365 days and 6 hours" and that "from these six hours one day was made every four years, and so that they had every four years the year of 366 days." In 1910, C. P. Bowditch laid to rest the notion of the existence of intercalary days without denying Maya knowledge of the tropical year. John Teeple (1930) believed

Table 2.2.
Maya Month Names, Including the Period Designated Uayeb

Pop
Uo
Zip
Zotz'
Zec
Xul
Yaxkin
Mol
Ch'en
Yax
Zac
Ceh
Mac
Kankin
Muan
Pax
Kayab
Cumku
Uayeb *(5 days without a name)*

he had found evidence of this knowledge as a result of his discovery of integral multiples of tropical years in intervals separating Maya dates. While subsequent scholarship has undermined Teeple's elaborate determinant theory (see Proskouriakoff 1960), it has, at least, continued to uncover in the inscriptions integral multiples of the true tropical year. Kelley and Kerr (1974) have published the most recent efforts in this area.

A variety of evidence equal to that which contributed to an uncertain beginning of the ritual day similarly complicates attempts to specify the beginning of a day of the Vague Year. Indeed, some Americanists (including Thompson 1931*b*) have suggested that, where the 260-day count began at sunrise, the 365-day count may have begun at sunset.

The Calendar Round

At an unknown point in their respective histories, the 260-day count and the 365-day count were combined to uniquely designate a relatively large number of days. The recognition that a given combination of (*1*) ritual day number, (*2*) ritual day name, (*3*) day of the month, and (*4*) month name (e.g., 1 Ahau 18 Kayab) would recur only every 18,980 days represented a significant step in the development of the calendar system. There is no known Maya term for the period. The appropriate Nahuatl term is *xiuhmolpilli*. Modern scholars refer to the count as the Calendar

Round. In commenting on the Calendar Round in 1914, S. G. Morley placed in proper perspective what might otherwise be interpreted as extravagant praise of native American calendrics: ". . . by conceiving the Calendar Rounds to be in endless repetition from a fixed point of departure, and measuring time by an accurate system, the Maya were able to secure precision in dating their events which is not surpassed even by our own system of counting time" (p. 59). It is in this context that all comparisons between Maya and modern calendars should be understood.

The Long Count

Linton Satterthwaite (1965, p. 606) is one of the few scholars willing to discuss the origins of the so-called Long Count, the third and apparently most recent aspect of Mesoamerican calendric practice. He writes that "the periods of the Long Count appear to have been a Protoclassic (A.D. 150–300) addition to those of the Calendar Round." Evidence of the use of the Long Count is confined entirely to the Maya area. It is a count separate from but concurrent with the Calendar Round, and it appears to have been developed to distinguish dates separated from each other by more than 18,980 days.

The Long Count divides elapsed time into kins, uinals, tuns, and multiples of tuns. Many students of calendric practice—myself included—have found it convenient to interpret Long Count dates like numbers in a modified place-value system. It is an analogy of limited applicability, however, for it is likely to emphasize the uinal (or 20-day interval) as the fundamental unit of the Long Count when "overwhelming" evidence points to the tun (or 360-day interval) as the "Maya chronological unit" (Thompson 1960, p. 141).[5] Thompson's (1960, p. 151) speculations on the reasons for a calendric unit of 360 days are most interesting because they hint at the variables which must always be considered in assessing the significance of numbers in Mesoamerican culture: "I am inclined to think that the period of 360 days was chosen because the Maya desired a formal year which would invariably start with Imix and end with Ahau. To fulfill that condition, 360 days was the logical choice, for 380 days (it had to be a number divisible by 20) are nearly 15 days beyond the true length of the year."

A typical Long Count date might be transcribed as 9 baktuns 9 katuns 9 tuns 16 uinals 0 kins. Translation into mathematical language leads to:

$$9(20^2 \cdot 360) + 9(20 \cdot 360) + 9(360) + 16(20) + 0(1),$$

where the penultimate addend may not exceed 360 and the ultimate addend may not exceed 20. The fundamental nature of the 360-day interval, the tun, should be apparent from the translation. Uinals and kins are necessary to designate intervals between tuns. Since the Long Count marks elapsed time, it presumes a beginning, or zero point, somewhere in the already existing Calendar Round. All known Long Counts relate to some distant 4 Ahau 8 Cumku. The interlocking nature of the calendar forces this inevitable conclusion. The complete Maya date 9.9.9.16.0 1 Ahau 18 Kayab is 1,364,360 days (3,789 tuns and 320 days) after the zero point.

It is 71 Calendar Rounds and 16,780 days after 4 Ahau 8 Cumku.

Readers familiar with the development of Old World calendars have surely noted the lack of any reference to the lunar month in the foregoing discussion of the Mesoamerican calendric system. In fact, the role of so obvious an astronomical body in marking time is not apparent in any of the aspects of the calendar so far discussed. Both the uinal of the Long Count and ritual calendar and the unnamed 20-day division of the Vague Year can easily be explained as fundamental extensions of a vigesimal number system.

To get a clearer picture of the lunar influences on Maya timekeeping, one must go beyond the system so far discussed. According to Landa (Tozzer 1941, p. 133), the Maya year was divided into "two kinds of months, the one kind of thirty days and called U, which means 'moon,' and they counted it from the time at which the new moon appeared until it no longer appears." The full significance of Landa's statement was realized in 1925 when John E. Teeple recognized day counts of the kind Landa described in a series of hieroglyphs frequently appended to a combination of Long Count and Calendar Round. Some elements of the Lunar Series, as it came to be called, are found with the earliest inscribed Long Counts, so that apparently a lunar count had long been associated with calendric matters. In fact the inscriptions indicate that the lunar month as recorded by the Maya had either 29 or 30 days, a circumstance which suggests that the counts were intended to reflect astronomical reality.

In 1843, John Lloyd Stephens published Pio Perez's suggestion that the 30-day month, later associated with the Lunar Series, actually preceded components of the Calendar Round. The notion that the 20-day grouping conventions of the formal calendar may somehow have been derived from an older lunar count is kept alive by the linguistic analysis of the term *uinal* and its glyphic representation (see Thompson 1960, pp. 47, 143–144). The lunar associations of a 20-day period can hardly be denied on those occasions when the moon glyph is used as a sign for 20. Such a convention is always employed in the Lunar Series. It may be used in combination with other glyphs to express the length of time separating two Long Count dates, when that time is between 20 and 39 days.

The best evidence that the Maya knew and used the synodic month can be found on pages 51–58 of the Dresden Codex. At the turn of the century, Forstemann (1906, pp. 200–215) recognized that the ritual calendar dates on these pages recorded intervals of 177 (or 178) days (6 lunations of length 29.5 days) and 148 days (5 lunations of length 29.6 days). As a result, this section of the Dresden has long been designated a lunar table. By 1913 it had earned the alternate designation of eclipse table. The full implications of this latter designation continue to be explored.

No discussion of calendric custom in Mesoamerica would be complete without some reference to the synodic period of Venus. In Landa's (Tozzer 1941, p. 133) words, the Maya "used as a guide by night, so as to know the hour of the Morning Star, the Pleiades and the Gemini." Knowledge of the hour of Venus as morning star was apparently as important to Nahuatl speakers as it was to the Maya (see Codex Chimalpopoca 1945, par. 51). Pages 24 and 46–50 of the Dresden Codex contain columns of ritual dates which have been recognized, again since Forstemann's (1906, pp. 182–196) work, as components of a Venus table. The intervals repeatedly recorded on these pages—236, 90, 250, and 8 days—add up to 584 days, the latter being an excellent approximation of the mean synodic period of the planet Venus. In fact, the average interval between successive first appearances of Venus as morning star is 583.92 days. That the Maya are well aware of and compensated for the effects of calculating with the nearest whole-day approximation of the true interval was first suggested by John Teeple in 1926. He based his conclusions on interpretations of the structure of the table which may prove vulnerable to recent challenges (see M. Closs's paper in this collection).

Astronomy through Correlation

Astronomers have long recognized the value of a continuous systematic count of days. In the most recent effort at uniformity, they agreed to assign Julian Day numbers, in order, to successive days beginning with 0 = 1 January 4713 B.C., and ignoring the vagaries of local calendric custom. Contacts between Maya scholars and astronomers in the early part of the twentieth century led both to recognize what each was certain would be useful similarities between modern astronomical practice and Maya methods of timekeeping. S. G. Morley (1920, p. 465), encouraged by his astronomer-colleague R. W. Willson, was one of the first Maya scholars to appreciate the analogy between the Maya Long Count and the Julian Period. He naturally hoped that the two parallel counts might be related and suggested in 1920 that astronomy would provide the link: ". . . it appears highly probable that actual astronomical phenomena of determinable nature are recorded in the Maya inscriptions; and it only awaits the exact identification of any one of these, such as any particular solar or lunar eclipse which was visible in northern Central America during the first six centuries of the Christian Era for example, to make immediately possible an exact correlation of Maya chronology with our own Gregorian calendar."

Morley's conviction that astronomy could provide the basis for a correlation between Maya and Christian chronology does, of course, rely on the assumption that the Maya observed and recorded in their Long Count identifiable celestial events. Morley challenged his colleagues to look for astronomically relevant dates in the inscriptions. Most of them wisely ignored the vast amount of evidence he provided (in the "Inscriptions at Copan" and the "Inscriptions of Peten") in favor of studying the tables of dates in the Dresden Codex. For many years following Morley's challenge, Maya astronomy was discussed only in the context of the correlation question. Attempts to answer the question can, then, be examined with a view to discovering how Mesoamerican calendrics has been considered evidence of astronomical activity.

In his "Astronomical Notes on the Maya Codices" (published posthumously in 1924), Robert Willson established a long-lived tradition of viewing pages 51–58 of the Dresden Codex as a list of ritual calendar dates on which solar eclipses could occur. Table 2.3 gives a transcription of a portion of the table showing the placement of the first three of ten interspersed pictures. Willson began his work

Table 2.3.
Transcription of the Beginning of the Eclipse Table in the Dresden Codex
(Numbers in brackets are corrections to the original. Pictures fall between columns
502 and [679], 2244 and [2422], 3278 and 3455.)

177	[354]	502	[679]	856	1033
6 Kan	1 Imix	6 Muluc	1 Cimi	9 Akbal	4 Ahau
7 Chicchan	2 Ik	7 Oc	2 Manik	10 Kan	5 Imix
8 Cimi	3 Akbal	8 Chuen	3 Lamat	[11] Chicchan	6 Ik
177	177	148	177	177	177

Page 53a

[2422]	2599	2776	2953	3130
2 Muluc	10 Cimi	5 Akbal	13 Ahau	8 Caban
3 Oc	11 Manik	6 Kan	1 Imix	9 Etz'nab
4 Chuen	12 Lamat	7 Chicchan	[2] Ik	10 Cauac
[178]	177	177	177	177

Page 55a

with the suspicion that the intervals of days which separated the pictures on Dresden 51–58 (2,244 − 502 = 1,742; 3,278 − 2,244 = 1,034, etc.) could be matched with a unique set of intervals separating nine solar eclipses visible in Central America. Although he found numerous strings of visible eclipses, Willson failed to find a suitable series of nine and he abandoned a study of intervals in the eclipse table in favor of attempting to associate three Long Count dates in the Dresden with specific celestial events. Willson assumed that the Long Count date which opened the Venus table, 9.9.9.16.0. 1 Ahau 18 Kayab, was associated by Maya astronomers with a first appearance of Venus as morning star four days after inferior conjunction with the sun. He then felt justified in identifying one of the Long Count dates which open the eclipse table, 9.16.4.10.8 12 Lamat 1 Muan, with a visible solar eclipse. Hoping to find *the* correlation, Willson searched existing planetary tables for Julian-numbered dates separated by 48,488 days which would satisfy the Dresden criteria as he interpreted them. He found twenty-two satisfactory combinations of dates and recognized a need to introduce further astronomical evidence.

Willson's assumption that pages 43–45 of the Dresden represent a Maya attempt to follow the motion of Mars never received the blessing of his colleagues. It did, however, enable him to designate a single link between Maya and Christian

1211	1388	1565	[1742]	1919	[2096]	2244
13 Etz'nab	8 Men	3 Eb	11 Muluc	6 Cib	1 Akbal	6 Chuen
1 Cauac	9 Cib	4 Ben	12 Oc	7 Caban	2 Kan	7 Eb
2 Ahau	10 Caban	5 Ix	13 Chuen	8 Etz'nab	3 Chicchan	8 Ben
[178]	177	177	177	177	177	148

Page 54a

3278	3455	3632	3809
13 Chicchan	8 Ik	3 Cauac	2 Cib
1 Cimi	9 Akbal	4 Ahau	3 Caban
2 Manik	10 Kan	5 Imix	4 Etz'nab
148	177	177	177

Page 56a

chronology. In Willson's view, the Long Count date 9.19.7.15.8 3 Lamat 6 Zotz (inferred from numbers of p. 43) represented some "noteworthy configuration of Mars with respect to the sun," specifically, a stationary point preceding conjunction. The addition of a Mars criterion enabled Willson to considerably narrow his search for an appropriate series of Julian Day numbers corresponding to 9.9.9.16.0, 9.16.4.10.8, and 9.19.7.15.8. He found only one satisfactory group of three and concluded that the Julian Day number of the 4 Ahau 8 Cumku which initiated the Long Count must be 438,906.

Robert Willson's astronomical solution to the correlation problem proved no more "exact" than any of the solutions based solely on the historical evidence provided by the Book of Chilam Balam (for examples, see Morley 1910). Problems with the result of his efforts, however, did not diminish the influence of Willson's assessment of the evidence for Maya astronomical activity. Consider the picture he presented: "A comparatively small acquaintance with the Maya literature will probably result in the belief that, at the time of which we have their records, they must have made use of some method of dividing the day. . . . It is not known what theories the Mayas had concerning the nature of the universe but they measured celestial movements and recorded the movements of heavenly bodies. . . . It is likely that the Mayas knew that the length of the year so determined by heliacal rising of stars was about 365¼ days" (p. 5). Willson's work served primarily to emphasize the evidence for Maya recognition of the periodicity of solar eclipses and synodic phenomena.

In volume 6 of the *Papers of the Peabody Museum, Harvard University* (1924), Willson's "astronomical notes" are followed by Herbert Spinden's lengthy monograph "The Reduction of Mayan Dates." In it Spinden presents and justifies *his* preferred correlation; and while his link was not suggested by astronomical assumptions, it was, in his view, considerably strengthened by the astronomical evidence it revealed. Spinden's correlation was based upon a comparison of inscribed and written evidence from Yucatan first described by Morley in 1910. By building on Morley's assumption that a Long Count date found in the old portion of Chichen Itza was inscribed soon before the abandonment of that city, reported with accompanying abbreviated date (Katun 10 Ahau) in the books of Chilam Balam, Spinden was led to suppose that the Katun 13 Ahau associated with the 1536 date of the conquest was 12.9.0.0.0. Such an assumption assigns the Julian Day number 489,384 to the 4 Ahau 8 Cumku beginning of the Maya Long Count.

The limited inspiration Spinden found in the Dresden Codex was equalled by the limited support it provided for his chosen correlation (see Thompson 1935, pp. 78–79). He did, however, share Morley's faith in the astronomical context of the inscriptions; and when an exhaustive application of his correlation to Morley's inscriptions produced an impressive number of astronomically interesting dates, Spinden felt that the correctness of his solution had been firmly established. What had been established simultaneously was Spinden's own impression of the nature of Maya astronomy.

Maya inscriptions, interpreted via the Spinden correlation, reveal a familiarity with the tropical year and indicate that the classic Maya recorded dates of astronomical and agricultural significance within the solar cycle. For example:

Stela 10 at Copan: September 6   (beginning of the "agricultural year")
Stela 5 at Copan: March 22   (vernal equinox)
Stela N at Copan: December 22   (winter solstice)
Lintel 25 at Yaxchilan: September 23   (autumnal equinox)

The efforts of Willson and Spinden represent two aspects of the classic view of the relationship between Mesoamerican calendrics and evidence of astronomical activity in the New World. In general, the latter is viewed only as inspiration or support for attempts to place the former in the context of Old World chronology. The picture of Maya astronomy developed by the correlationists invites criticism. For it is based either on what seem like ad hoc assumptions or on what can only be considered tenuous identifications of astronomical records.

Astronomy without Correlation

In 1930, John E. Teeple published what must still be considered the most lucid account of astronomical practice in the New World. The conclusions he reaches are entirely independent of the correlation question. They are based solely on an examination of intervals separating Maya dates on the monuments and in the codices. Teeple's major contribution is his assessment of the astronomical evidence in the so-called Lunar Series which often supplements the calendric information provided by the Long Count and Calendar Round. Teeple first determined that elements of the Lunar Series recorded the "age" of the moon (counted from new moon) and the length of the current lunar month. Random errors in the recorded ages suggested to him that the inscribed moon ages were records of observations and not products of formalized computation (p. 51). On the other hand, a systematic relationship between the inscribed length of the current month (Glyph A) and its position within the lunar half year (Glyph C) convinced Teeple that the recorded month length was a "predicted and not an observed figure" (p. 63). Thus, Teeple's evaluation of the internal evidence supplied by calendrics reveals a simultaneous program of lunar observations and predictive calculation. His conclusions do not suffer by their association with a particular correlation.

Historians of astronomy find Teeple's approach particularly appealing. His influence is obvious, for example, in the work of Alexander Pogo reported on in the 1937 *Yearbook* of the Carnegie Institution of Washington. Pogo compares the intervals between ritual dates on pages 51–58 of the Dresden with intervals separating the dates of lunar eclipses actually observed in Maya territory and concludes (in contrast with Willson) that "the tabular framework . . . is based on lunar, and not on solar, eclipses actually observed by the Maya."

To my knowledge, a Pogo-like analysis of the Venus tables in the Dresden has never been attempted, possibly because on the surface most of the intervals in the table seem curiously unrelated to astronomical reality. Consider the last entry in each column of ritual dates on pages 46–50 (table 2.4). The 584-day interval separating every fifth entry is a close enough approximation to the synodic period of Venus to suggest that one should examine the motion of this planet for an explanation of the subintervals (90, 250, 8, 236) which appear. Indeed the recorded 8-day interval can justifiably be identified with the brief period of disappearance of Venus at inferior conjunction. The possibility that the dates 5 Kan, 4 Lamat, 3 Eb, 2 Cib, and 1 Ahau each represent the first appearance of Venus as morning star has consistently led to attempts to identify the other entries in the table with the remaining horizon phenomena typical of Venus: last appearance as morning star, first appearance as evening star, and last appearance as evening star. Table 2.5 shows these four synodic phenomena with the intervals which would separate them if identified with the entries in the Dresden table and with the intervals which separate these phenomena as recorded by modern observations (A. F. Aveni, private communication). Several interpretations of the evidence are possible:

1. The Maya only observed the disappearance of Venus at inferior conjunction.
2. The intervals recorded on pages 46–50 of the Dresden result from a still misunderstood combination of astronomical conditions.
3. The seemingly unnatural intervals in the Venus table are the product of the same calendric, ritualistic, and astronomical influences which Thompson believed led to their choice of a fundamental calendric unit of 360 days (see Thompson's [1960, p. 151] earlier quote).

Table 2.4.
Last Entry in Each Column of Ritual Dates on Pages 46–50
of the Dresden Codex with Intervals Separating Entries

Page of Dresden	Last entry of each ritual column		Interval of days separating columns
	8 Cib		
		90 days	
	7 Cimi		340 days
46a		250 days	
	10 Cib		
		8 days	
	5 Kan		
		236 days	
	7 Ahau		
		90 days	
	6 Oc		340 days
47a		250 days	
	9 Ahau		
		8 days	
	4 Lamat		
		236 days	
	6 Kan		
		90 days	
	5 Ix		340 days
48a		250 days	
	8 Kan		
		8 days	
	3 Eb		
		236 days	
	5 Lamat		
		90 days	
	4 Etz'nab		340 days
49a		250 days	
	7 Lamat		
		8 days	
	2 Cib		
		236 days	
	4 Eb		
		90 days	
	3 Ik		340 days
50a		250 days	
	6 Eb		
		8 days	
	1 Ahau		

Table 2.5.
Intervals Separating Entries in the Dresden Venus Table
Compared with Observed Intervals between Horizon Phenomena
as Recorded in "Sky and Telescope"
(Averaged figures for modern observations compiled by A. F. Aveni)

Venus phenomena	Intervals separating phenomena	
	Dresden	Modern observations
First appearance as morning star		
	236 days	263 days
Last appearance as morning star		
	90 days	50 days*
First appearance as evening star		
	250 days	263 days
Last appearance as evening star		
	8 days	8 days
First appearance as morning star		

*Further specification:
viewing simple: 70 days
viewing possible if careful: 62 days
viewing difficult: 46 days

The second of these several interpretations is examined by David Kelley in another essay in this collection. It may prove useful to consider here the implications of the third.

Regular observations of the first appearance of Venus in the east would quickly show that it consistently occurred on days of the 260-day count having one of five names. The structure of the ritual portion of the Venus table suggests that at the time it was devised these five important day names were

Kan, Lamat, Eb, Cib, and Ahau.

The creator of the Venus table shows a clear preference for these days as well as for days in the name list midway between any two crucial days (see table 2.1):

Cimi, Oc, Ix, Etz'nab, and Ik.

The table consists entirely of dates involving these ten names. Circumstances strongly suggest that the astronomical significance of dates in the upper registers of pages 46–50 may be disguised by ritualistic concerns.

How does the assumption that the columns of the Venus table designate ritualistic events associated with that planet affect our impression of Maya planetary astronomy? It would seem, at first glance, to reduce the value of the table as

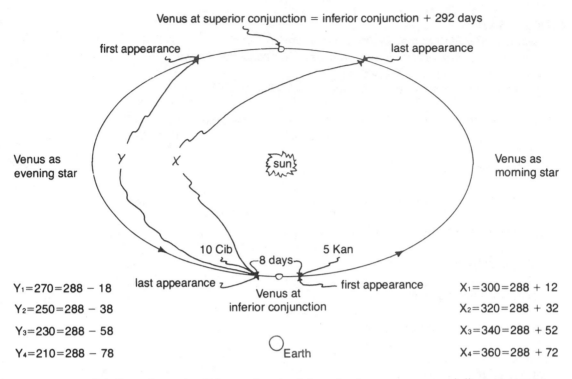

Venus at superior conjunction = inferior conjunction + 292 days

first appearance

last appearance

Venus as
evening star

Y X

{sun}

Venus as
morning star

10 Cib

5 Kan

−8 days−

$Y_1 = 270 = 288 - 18$

last appearance

first appearance

$X_1 = 300 = 288 + 12$

$Y_2 = 250 = 288 - 38$

Venus at
inferior conjunction

$X_2 = 320 = 288 + 32$

$Y_3 = 230 = 288 - 58$

$X_3 = 340 = 288 + 52$

$Y_4 = 210 = 288 - 78$

Earth

$X_4 = 360 = 288 + 72$

2.1. *Synodic cycle of Venus showing intervals of appearance and disappearance.*

astronomical evidence. It need not do so, as the following analysis reveals.

Consider the synodic period of Venus as illustrated in figure 2.1. As the diagram shows, minimum astronomical reality requires that 292 days separate inferior and superior conjunction. Data from table 2.5 indicate that an 8-day disappearance interval (4 + 4) encloses inferior conjunction. The interval of disappearance at superior conjunction averages 50 days but can conceivably extend to about 70 days. By combining evidence from the Codex Chimalpopoca and Landa's *Relacion* with astronomical reality, we can assign dates in the columns separated by 8 days to the events of last appearance as evening star and first appearance as morning star: for example, 10 Cib and 5 Kan.

Dates from other columns in the Dresden may not be as readily placed on the diagram unless certain assumptions are made. It is possible that the creator of the Venus table wished to include a column of ritual dates relating to the last appearance of Venus as morning star. If he did so, it is also possible that he included ritual dates which would anticipate the event. (La Farge and Byers's account of the ceremonial year at Jacaltenango [1931, pp. 173–175] includes a number of anticipatory ritual dates.) A second appropriate constraint might have been the requirement that ritual associated with disappearance (in east or west) should take place on days of the same name. Satisfaction of the combined conditions would have resulted in a column of ritual dates separated from dates relating to last appearance in the evening (10 Cib, 9 Ahau, 8 Kan, etc.) by an interval X greater than 288 (292− 4) and divisible by 20. Some possible values for X are given on the right in figure 2.1. Note that X_3 is the one interval which guarantees a ritual date close to but not after disappearance. It is the interval characteristic of the Dresden table.

If ritual associated with first appearance in the west had to occur on a day name falling midway in the ritual-day list between day names of adjacent last appearances (see table 2.1), then the interval Y separating two columns in the Dresden table would be an integer which gives remainder 10 upon division by 20. Assuming the ritual had to take place while Venus was visible (as did the disappearance ritual), then the interval integer would also have to be less than 288. Some possible values for Y are given on the left in figure 2.1. The interval Y_2 would guarantee celebration of the appearance ritual closest to but not before first appearance as evening star. It is also the interval characteristic of the Dresden table.

The seemingly unnatural intervals in the Dresden table need not necessarily preclude Maya observations of Venus at superior conjunction. In fact, the intervals of 250 and 340 days can be considered to evidence astronomy tied to ritual. The columns of the Venus table may conceivably be interpreted as consisting of dates separating ritual which would occur as close as possible to the events of last and first visibility without taking place during disappearance.

An analysis of the curious subintervals in the Dresden Venus table has been offered here primarily to emphasize the difficulties inherent in any evaluation of evidence of Maya astronomy supplied by calendric material. Indeed, the conclusion that astronomical knowledge lies hidden under ritualistic constraints may prove a facile explanation for the structure of the Venus table. Still, a dual devotion to calendric ritual and astronomical pursuits remains the distinctive attribute of Mesoamerican culture. The work of the historian of native American astronomy must begin with an understanding of the nature of these interrelated concerns.

Notes

1. Examples of these include Landa's *Relacion* (see Tozzer's 1941 edition) and the Florentine Codex or *A General History of the Things of New Spain* by Fray Bernardino de Sahagun (see Dibble and Anderson's edition).

2. In the 1930's and early 1940's a series of ethnographic accounts of existing Maya calendars were published by Burkitt, Gates, LaFarge, Lincoln, Lothrop, Scholes, Thompson, and others. Brockington and Paddock are currently engaged in similar studies of existing Zapotec calendars.

3. For recent reproductions of these manuscripts see Villacorta and Villacorta 1930 and Thompson 1972.

4. The best comprehensive collection of drawings of Maya inscriptions remains A. P. Maudslay's appropriately monumental *Archaeology, Biologia Centrali-Americana*, first published between 1889 and 1902 and recently reissued by Arte Primitivo, New York. For the most recent considerations of the significance of dates in the inscriptions see Proskouriakoff 1960 and Mathews and Schele 1974.

5. Michael P. Closs was the most recent alert listener to remind me of the dangers of the place-value analogy.

Astronomical Signs in the Codices Bodley and Selden

Horst Hartung

One of the main objectives of investigation in archaeoastronomy is to check the existing ancient monuments for directions and alignments which may correspond to an astronomical reference. Some of the methods, possibilities, limitations, and results of these studies have been presented elsewhere (Aveni, ed., 1975).

Scholars of related sciences have become increasingly interested in collaboration in this new field. But there is an urgent need to obtain evidence from these investigators to confirm or reject the proposed results of the astronomical measurements.

One such investigation relates to the ancient codices, a limited number of which have escaped destruction. Over seventy years ago Nuttall (1906) published an article which dealt primarily with astronomical drawings in the codices. No further similar study has been published since.

Except for the three (or four) known Maya codices, all are from Central Mexico. The two codices selected for this study, Codex Bodley and Codex Selden, come from the Mixtec highlands. Both codices exist in facsimile with detailed commentaries by Caso (1960 and 1964). His interpretations and the codices themselves deserve further investigations.

This study is concerned primarily with two signs appearing in these documents: the so-called crossed sticks and crossed legs. The former sign is regarded as representing the astronomical device used by astronomers in Mesoamerica to observe the movements of the stars. Caso interprets this sign as "Observatory" or "astronomical instrument." The meaning of the crossed legs is not clear, although pictorially they seem to function in the same manner as the crossed sticks (Smith 1973, p. 60). The crossed legs do not appear in the Codex Selden.

The aforementioned symbols can be separated into two categories based on their use: place signs of towns and personal names of individuals.

A preliminary analysis of the crossed-sticks and crossed-legs signs in the

6-II

15-II

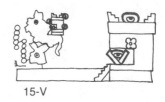
15-V

16-IV

16-V

19-II

19-III

20-II

21-II

21-III

22-II

22-III

23-III

23-IV

26-I

28-I

30-V

32-IV

35-II

38-II

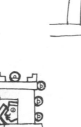

3.1. *Drawings of all crossed-sticks and crossed-legs signs in the Codex Bodley. They are presented with the contours of individuals, platforms, and temples nearby. The arabic numbers refer to the page, the roman numbers to the line of the corresponding page of the codex.*

Codices Bodley and Selden shows the following characteristics: there are twenty-six drawings in both codices which contain one or two astronomical signs, twenty in the Bodley (fig. 3.1) and six in the Selden (fig. 3.2). In 1906 Nuttall discussed only fifteen of these in both codices.

Twenty-one signs are represented by crossed sticks and eleven by crossed legs. Seven of these signs are visible in the doorway of a temple; only one is of the crossed-legs type (fig. 3.3). Another one is marked in the "house" sign belonging to a personal name (Bodley 15-V). Four signs are situated on platforms (Bodley 6-II, 15-II [two], 35-II). One sign is represented on top of a temple (Bodley 28-I). Seven signs are between people sitting opposite one another. Of these, three signs (Bodley 21-II, 22-II, 23-III) refer to a site called "Observatory" by Caso, one sign corresponds to a personal name (Bodley 38-II), and for three signs there is no special discussion by Caso (Bodley 20-II, 21-III, 22-III).

The largest number of signs, thirteen, corresponds to personal names of individuals (Bodley 15-V, 16-V, 19-II, 19-III, 23-III, 23-IV [two], 38-II and Selden 5-III, 5-IV, 13-III, 13-IV [two]). One of these (Bodley 15-V) mentioned by Caso as "house" has crossed sticks in the doorway and must refer to an observatory.

Caso mentioned, or directly implied, "Observatory" in fourteen cases. In one of these cases (Bodley 15-II), two signs apparently refer to the same place called "Observatory." These are Bodley 6-II, 15-II, 15-V, 16-IV, 20-II, 21-II, 22-II, 23-III,

3.2. *Drawings of all crossed-sticks signs in the Codex Selden. In order to distinguish these signs from those of the Codex Bodley, the former have an "S" (= Selden) before the numbers.*

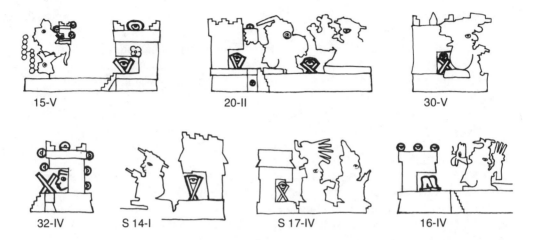

| 15-V | 20-II | 30-V |
| 32-IV | S 14-I | S 17-IV | 16-IV |

3.3. *Seven drawings show the "astronomical instrument" inside the doorways of buildings (temples ?). Sign 32-IV even presents a head looking through the device from inside the temple; in this case there is no eye between the sticks as in the other five examples. Sign 16-IV demonstrates the only example with the crossed legs (without an eye) in the doorway.*

28-I, 30-V, 32-IV, 35-II and Selden 14-I, 17-IV. There is no astronomical sign reference for the crossed sticks in Bodley 26-I.

In 1960 Caso listed the names of eight towns whose place signs had been identified (p. 18). In 1973 Smith mentioned twenty-three names as securely identified and several others which still needed more definite proof (pp. 80–82).

Of interest was Smith's alternative hypothesis for the place sign of Tlaxiaco, an important town in the Mixteca Alta. Tlaxiaco is a Nahuatl name which means "place of the ballcourt outside the town"; the Mixtec name is usually given as Ndisi (obvious, visible) Nuu (face, stars, and eyes) and this might be translated literally as "visible face" or less literally as "clearly seen." "Given a translation of *Ndisi Nuu* as 'clearly seen' or 'clearly visible,' . . . it is possible that the place sign usually described as 'Observatory' may be the place sign of Tlaxiaco" (Smith 1973, p. 60).

The concept expressed in the "Observatory" sign resembles very closely the idiomatic translation of Ndisi Nuu as "clearly seen," and the specific motif of an eye that is visible between two crossed sticks or above crossed legs reflects a literal translation of Ndisi Nuu as "visible eyes." This interpretation would seem to be confirmed by a sign that represents one of the personal names of a ruler who appears in Codex Muro. This sign consists of an eye inside a flame motif, which rests on a bowllike base. The final two words of the gloss are Ndisi Nuu, the same two words which comprise the Mixtec name of Tlaxiaco (Smith 1973, pp. 60, 89). If the above consideration is valid, the flame motif with an eye, drawn as a torch as in Selden 14-IV (also in fig. 3.2) may have an astronomical implication.

The Mixteca Alta is one of the less well studied archaeological zones of Mesoamerica. Excavations could reveal some very interesting data, which may coincide with the written historical references in the codices. The frequently noted astro-

nomical signs must refer to existing places and possibly even to particular buildings. A reference to the occupation of a particular individual or his birthplace could
have been substituted for a personal name. It may be of interest that Spores
(1967, p. 55) noted that the town of Tlaxiaco is surrounded by a number of un-
surveyed and unexcavated archaeological sites, for example, the hilltop site of
Cerro Encantado, located about one kilometer to the northeast.

Possibly one day an astronomical observatory will be excavated in the Mixteca Alta which would enlarge our understanding of the nature of astronomical
practice in ancient Mesoamerica. Given the written evidence, we have only to dig
and excavate at the right place, as did Schliemann at Troy.

Acknowledgments

My thanks to Emily Rabin for valuable advice and to Federico Solorzano for
allowing me to use his bibliographic material.

4

Palenque: The House of the Dying Sun

Linda Schele

This paper will consist of two parts: a brief description of the iconography of the Tablet of the Cross (TC) and the Temple of Inscriptions (TI) sarcophagus lid and an analysis of the skull variant emblem glyphs of Palenque. The detailed analysis of the iconography of the TC and the TI sarcophagus lid was presented at the Segunda Mesa Redonda de Palenque (Schele 1976). It is necessary to briefly summarize those findings in order to discuss the full implications of the emblem glyphs of Palenque.

The Temple of Inscriptions is the funerary monument of Lord Shield-Pacal (born 9.8.9.13.0 8 Ahau 13 Pop, acceded 9.9.4.2.8 5 Lamat 1 Mol, and died 9.12.11.5.18 6 Etz'nab 11 Yax). The Temple of the Cross is the accession monument of Lord Chan Bahlum (born 9.10.2.6.6 2 Cimi 19 Zotz', acceded 9.12.11.12.10 8 Oc 3 Kayab, and died 9.13.10.1.5 6 Chicchan 3 Pop) (Mathews and Schele 1974). Both tablets (figs. 4.1 and 4.2) occupy the dominant place in each monumental space and both portray essentially the same iconographic theme. A cross image is formed by three levels of dragon heads; the upper is square nosed and jewelled, the middle is fleshed, and the lower is skeletal but identical in anatomical detail to the middle form. The three dragons form a stacked model of the vertical universe with the jewelled dragons representing the celestial level, the fleshed the middle level, and the skeletal the underworld. At the base of each cross, but isolated from it, is the rear head of the celestial monster. In the TI the rear head is isolated between the doubled jaws of the underworld dragon and in the TC it is suspended half above and half below a sky band, which on the left (western) side is composed of night signs and on the right (eastern) side of day signs. In both cases the monster above the nose is fleshed and below is skeletal.

4.1. *Sarcophagus lid from the tomb of the Temple of Inscriptions. (Courtesy of Merle Greene Robertson.)*

4.2. *The Tablet and Sanctuary Jamb Panels from the Temple of the Cross. Sections enlarged on following pages.*

L.Schele '75

L.Schele '75

In the TI, Pacal, the dead ruler, is shown above the monster in a falling position. His state of movement is emphasized by his unbalanced position and the disarray of his clothes. Both he and the monster are shown to be entering the jaws of the underworld. The act of entrance is emphasized by the inward closure of the skeletal jaws. In the TC the monster is isolated from the adjacent figures. The left (western) figure is Pacal, who by iconographic detail and scale is shown to be dead. The right (eastern) figure is Chan Bahlum, the son and acceding ruler. Pacal holds a scepter which is the same rear monster seen at the base of the cross image in both tables.

The identification of the cross monster in question should be reconfirmed here by the following list of his attributes:

1. A badge of three elements is always present above his head. It consists of a cross-section shell, a sign of the underworld; a stingray spine (Joralemon 1974), a sign of the middle world and blood letting; and the crossed-bands cartouche, a sign of the celestial world.

2. The monster has a helmet devised on his forehead with a *kin* infix. Among the meanings of *kin* are time, day, and sun.

3. The monster is shown in the TC suspended between signs of night in the west and day in the east. In the TI he is shown entering the jaws of the underworld by falling from the level of the middle world. The portrayed instant corresponds to sunset in the daily cycle and to winter solstice in the yearly cycle.

4. The monster is shown to be half skeletal and half fleshed, or in a state of transition from life to death.

5. In instances where the monster is shown in a full, double-headed saurian (e.g., in Temple 22 at Copan, in House E at Palenque, and in the niched stelae at Piedras Negras), he is shown in an arched form heading, in the majority of cases, in a westerly direction. In other words, he follows the motion of the sun from east to west. At Copan, the easternmost site, he is shown as a fleshed monster with the tropical year passage of the sun as a body. He is supported by bacabs under which is a ground line over skulls. At Palenque he is shown with a body composed of the sky band, above which perches the screech-owl variant of the serpent bird, identified by Bardawill (1976) as an underworld god.

In summary, the rear monster's identity must satisfy the following criteria: identification with celestial, middle, and underworld planes of existence, and the capability to change from fleshed to skeletal states, to be suspended between night and day and the middle and underworlds; and to form an arc which can travel either in the heavens or the underworld. The monster is identified by the sign *kin*-sun on his forehead. If the monster were a manifestation of any other heavenly body, I doubt seriously if it would have been so consistently identified as *kin*-sun.

The identification of the rear monster as the sun becomes tremendously important when the program for power transfer portrayed in the TC is investigated. The entire program shows a literal transfer of power from the dead king to the living as a physical, explicit act. The action begins on the inner tablet with the acceding ruler standing on the eastern side of the image which describes the power involved in the transfer. He is dressed simply and carries a reclining jester god. The dead king stands in the west and acts in a supernatural context. He holds the sun monster with a *caan*-sky sign infixed in its forehead and with water pouring from the mouth.

The action concludes on the sanctuary jambs with Chan Bahlum, who has acceded to office, standing literally in the place of his father, the dead king. He is dressed in the uniform worn by rulers after accession at Palenque. He holds in his hand the sun-monster scepter inverted and with a *kin*-sun infix. He offers the scepter to God L who stands on the eastern jamb panel. Coe has not only identified God L as one of the chief gods of the underworld, but also emphasized that the TC East Jamb is one of the two known occurrences of God L in a monumental stone tablet (Coe 1975*a*). The other is the Tablet of the Sun, involved in the iconographic triptych of the Group of the Cross. God L's occurrence here is especially significant when viewed in the context of his frequent appearance on funerary pottery. Notice that on the inner tablet before the act of transfer Pacal stands on the subordinate side, perhaps because he is dead. But on the outer tablets after the transfer the living ruler, Chan Bahlum, stands on the subordinate side and God L stands on the dominant east. The sun monster at the base of the cross is half fleshed, half skeletal, and suspended between night and day. The same god is offered by the ruler at accession to one of the chief gods of the underworld.

The extraordinary significance of the iconography described above is magnified by the hierophanies associated with both the TC and the TI. The iconography defines the critical instance in the daily passage of the sun as the moment of transition between the middle world and the underworld, or sunset. The architectural hierophanies specify the critical instant in the tropical year as the winter solstice. Two events of powerful significance occur at the setting of the winter solstice sun. From the top floor of the Tower and indeed from most locations in the Palace, the sun at about three in the afternoon of winter solstice is seen to enter the earth (the ridge behind the inscriptions) over the approximate center of the TI. The angle of entrance appears to be very close to the angle of the first flight of stairs to the tomb. In other words, the winter solstice sun enters the underworld through Pacal's tomb, and the event portrayed symbolically on the sarcophagus lid is reproduced literally on each winter solstice.

Another kind of hierophany which may be even more impressive occurs in the Temple of the Cross. The site is arranged in such a way that, when the sun disappears behind the inscriptions ridge, the main center—including the TI, Palace, Temple 11, etc.—is covered with an advancing shadow (fig. 4.3). A depression in the ridge allows the sun at the same time to shine fully on the Group of the Cross. The effect is very much like a spotlight. The sunlight falls at an oblique angle across the front of the Temple of the Cross and, because of the placement of the TC, it is only at this time of the year that direct sunlight ever hits the front of the temple or its interior (fig. 4.4). The piers in front are arranged in such a manner that pier b (left of figure) casts a long oblique shadow creating a shaft of light adjacent to it. As the sun sinks lower, the light is isolated onto God L. If the lintel over the pier were in place, the shadow would form an angled light terminating near the top of the God L jamb. The shaped light travels down the jamb toward the lower right-hand corner. The last direct sunlight of the winter solstice to hit the main center falls on the feet of God L.

4.3. *An aerial photograph of Palenque taken from the north near winter solstice. Note the TI is in a shadow which has advanced along the western face of the Palace. The Group of the Cross is in full light with the northern, rear face of the TC in shadow.*

4.4. *A photograph of the sanctuary and center wall of the Temple of the Cross taken on the evening of December 24, 1974. Note the light is fully illuminating the east, God L panel. The broken line corresponds to the approximate location termination caused by the missing lintel. The motion of the shadow had been from left to right, up to down during the afternoon.*

The two hierophanies are arranged to occur successively beginning at about 2:30 P.M. and concluding at about 5:30 P.M. In both cases the events are extraordinarily vivid and must have been designed to reproduce the occurrences portrayed symbolically on the tablets. I do not believe that either hierophany was structured to produce the kind of astronomical observations evident in the Dresden Codex; both experiences are too broadly structured for precise measurement. Instead, I think the function was perhaps more significant and designed to make the site itself or perhaps the universe reproduce, for all to see and understand, the cosmological foundation of rulership. Who could argue with the divinity of the Palenque dynasty if the sun god entered the underworld through the tomb of Pacal? The events could be reconfirmed for Pacal, Chan Bahlum, and their descendants each year, even until this day.

The emblem glyphs (EG) of Palenque reinforce the interpretation of the icon-ography presented above. Palenque's emblem glyphs appear in three distinct forms, with the main sign being, respectively, a bird variant (T793a) (Thompson 1962) (fig. 4.5b), a bone with the sutures shown (T570) (fig. 4.5a), and a skull (T1045) (fig. 4.5c). The species of the bird has not been identified but it appears in full-figured variant in the Palace Tablet at C6 (fig. 4.5b). The T570 bone variant is best seen in the Jonuta Tablet where the upper and lower circular elements are carved in relief, indicating that they are negatives. The death associations of the bone as an EG main sign have been pointed out by Coe (1975a).

The skull variant is the most important EG for the discussion in this paper. The EGs of Palenque occur in the known tablets ninety-six times, of which 23 percent of the occurrences are the bird variant and 38.5 percent each are the bone and skull variants. There is no presently discernible pattern in the occurrences of the vari-ants, but if frequency is important, 77 percent of the known EGs are the bone or skull variants. The skull used in the EG is subject to a degree of variation in its de-tailing, but there are two characteristics that are consistently present. Normally, two prominent incisor teeth (fig. 4.6) appear at the front of the upper jaw, although in the examples from the Tablet of the 96 Glyphs (fig. 4.7a) and TI II (fig. 4.7c) the teeth are missing. Second, a long vertical element always appears at the rear of the head with round shapes infixed. In most cases one or more of the infixed shapes are crossed hatched, indicating black. These spots are like those elements Coe (1975a) has termed death spots and were used to indicate that the object por-trayed is dead, or in the underworld. Their presence in the EG skull indicates a state of death for the animal, reinforcing the meaning of skull as a death sign.

The question remains of why the Palencano scribes felt obligated to place death spots, a sign of putrifying flesh, on an object which was already in a skeletal state. I believe the death spots were necessary because the object is an ear, which would normally not be present on a skull. The death spots were used to show that, while it was necessary to portray the ear of the animal, it was equally imperative to show that the ear had also succumbed to the effects of death. If such is the case, the ear was of primary importance to the identification of the species and the species of the animal was vital to the specific meaning of the EG.

The ear is long and limp and hangs along the side of the head. Two animals appear in Maya glyphs and iconography repeatedly with this kind of ear—the deer and the rabbit. The confirmation of the deer and its mythological meaning is to be found in T765d, a glyph frequently found at Palenque and other sites as a substi-tute for the *kin* glyph in distance numbers (fig. 4.7a–c). To my knowledge the spe-cific animal of the distance number glyph has not been identified to date, but an extraordinarily clear example of it found on a stone fragment in the Palenque Bodega in 1974 (fig. 4.7a) has allowed the identification of the animal. The animal in this glyph has a long sloping nose and crossed bones in the eye. The critical element is the trilobed element at the forehead, which can be identified as a horn by comparing it to the crouching deer below the right figures in the Tablet of the Slaves (fig. 4.8d). The brocket deer, indigenous to the Palenque area and Yuca-tan, has very short horns similar to the horn of the glyphic deer. The *kin* animal is a deer. Because it substitutes for the *kin* glyph, the deer, especially when it appears

a. T570   b. T793a   c. T1045

4.5. *The emblem glyphs of Palenque.*

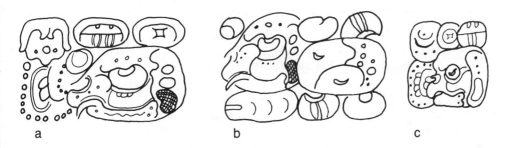

fleshed rabbit,
Pal. Tab. P3

4.6. *The rabbit skull variant of the T1045 emblem glyph.*

a   b   c

4.7. *The deer skull variant of the T1045 emblem glyph and a title.*

with the crossed-bones element, is the sun. Thompson (1950, 1967) points out the rich Maya data associating the deer with the sun (fig. 4.8).

The second animal frequently appearing with a long downturned ear is the rabbit. The square format of the glyph block caused the scribes at Palenque to vary the position of the rabbit's ear according to the imperatives of available space. A beautiful rabbit appears at P3 in the Palace Tablet with a long downturned ear identical to the skull of the emblem glyph (see fig. 4.6). The long incisor teeth of the rabbit appear as prominent characteristics of the skull (fig. 4.10).

Nicholson (1971, p. 402) shows the Mexican association of the rabbit with the moon, especially in the story of the conflict upon the creation of the sun and the moon who were of rival brilliance. In a fit of jealousy a rabbit was thrown in the face of the moon, forever dimming and engraving the outline of the unfortunate rabbit

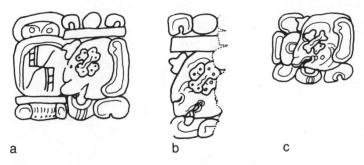

a   b   c

distance number *kin* head variant

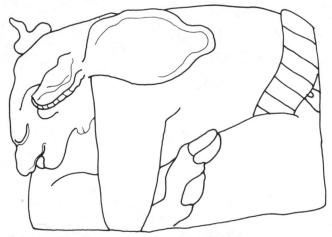

d. deer bearer from the Tablet of the Slaves

4.8. *The deer as a head variant of* kin *in distance numbers.*

on its face. The shape of the rabbit is very obvious even to western eyes in the dark area of the moon.

Three objects for the Late Classic period confirm the association of the moon and the rabbit in Maya thought. In February 1975, Jeff Miller sent me a drawing of an eccentric flint from the Museo Nacional de Guatemala (fig. 4.9*b*). The flint has an incised drawing of a three-quarter moon in which sits the moon goddess holding a rabbit. The same composition is repeated in Bonampak Altar II in which the lunar *u* nearly closes a circle. Within the moon sign sits a deity with confused characteristics. It may in fact be the moon goddess, but the identification is too uncertain at present. A rabbit is held in the deity's arms (fig. 4.9*c*).

The final example of the moon and rabbit appears at D5 in the Tablet of the 96 Glyphs (fig. 4.9*a*) in an example of the humor of the Maya scribes at Palenque. The entire glyph block is the seating compound for the accession of Lord Hok. The compound is transcribed as T644a:140.181. The T181 lunar postfix was recorded by Landa as the phoneme *ah* and is accepted by Lounsbury and Kelley (personal communication) as the past tense suffix for the verb, which is read as *culah*, "was

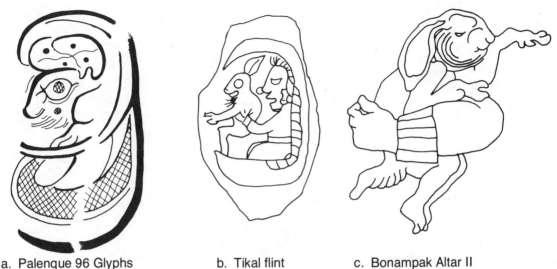

a. Palenque 96 Glyphs   b. Tikal flint   c. Bonampak Altar II

4.9. *The moon and the rabbit.*

seated." A delightful rabbit head with its ear flipped over its head is infixed into the negative of the lunar postfix. The rabbit has absolutely no morphemic or phonemic function in the glyph compound and indeed, to my knowledge, a similar configuration does not occur anywhere else in Maya writing. I believe the rabbit in this instance is an example of the play on meaning by the scribe. The moon has a rabbit engraved on its face in reality, so it was put in the postfix which was the moon graphemically but not morphemically.

The ear with the death spots becomes understandable when the two possible species of the skull are identified. One of the most obvious characteristics of the deer and rabbit is the ear. The skull without the ear is not identifiable glyphically. Even the incisor teeth of the rabbit are shared by rodent species. The ear ensures the identification of rabbit and deer and, I believe, the secondary meaning of each species, the moon and sun.

Thompson (1967) recorded a number of myths from various Maya groups which include a pan-Maya belief in the moon and sun as twins. The myth of the twins is variable in its identification of the twins as moon and sun or Venus and sun. The deer and rabbit are associated similarly as twins throughout Mesoamerica. Peter Furst has related a number of Huichol stories about the adventures of the twins, Rabbit and Deer. The animals are quite different in scale but otherwise remarkably similar in form. Both have long, floppy ears and short active tails, and the forms of their mouths are similar. Significantly, the excrement of both animals looks almost exactly the same, except for size.

The rabbit is certainly identified as one of the EG skulls by the presence of the typical incisor teeth, but in the case of the EG variant from the Tablet of the 96 Glyphs and the TI II, the teeth are missing. Significantly, the deer lacks teeth in the front upper part of his mouth, making the presence or lack of teeth a critical identifying element to the specific animal (fig. 4.10). A characteristic of such impor-

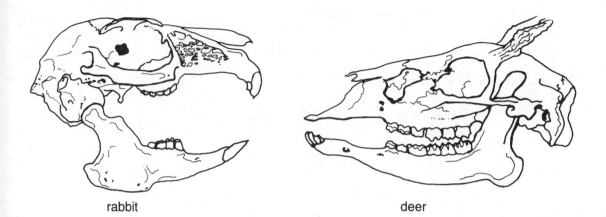

rabbit   deer

4.10. *Skull configurations of the rabbit and deer.*

tance is not likely to have been ignored by the scribes. Furthermore, a slight knob occurs on the forehead of all of the 96 Glyphs EGs, but is absent from all but one of the EGs with incisors. I believe the knob represents the horn of the brocket deer and was used to ensure the differentiation of the deer from the rabbit.

The skull variant EG thus can be paraphrased "the place of the dead rabbit" and ". . . deer" and by extension "the place of the dead moon" and ". . . sun." It is exactly this meaning which is detailed as the principal power and responsibility of the ruler of Palenque in the TC and tomb-lid tablets. The precise pattern of the physical configuration of the city was carefully designed to produce repeatedly spectacular hierophanies to expound cosmologically the same definitions. The Palencanos called their city the "place of the death of the sun and moon" and they arranged their architecture so that the sun and moon literally did what they said.

In conclusion, the interpretation of the skull variant EG of Palenque as a dead rabbit and deer or the dead moon and sun is supported by the picture of the power and responsibility of rulership that the Palencano Maya structured for themselves and left as witness to their beliefs. The patterns of stones, of buildings, of space, of the physical experience of human beings, and of the universe were designed to reproduce the definitions contained in names and myths. The detailed interrelationship of the name, the mythology, and the physical identity of the city in cosmological terms strongly suggests that the skull variant EG of Palenque was the name of the place and not the lineage so far as the lineage can be defined as a thing separate from the place. The place of Palenque seems to have been defined in terms of Late Classic Maya geography and cosmology as the western portal of the underworld, where the sun, the moon, and the cyclic gods died.

Maya Astronomical Tables and Inscriptions

David H. Kelley

Although I do not believe that more than about a tenth of the Maya glyphs can yet be read with any assurance, we are beginning to understand the general tenor of many formerly obscure texts. Astronomically, the emergent picture suggests that the Maya rulers consciously and directly linked events of their own lives with eclipses and planetary movements. Personal astrology, in the strictest sense of the word, played a crucial role in what was inscribed on the mountains. At Palenque, Pacal's great inscription links his own reign with the accession of a ruler who was probably a planetary god nearly a million and a quarter years earlier. The problems posed by our limited understanding of the glyphs are well illustrated by the name glyphs of his son and successor. The most constant of these is the head of an animal which combines the characteristics of a snake and a jaguar. For this reason, Kubler called him Snake Jaguar and the scholars at the first Palenque Mesa Redonda agreed to call him Chan Bahlum, a Chol translation of Snake Jaguar. A frequently occurring alternate name for him is an Ahau glyph, partially covered by irregular spots of the kind used to represent a jaguar skin, preceded by a bone glyph. Spinden (1924, pp. 151–152) pointed out the apparent substitution of this glyph in a text at Palenque for a half-darkened *kin* glyph. *Kin* means 'sun' or 'day', and Ahau, 'lord', has usually been recognized as a title for the Sun God. Spinden went on to suggest that this half-darkened sun or Ahau meant 'equinox'. I recently made the alternate suggestion (Kelley and Kerr 1973, pp. 190–191) that the half-darkened *kin* was an eclipse glyph, and in my preliminary studies of the correlation of glyphs with astronomical events, I innocently attempted to link various dates in the life of Chan Bahlum with eclipses simply because the dates were associated with the covered-Ahau glyph, which I did not recognize as a name glyph until it was demonstrated to me by Linda Schele and Peter Mathews. I would now read the prefix as *bac*, which is a general Mayan word for 'bone' and which I would read in this context as the homonym *bac*, known from Yucatec as a word for child. The general interpretation derives from an idea of Linda Schele. I believe that the jaguar skin here represents the root *bal*, 'hide' (cf. *balam*, 'jaguar') and that the name is to be read as "Child of the Hidden Lord" (i.e., of the Eclipsed Sun). This interpretation, in turn, derives partly from the fact, which Floyd Lounsbury pointed out to me, that the date of Chan Bahlum's birth, in the 584,283 or revised Thompson correlation, preceded an eclipse syzygy by three days, although this was not an eclipse visible in Mesoamerica. Naturally, some other correlations which put the base of the Dresden Codex lunar table at or near an eclipse will also make Chan Bahlum's birth at or near an eclipse syzygy. Thus, the Makemson correlation puts his birth the day before an eclipse visible across central Africa, and the Dittrich correlation puts it seven days before an eclipse equally invisible in Mesoamerica. Recognition of the same glyph allows us to associate the glyph with the one really relevant date (with which it does not occur) and to exclude the many other dates with which the glyph does occur.

I am going to try to demonstrate how such inscriptional evidence as that referring to the birth of Chan Bahlum may be correlated with the lunar and Venus tables of the Dresden Codex. Although the general structure of these tables has long been recognized, only Spinden (1928, 1930) has formally attempted to match information from the tables with inscriptional evidence, and he did so in terms of his own correlation. Figure 5.1 shows a number of inscriptions whose dates tie them to specific positions of the Dresden Venus table. The Venus table is found on pages 46–50 of the Dresden (directly following a preamble on page 24 in the original which should have been paginated successively). The preamble gives a brief text, some dates, and a multiplication table for use with the main table. The latter is divided into five sequent sections, with dates, intervals, and running totals. Each page totals 584 days, divided in 236, 90, 250, and 8 days, in three parallel sets of dates. The five pages together total 2,920 days (which equals both 5 × 584 and 8 × 365). Since the true average length of a Venus synodic period is now calculated at 583.92166, the interval of 584 days is by far the best possible whole-day approximation. Since the actual interval varies from 579.6 to 588.1 within each eight-year period but averages out over that period, the figures must be considered a table of mean motion. The early colonial literature indicates that Venus was supposed by the Mesoamericans to disappear for eight days at inferior conjunction and it has generally been supposed that the 90-day period indicates a comparable period of invisibility at superior conjunction, with a not quite symmetrical distribution of the intervening periods of visibility. However, 90 days is unrealistically long for invisibility at superior conjunction and the probability is high that this period has other properties, not yet recognized, in which the Mayas were interested.

The structure of the table proper may be seen most easily and clearly in Thompson (1950, p. 222; 1972, p. 66) and the structure of the preamble is shown by Spinden (1930, p. 89). By repeating the day names with their 13 numbers in each of the possible year positions, a longer cycle of 13 × 2,920 is created. This is 37,960 days or 104 years of 365 days each. Over this period of 65 Venus cycles, the table will accumulate an error of 5.20 days. It is generally believed that variations in the table of multiples in the preamble may be connected with corrections. The table is divided horizontally into three sets of month names and it has been suggested that shifts from one set of these to another were a means of making corrections.

The base of the table is a day (1) Ahau, associated in the top line with a date 13 Mac, in the middle line with a date 18 Kayab, and in the bottom line with a date 3 Xul. The preamble to the table gives the date 9.9.9.16.0 1 Ahau 18 Kayab, counted over a period of 1,364,360 days from 12.19.13.16.0 1 Ahau 18 Kayab, 2,200 days before 4 Ahau 8 Cumku. This is the only clear suggestion of the position of any of the base dates. Given the structure of the table, it was early assumed that the date 9.9.9.16.0 1 Ahau 18 Kayab should be placed in real time about 4 days after an inferior conjunction of Venus and the sun. Investigating this, Dittrich (1936) found that the only occurrence which would fit the colonial and modern evidence for the 52-year cycle was Julian Day 2062524 or 2062525, 24 or 25 November 934 A.D. (Gregorian) or 20 or 21 November (Julian). His correlation simply identifies this date as 9.9.9.16.0 of the Maya era. Other correlations have involved either rejection of the evidence for the 52-year cycle or denial of its applicability to the Classic period (as in Smiley's correlation) or placement of 1 Ahau 18 Kayab at a different point in the Long Count, due to some sort of correction. Thus, Spinden (1928, p. 15) put 1 Ahau 18 Kayab at 10.18.9.15.0 which, in his correlation, is 20 November 934 (Julian). Thompson (1972, p. 63) puts it at 10.10.11.12.0 which, in his correlation, is the heliacal rising of October 1038, one cycle of 104 years after the one accepted by Dittrich and Spinden.

I think we must accept that one of the three intended table bases is either 9.9.9.16.0 1 Ahau 18 Kayab or, just possibly, 12.19.13.16.0 1 Ahau 18 Kayab. The nearest possible occurrence of any day 1 Ahau 3 Xul to any day 1 Ahau 18 Kayab is 9,360 days earlier and the first occurrence of a day 1 Ahau 13 Mac after a day 1 Ahau 18 Kayab is 11,960 days later. Since 54 eclipse seasons are 9,358.60 days and 317 lunations average 9,361.20 days, the interval of 9,360 is, on the average, one day off from a very good eclipse interval. The interval of 11,960 days is the length of the eclipse table proper, to be discussed shortly. Over the combined interval of 21,320 days, the lunation error is slightly reduced and the error on node passage is increased to 3 days. These intervals will, of course, apply to all the dates in the three lines. If any date in the bottom line is an eclipse, there would be a good chance that an eclipse would occur at the date above it in the middle line and also a good chance that there would be a third eclipse in the top line. If these are the correct placements of the three lines, then only one of the three can actually refer to a normal pattern of Venus movements, if, indeed, any of them do. Accepting the vertical interval between the bottom and middle rows as 9,360 days, this is 16 days more than 16 Venus revolutions. The interval between the middle and top rows, 11,960 days, is 280 days over 20 Venus rounds, so that the whole interval is 296 days more than 36 Venus rounds. This is 4 days more than half a Venus revolution. The effect of this is that the top and bottom rows differ by 52 years and 4 days. Put differently, a date in the bottom row which is a standard Venus interval from 1 Ahau 3 Xul will be followed after 4 days by a date which is 292 days after a standard Venus interval from 1 Ahau 13 Mac. The relationship to the middle line is such that a "standard" heliacal rising position of the 3 Xul line (at 19 Kayab, 13

Yax, 7 Zip, 6 Kankin, and 0 Yaxkin) precedes by 364 days a "standard" heliacal rising position of the 18 Kayab line (at 18 Kayab, 12 Yax, 6 Zip, 5 Kankin, and 19 Xul). The calculating uses of this device, though not entirely clear, are much more obvious than any observational pattern.

The accompanying figures 5.1–5.4 strongly suggest that observations were formulated in terms of patterns which approximate those of the Dresden Venus table in some way which utilized all three table bases concurrently rather than as successive corrections, as has usually been supposed. Before considering the inscriptional material, the interpretation of the Dresden lunar table must also be examined. It is generally believed that the lunar table is a table of lunar months arranged to mark intervals between 69 successive solar eclipse syzygies, most of which would not have been locally visible. Smiley regards it as a Solar Eclipse Warning Table marking new moons which will be followed after either one or two lunar months by an eclipse (see especially Smiley 1975) and Owen (1975) regards the eclipses as lunar. Just prior to the table proper are four dates, in two columns. The first column has one date, incorrect as it stands and with no generally accepted correction, and another which is 9.16.4.11.18 3 Etz'nab 11 Pax. The second column contains the dates 9.16.4.10.8 12 Lamat 1 Muan (in black) and 9.16.4.11.3 1 Akbal 16 Muan (interwritten in red). It will be seen that 12 Lamat is followed in 15 days by 1 Akbal and in another 15 days by 3 Etz'nab. The table then starts by counting forward 177 days to the successive days 6 Kan, 7 Chicchan, and 8 Cimi. Subtracting 177 days from these takes us back to 11 Manik, 12 Lamat, and 13 Muluc. It seems to me most unlikely that this 12 Lamat is anything but the recorded 9.16.4.10.8 12 Lamat 1 Muan in the preceding column. The table then continues forward by intervals of 177, 178, or 148 days. The 148-day intervals precede pictures which interrupt the text and which seem to refer to both solar and lunar eclipses. From the position of these intervals, Teeple (1930) worked out the positions of draconitic node passage and concluded that the base of the table was probably a day 11 Manik at node passage. Since the date 9.16.4.10.8 12 Lamat 1 Muan (the day after 11 Manik) was an eclipse syzygy in the Thompson correlation but was about as far as possible before a node passage, Teeple concluded that the 12 Lamat table base was *not* the immediately preceding 12 Lamat date. Later, Makemson (1943, p. 189) suggested that the three dates were a lunar eclipse between two solar eclipses (one of which would be locally invisible, if not both). This would necessarily mean that the node passage was near the middle date, 9.16.4.11.3 1 Akbal 16 Muan, and that that date should be a lunar eclipse. The unrevised Thompson correlation (584,285) makes this date the equivalent of Julian Day number 1997148, 23 November A.D. 755 of the Julian calendar, which was the date of a lunar eclipse.

It seems to me utterly contrary to Maya writing practices to accept the separation between the date and the accompanying table which is demanded by the Makemson and Teeple suggestions. If Teeple's location of the node passage position is correct, then the Thompson correlation must be incorrect. If the Thompson correlation is correct, then Teeple's seemingly lucid demonstration that node passage was at 11 Manik of table base must be rejected. Owen (1975) offers one possible alternate explanation but, since this makes 9.16.4.10.8 a full moon rather than a new moon, it cannot be adapted in any way to the Thompson correlation. In this particular, the Thompson correlation fares better than hers, for the Maya inscriptions count the days of the lunar month from a base marked either by a hand (probably to be read *lah* 'end' and referring to disappearance before conjunction) or by a frog-head glyph which is almost certainly to be read *pok* 'be born' and which refers to the first appearance of heavenly bodies after conjunction, hence, in this case, to new moon. The date 9.16.4.10.8 12 Lamat 1 Muan can be calculated from dated inscriptions as corresponding approximately to this "end/be born" interval which seems in flat contradiction to the Owen view.

Strangely, no one seems previously to have calculated the Long Count positions of the eclipse table dates on the straightforward presumption that they were counted from 9.16.4.10.8. When this is done, some dates in the table also appear in the inscriptions, and one also finds a surprising degree of approximations to positions in the Venus table. These are shown in table 5.1, which lists the middle date of the three successive days given by the Dresden eclipse table. Thus, for the eighteenth eclipse, the Dresden shows 8 Caban, 9 Etz'nab, 10 Cauac; counted from 9.16.4.10.8, they would be 9.16.13.4.17 8 Caban 5 Yaxkin, 9.16.13.4.18 9 Etz'nab 6 Yaxkin, and 9.16.13.4.19 10 Cauac 7 Yaxkin. The first of these days appears as the Initial Series of Stela D at Quirigua, where it is the second katun anniversary of 9.14.13.4.17 12 Caban 5 Kayab. At first sight, this suggests that the coincidence of the Stela D date with the Dresden eclipse table is entirely accidental. However, two katuns is close to an eclipse interval and, if 9.16.4.10.7 was at node passage, then node passage would have occurred at about full moon, five days after 9.14.13.4.17 and this full moon would have had to be eclipsed. I have previously suggested that this date was the birth date of a ruler whose name glyphs include the smoke prefix, the *haab* or Cauac glyph, the sky glyph, and two appendages, interpreted by Thompson (1950, fig. 2, pp. 47–49) as inverted legs although they look at least as much like upraised arms. He called the glyph "two-legged sky," which I adopted as a mnemonic name for this ruler (Kelley 1962, p. 328). I had not then realized that the glyph block appearing on Quirigua Stela E, west, at A6 was either a G7 variant of the glyphs of the Nine Lords of the Night (as in Thompson 1950, fig. 34, no. 38) or another glyph replacing the G series. The drawing given by Thompson is markedly different from Annie Hunter's (Maudslay 1889–1902, 2: pl. 31), the latter showing the upturned arms or legs which appear in the "Two-legged Sky" glyph. Examination of photographs of the monument indicates that Annie Hunter is correct on this point and I think we may safely conclude that the glyph incorporates some astronomical event and that it was from this that "Two-legged Sky" took his name. I have previously argued that G7 corresponds to Saturn (Kelley 1972, p. 59), but these glyphs include none of the usual G7 glyphs and I think this may well be an inserted directly astronomical reference. The bottom glyph of this glyph block includes a crossed-band element. Although I cannot demonstrate this, I suspect that these cross bands may refer here to the forthcoming lunar node passage.

The 8 Caban 5 Yaxkin date of Quirigua is only two days after the doubtfully read date 9.16.13.4.15 6 Men 3 Yaxkin on Stela N at Copan (Morley 1920, p. 286), which, in turn, is three days after 9.16.13.4.12 3 Eb 0 Yaxkin, a formal date of the

Table 5.1.
Interlocking Dates of the Eclipse Table and Venus Table

Number in table	Presumed eclipse syzygies (assuming 9.16.4.10.8 12 Lamat 1 Muan as table base)	Formal positions of the Venus table (assuming 9.8.3.16.0 1 Ahau 3 Xul, 9.9.9.16.0 1 Ahau 18 Kayab, 9.11.3.2.0 1 Ahau 13 Mac)
0	9.16.4.10.8 12 Lamat 1 Muan	
		9.16.4.10.14 5 Ix 7 Muan (13 Mac)
		9.16.5.17.8 5 Lamat 11 Zip (13 Mac)
3	9.16.5.17.10 7 Oc 13 Zip	
8	9.16.8.7.16 9 Cib 9 Zac	9.16.8.7.16 9 Cib 9 Zac (18 Kayab)
		9.16.11.4.4 8 Kan 2 Kayab (3 Xul)
15	9.16.11.4.7 11 Manik 5 Kayab	
		9.16.13.4.12 3 Eb 0 Yaxkin (3 Xul)
18	9.16.13.4.18 9 Etz'nab 6 Yaxkin	
25	9.16.16.11.9 11 Muluc 2 Mac	
		9.16.16.11.12 1 Eb 5 Mac (13 Mac)
27	9.16.17.9.14 11 Ix 2 Zac	
		9.16.17.10.6 10 Cimi 14 Zac (13 Mac)
		9.16.19.17.18 11 Etz'nab 16 Cumku (3 Xul)
32	9.17.0.0.0 13 Ahau 18 Cumku	
		9.17.2.6.16 11 Cib 19 Xul (18 Kayab)
37	9.17.2.6.17 12 Caban 20 Xul (0 Yaxkin)	
		9.17.4.13.12 9 Eb 5 Mac (13 Mac)
42	9.17.4.13.13 10 Ben 6 Mac	
45	9.17.6.4.4 8 Kan 7 Zip	
		9.17.6.4.4 8 Kan 7 Zip (3 Xul)
		9.17.7.3.12 5 Eb 10 Uo (3 Xul)
47	9.17.7.3.18 11 Etz'nab 16 Uo	
		9.17.8.1.18 6 Etz'nab 16 Cumku (3 Xul)
49	9.17.8.2.3 11 Akbal 1 Uayeb	
52	9.17.9.10.15 11 Men 3 Ch'en	
		9.17.9.11.4 6 Kan 12 Ch'en (13 Mac)
		9.17.12.0.16 7 Cib 14 Pax (3 Xul)
57	9.17.12.1.0 11 Ahau 18 Pax	
		9.17.15.7.10 12 Oc 8 Zotz (13 Mac)
64	9.17.15.7.11 13 Chuen 9 Zotz	
		9.17.17.13.12 9 Eb 20 Ch'en (0 Yax) (13 Mac)
69	9.17.17.14.6 10 Cimi 14 Yax	

3 Xul section of the Dresden Venus table. Although I have found no clear glyphic indications of astronomical interest in this Stela N date, the fact that two monuments at different sites fall in the short interval between the formal Venus date and the formal eclipse date is suggestive of deliberate astronomical intent.

A widely marked date of the eclipse table is that of the thirty-second eclipse, 9.17.0.0.0 13 Ahau 18 Cumku, falling two days after 9.16.19.17.18 11 Etz'nab 16 Cumku, a formal position of the 3 Xul table of Venus. In the Thompson correlation (584,283), this was 11 days past a superior conjunction of Venus and the sun (at 289°, 5 January 771, Julian). In the 584,283 correlation, 9.17.0.0.0 was two days before an eclipse but coincided with the eclipse in the 584,285 correlation, as will be discussed at greater length in a forthcoming paper. Among the monuments marking this date is Temple 21a of Copan, with its repeated giant star glyphs which led Morley to name it the Temple of Venus. In the Spinden correlation, the date is within one day of inferior conjunction of Venus and the sun (at 6°, 25 March 511, Julian).

On Tortuguero Monument 6, we find the date 9.10.16.13.6 8 Cimi 9 Mol associated with the *batcah* (descent?) verb (Kelley and Kerr 1973, p. 192) and with a dotted circle containing a hand clasped on a cross band. The interval to 9.16.4.10.7, postulated as node passage, is 38,821. The half eclipse season is 173.31 and 224 times this is 38,821.44, so that both dates would be at node passage. Below the dotted circle-hand-cross-bars glyph appears the double Cauac glyph which I read *cuc*, 'cycle'. The dotted circle surrounding a circle is the glyph for the month Mol and the word *mol* includes the meanings 'join together, congregate'. In astronomical usage, I suspect that the dotted circle infixing another glyph is to be read as *mol*, with the technical meaning of conjunction, though perhaps used somewhat differently than by western astronomers.

The Hieroglyphic Stairway at Naranjo has on block 5 the date 9.10.10.0.0 13 Ahau 18 Kankin with the half-darkened sun glyph as G9 of the Lords of the Night and followed by a hand glyph with infixed cross bars. The hand is in a different position, which is probably significant. The interval from 9.10.10.0.0 to 9.10.16.13.6 is 2,426 days and 14 × 173.31 = 2,426.31. Hence, this date was also apparently within one day of node passage. It is about 7 days after a new moon which should have been a solar eclipse and about 8 days before a new moon which should have been a lunar eclipse. Despite the suggestive appearance of the half-darkened sun in this variant of G9, other occurrences of a darkened or partially darkened sun glyph as G9 do not fit any presently discernible eclipse pattern.

The crossed bands also occur, in the same passage with a knife and shield combination (also found on Tortuguero Mon. 6), on Stela 23 at Naranjo at the date 9.13.19.6.3 3 Akbal 16 Zip. This date was about 7 days after node passage and had an average lunar age 15 days greater than 9.16.4.10.8; hence, it was probably a full moon and a lunar eclipse. Although the date is not that of node passage, a reference to node passage in an eclipse context seems to me entirely reasonable.

Figure 5.1 shows still another occurrence of the cross bands, here with a smoke prefix, on the Hieroglyphic Stairway at Naranjo (block 6) at 9.9.17.16.3 7 Akbal 16 Muan and at the same date on Caracol Stela 3. The interval between 9.9.18.16.3 and 9.10.16.13.6 is 6,423 days which is (37 × 173.31) + 11.53 days;

10.19.14.17.0
6 Ahau 18 Kayab

Dresden Codex Venus table positions from 9.9.9.16.0—standard parameters
236-90-250-8

9.9.9.16.0
1 Ahau 18 Kayab

9.9.18.16.3
7 Akbal 16 Muan

9.9.18.16.6
10 Cimi 19 Muan

Caracol St. 3

Naranjo hieroglyphic stairway

9.10.16.13.6
8 Cimi 9 Mol

9.10.16.13.10
12 Oc 13 Mol

Tortuguero Mon. 6

Tortuguero Mon. 8

9.11.19.3.16
12 Cib 9 Zac

9.11.19.4.3
6 Akbal 16 Zac

Tikal bones text

9.14.0.0.0
6 Ahau 13 Muan

headdress, Tikal St. 16

Copan St. C

9.14.0.0.6
12 Cimi 19 Muan

9.15.4.6.4
8 Kan 17 Muan

Aguateca St. 2

Dos Pilas St. 16

9.15.4.6.6
10 Cimi 19 Muan

9.18.8.7.14
3 Ix 7 Pop

(9.18.8.7.16?)
5 Cib (9?) Pop

direction of reading

Copan TII, Ca3–Cb4

9.18.9.4.4
7 Kan 17 Muan

9.18.9.4.6
9 Cimi 19 Muan

Palenque Initial Series pot
forward was installed as ruler

Earth Star
(names or titles)

5.1. *Approximations to Dresden Codex Venus table positions in Maya inscriptions.*

that is, if node passage was at the second date, it would be 11 or 12 days after the first date. These two dates also bring us back to the Dresden Venus table, for 6,423 days is (11 × 584) − 1 and the dates approximate dates given in that table. No star glyph is found with the 8 Cimi 9 Mol date of Tortuguero Monument 6, but there is a count forward of 148 days to 9.10.17.2.14 13 Ix 17 Muan which is followed by a dotted star glyph combined with shell and earth (fig. 5.1). In my first attempts to relate glyph and dates, I assumed that the dotted-star, earth, shell should be associated with the latter date. However, this glyph block contains the affix T125 (probably equatable with T126) which normally appears indicating a reference to a previous event and seems to be roughly translatable as 'from'. In that case, the entire relevant passage might be approximately transcribed "148 days from [undeciphered] [to] 13 Ix 17 Muan, from 'dotted-star-earth-shell.'" This interpretation would associate "shell-star" with 8 Cimi 9 Mol rather than with the date which it directly follows and, on the sole basis of this monument, I would be inclined to regard it as the best explanation. However, Tortuguero Monument 8, in a drawing kindly supplied by Berthold Riese, shows the star-dot-earth compound, without the shell and without the "from" affix, associated with the date 13 Ix 17 Muan. This seems to put us back where we started. Until we have a much fuller understanding of such apparently minor affixes, we will continue to be plagued by difficulties of interpretation. In the present situation of rather fumbling attempts at decipherment, it seems desirable to note such alternative possibilities.

Panel 4 at Altar de Sacrificios (Graham 1972, p. 91) has a date 12 Ix 17 Muan which also includes star, earth, the dotted prefix, and the "from" affix. The date may be either 12 or 64 Maya years after 9.10.17.2.14 13 Ix 17 Muan which, in turn, is 18 Maya years and 1 day after the 9.9.18.16.3 7 Akbal 16 Muan date of Caracol and Naranjo. Since 64 Maya years are 23,360 days and equal 40 Venus rounds of 584 days, the latter seems the more likely placement. Unfortunately, this panel is badly broken and eroded. No other dates have been recognized on the existing fragment and only the suggested Venus round associations place it in the Long Count.

One hundred four years and 1 day after the 7 Akbal 16 Muan dates of Naranjo and Caracol, we reach 9.15.4.6.4 8 Kan 17 Muan on Aguateca Stela 2 and its close parallel, Dos Pilas Stela 16. The dotted star and shell are accompanied by glyphs which I read as *ti haabil cuc*, 'at the cycle of the year', presumably referring in some fashion to the 104-year double cycle in which the 365-day year and the 584-day Venus cycle come back together. Going forward another 64 years (of 365 days) (40 Venus cycles of 584 days) we reach the date 9.19.9.4.4 7 Kan 17 Muan of the Palenque Initial Series pot. The text seems to say that at that date an individual was installed as ruler (presumably of Palenque) and indicates that he was the son of an otherwise unknown Pacal (presumably named after the great Pacal). Among the associated glyphs are star and earth, preceded by what looks like the number 9. Judging by the parallel texts, however, it is more likely to be a stylized version of the dotted prefix. The glyph is apparently one of the names or titles of the ruler installed at that date. Whether he took the name at the time of his installation because of its association with that date or whether one of the reasons for selecting this installation date was that he already had the name must remain unclear as long as we do not have other texts. This date is associated with a date of the 819-day count, 9.18.7.10.13 1 Ben 11 Zotz', which is 591 days earlier, some 9 days before a standard position of the 18 Kayab table. In the Thompson correlation, this 1 Ben 11 Zotz' is 13 days after superior conjunction at the spring equinox of A.D. 798. In the Spinden correlation, it was 8 or 9 days after inferior conjunction of Venus and the sun, 4 June 538, Julian.

A most interesting inscription from Copan Temple 11 gives the "great star" combination, typical in the codices for Venus but very rare in the inscriptions, together with a hand-and-mirror glyph group which is the normal verb of the Dresden Venus table. The shell element, which forms part of the glyph for "south" in the inscriptions, is found in a position of the text which corresponds to a direction glyph in the Venus table of Dresden although it is not the normal "south" glyph and may be the shell of the "shell-star" combination. The remaining glyph is a deity head with a cross band on it, presumably corresponding to a deity name found at the equivalent place in the codex. This is associated with a date 5 Cib 10 Pop. We would normally expect 9 Pop; however, there is some evidence that days of the 260-day cycle began at a different time of day (sunset?) from days of the 365-day year (sunrise?), in which case it is possible that 10 Pop had already begun while it was still 5 Cib. The Long Count position of this date is not certain, but the most likely placement is at 9.18.8.7.16; in this position, it is 2 days after 9.18.8.7.14 3 Ix 7 Pop, which is in the 326-day age position from 1 Ahau 18 Kayab, like all but one of the dates in table 5.1. The date is (91 × 173.31) + 17.79 days after 9.16.4.10.7, at the outermost limit from node passage for a solar eclipse, so it remains very doubtful whether the cross bands in the deity head refer to node passage.

Figure 5.1 also includes an animal skull glyph from Copan Stela C associated with the date 9.14.0.0.0 6 Ahau 13 Muan. The same rare glyph appears on Tortuguero Monument 6 in connection with the date 8.15.16.0.5 11 Chicchan 13 Muan. This is precisely 359 Maya years earlier than the date on Stela C and would have involved a shift of a quarter of a tropical year. The same skull appears as the headdress of a ruler on Tikal Stela 16, dated 9.14.0.0.0, where it has a "star" glyph attached to it. On Copan Stela C, a calculation goes backward to 10.19.14.17.0 6 Ahau 18 Kayab. The accompanying text is generally obscure but includes a "star" glyph. This date precedes the 18 Kayab date of the Venus table of Dresden by 4,352 years of 365 days. As pointed out long since by Spinden (1924, pp. 174–175), this interval is within a day of recovering the same day of the tropical year. Since 1,508 years of 365 days (29 Calendar Rounds) are equal to 1,507 tropical years, the period is three times this and an additional 8 years. The period is also 2,832½ Venus rounds of 584 days. At 583.92166 days to an average synodic revolution, we would compute the error over this period at 221.898+ days, but we have no way of knowing at this time what the Maya calculation was.

The one date in table 5.1 which is not in the formal 326 position of the 1 Ahau 18 Kayab table is the Calendar Round date 6 Akbal 16 Zac. This occurs on engraved bones from Tikal, showing canoe scenes, and one of the canoes has a simplified form of the "star" glyph on it. The figures in the canoes are animal deities and a corn god but the accompanying text refers to a historic ruler of Tikal. Satterthwaite, in a privately circulated note, has suggested the date 9.11.19.4.3 6

Akbal 16 Zac. This is 7 days after 9.11.19.3.16 12 Cib 9 Zac, which is a day 236 from the 1 Ahau 18 Kayab base.

Figures 5.2–5.4 show other texts, many of which suggest glyphically an astronomical interest and some of which are in accord with standard positions of the Dresden Venus table. There are also some other dates which do not show glyphic evidence of astronomical interest but which fit this pattern. The Initial Series of Caracol Stela 3 is 9.6.12.4.16 5 Cib 14 Uo. This date is 56 × 584 days earlier than 9.11.3.2.0 Ahau 13 Mac. The same stela also contains the date 9.7.10.16.8 9 Lamat 16 Ch'en which is 8 × 584 days earlier than 9.8.3.16.0 1 Ahau 3 Xul, previously suggested as the base of the 3 Xul table. This same monument contains the date 9.9.18.16.3 7 Akbal 16 Muan, which approximates the position of a formal date of the 18 Kayab series. When a single monument contains dates which are congruent with all three rows of the Dresden Venus table, it seems to me highly likely that all three rows were being used concurrently in some fashion which we do not yet understand.

What is true of Caracol Stela 3 is equally true of Monument 6 at Tortuguero. Attention has already been drawn to the date 9.10.16.13.6 8 Cimi 9 Mol of this monument which is 4 days before a date of the 1 Ahau 18 Kayab table. The date 9.10.15.0.0 6 Ahau 13 Mac is 5 × 584 days before 9.11.3.2.0 1 Ahau 13 Mac, although, since this is a 15-tun ending, it is expectable as a chronological marker; unfortunately, the text is damaged at this point and we cannot tell whether there is any glyphic indication of astronomical interest. The text also refers to the date 9.10.15.1.11 11 Chuen 4 Muan which is (31 × 584) + 236 + 90 (+1) days after 9.8.3.16.0 1 Ahau 3 Xul and hence 1 day after the 326 position of the 3 Xul table. The date is accompanied by the phonetic glyphs *ka-m(a)* and a smoke glyph within a dotted circle. *Kam* in Yucatec is 'to receive or accept' and I have already suggested that the dotted circle is read *mol* and refers to conjunction, but the entire meaning is unclear.

Another important text which fits the 1 Ahau 13 Mac base is that from the middle tablet of the Temple of Inscriptions at Palenque at 9.12.0.0.0 10 Ahau 8 Yaxkin, which was the contemporary katun of the inscription. This date is 4 days after 9.11.19.17.16 6 Cib 4 Yaxkin, which is in the age 236 position of the Dresden 13 Mac table. It should be noted that the date 1.18.5.4.0 1 Ahau 13 Mac is the Initial Series of the Temple of the Foliated Cross at Palenque, earlier by 3,016 Maya years, by 1,895 cycles of 584 days, and by 3,014 tropical years. It should be noted that x Ahau 8 Ch'en dates of the 3 Xul table follow by 236 days x Kan 17 Muan, and that Aguateca Stela 2 actually counts forward 236 days from 9.15.4.6.4 8 Kan 17 Muan to 9.15.5.0.0 10 Ahau 8 Ch'en; this is in the wrong 52-year cycle for the previously suggested placement of 1 Ahau 3 Xul, but because the 13 Mac table differs by 52 years and 4 days from the 3 Xul table it is 4 days before 9.15.5.0.4 1 Kan 12 Ch'en in the 576 position of the 13 Mac table. Sculptured Panel 1 of Altar de Sacrificios contains the dates 9.10.0.6.13 4 Ben 16 Zec and 9.10.11.13.0 9 Ahau 8 Ch'en. The interval between the two dates is (7 × 584) − 1 and the text contains an unidentified glyph with a prefixed number 7. The second is a formal position of the 3 Xul table but in the wrong 52-year cycle. The 16 Zec date is 3 days before 7 Cib 19 Zec of the 13 Mac table, and the 8 Ch'en date is 4 days before 1

Kan 12 Ch'en. The date 9.10.0.6.13 4 Ben 16 Zec is also 44,714 days before 9.16.4.10.7 11 Manik 20 Kankin (0 Muan) of the eclipse table, which would put 4 Ben 16 Zec at node passage if 11 Manik 20 Kankin is there. Whether by coincidence or not, it is worth noting that, by our calculation, the true average age of Venus at 9.10.0.6.13 was 4 days greater than 13.0.0.0.0 4 Ahau 8 Cumku. The same panel contains an intermediate date, 9.10.3.17.0 4 Ahau 8 Muan, which is not a standard position of any of the rows of the Venus table and which has no obvious glyphic evidence of interest in Venus. It is, however, (67 × 584) + 5 days earlier than 9.15.12.11.13 7 Ben 1 Pop of Tikal Temple 4, Lintel 2, which does contain the dotted-star combination with what may be a shell glyph with an unusual infix replacing the normal spiral.

Still another date which approximates the 13 Mac table is the Initial Series of Stela 15 at Altar de Sacrificios which is 9.16.18.5.1 5 Imix 4 Xul and which precedes by 3 days 9.16.18.5.4 8 Kan 7 Xul in the 584/0 position of the 13 Mac table. This monument, unfortunately, is extremely eroded and contains no worthwhile detail for present purposes.

It is, of course, obvious that if all three Venus tables were being used concurrently, as I think, then not more than one of them could be in step with the phases of Venus. If the 18 Kayab table was approximately in step beginning from a rising after inferior conjunction, as is usually assumed, then the most important position was first appearance as evening star at day 326 of the table. Most puzzlingly, inscriptional dates approximate but do not coincide with this table. This might suggest variation in observation, but the approximations continue over 167 years and in that period the observations should show more variation than they do because of the fact that the synodic period of Venus is just slightly less than 584 days. The Thompson correlation puts most of the emphasized dates a relatively short time after superior conjunction when Venus would still have been invisible behind the sun, at a point which has no obvious real astronomical significance. The Spinden correlation fares substantially better, putting many important dates of the inscriptions shortly after Venus appeared as morning star, the date which we know was most important to other Mesoamerican groups. One possible glyphic clue is provided by the middle tablet of the Temple of Inscriptions at Palenque. The passage (given in fig. 5.2) contains 6 glyph blocks. Dotted-shell-star appears here followed by "eastward," then by *tzukin*, then by "westward," by *tzukin* again, and by a figure of a headless body found elsewhere in astronomical contexts. I think that the normal structure of the texts would suggest that shell-star is here assigned to the east, that *tzukin* is assigned to the west, and that something else is happening to *tzukin*. This is certainly incompatible with the 18 Kayab table base. It rather suggests the 3 Xul table, for the Dresden assigns 0 Yaxkin to the east, but it is the wrong 52-year cycle for this, in my interpretation. In the 13 Mac table, 4 Yaxkin is assigned to the north. It is possible, however, that these directional assignments are ritual rather than astronomical.

I think enough material has been presented to show that the astronomical tables were used in ways which are substantially more complex than has usually been realized and that it is by no means clear that the 18 Kayab base refers to a first appearance after heliacal rising as has always been assumed. The indications

1.18.5.4.0
1 Ahau 13 Mac
Palenque, Temple of the Foliated Cross

9.6.12.4.16
5 Cib 14 Uo

9.6.12.4.16
5 Cib 14 Uo

Caracol St. 3

9.10.0.6.13
4 Ben 16 Zec

9.10.0.6.16
7 Cib 19 Zec

9.10.11.13.0
9 Ahau 8 Ch'en

9.10.11.13.4
13 Kan 12 Ch'en

9.11.3.2.0
1 Ahau 13 Mac

9.11.19.17.16
6 Cib 4 Yaxkin

9.12.0.0.0
10 Ahau 8 Yaxkin

Palenque, Temple of Inscriptions, middle tablet

9.15.5.0.0
10 Ahau 8 Ch'en

9.15.5.0.4
1 Kan 12 Ch'en

Aguateca St. 2

9.16.18.5.1
5 Imix 4 Xul

9.16.18.5.4
8 Kan 7 Xul

Altar de Sacrificios St. 15 (very eroded)

9.17.10.6.0 2 Ahau 3 Zotz
(much farther from table base)

9.17.10.7.0
9 Ahau 3 Zec

9.17.10.7.16
12 Cib 19 Zec

Los Higos St. 1

Piedras Negras Throne 1

5.2. *Approximations to Dresden Codex Venus table positions in Maya inscriptions. Base 9.11.3.2.0 1 Ahau 13 Mac.*

are that Venus movements were somehow used in predicting eclipses. The importance of astronomy in Maya culture is indicated by astronomical dates picked for the inauguration of rulers, by extensive monuments giving astronomical information, by the use of astronomical events to give names to individuals, and by the wearing of headdresses which contain star glyphs. The observational basis behind all this astronomy remains very obscure, but Digby (1974) believes that the highland year glyph derives from an astronomical instrument. It is apparently the same or a related instrument which is worn by the ruler depicted on Aguateca Stela 2 and Dos Pilas Stela 16. These monuments, with their emphasis on the cycle of years and on Venus, offer strong support to Digby's interpretation and further evidence of the importance of astronomy to the Maya. It may be pointed out that they also suggest an interest in eclipses, for if 9.16.4.10.7 was at node passage, 9.15.4.6.8 would be at node passage and within a day or two of an average full moon. It would, therefore, be a lunar eclipse between two solar eclipses (with no way of knowing whether either of them was locally visible). The monuments mention the days 9.15.4.6.5 and 9.15.4.6.11 but not 9.15.4.6.8.

The relationships of the various astronomical texts in figures 5.3 and 5.4 are considerably more obscure. Star glyphs on five separate monuments at four dates in figure 5.3 are separated by near or exact multiples of Venus periods. Two of the monuments, Tortuguero Monument 6 and Caracol Stela 3, show other dates consistent with the Dresden Venus table, one of them being directly linked to 9.10.17.2.14 13 Ix 17 Muan by an interval of 148 days. Although the interval suggests an eclipse interest, it seems incompatible with the positioning of the 148-day periods in the Dresden eclipse table. The inscription from Copan Altar R relates to the inaugural date of a ruler who took the probably astronomical name of "New-sun-at-horizon." The combination of *mol* with Venus and moon glyphs suggests Venus in conjunction with some specified lunar position. The date is 17 days after draconitic node passage at the extreme limit for an eclipse, if the Dresden eclipse table is taken as it seems to be intended. It is 14 days after the middle line date of the sixteenth eclipse of the table, which means that it is near full moon. However, it is outside the limits for a lunar eclipse.

In figure 5.4, the star headdress worn by the ruler shown on Quirigua Altar L again emphasizes the interrelationship of man and stars. Here the Calendar Round date is not fixed in the Long Count in any certain way. The most likely date is at 9.10.0.11.11, the day before a standard date of the 3 Xul table of Dresden; the archaeological context suggests that this is an early monument at Quirigua. The 14 Zec date is one of five dates of astronomical interest at 13, 14, or 16 Zec, like the 13, 16, and 17 Muan dates of figures 5.1 and 5.2. However, there is no obvious astronomical patterning of these dates. We are still far from understanding much of what the Mayas wrote, but some patterns are beginning to emerge. Particular day names and months were important for astronomical recording even when they show no clear relationships to each other.

Taking all the information together, I think it is very likely that the dates given as Initial Series in connection with the eclipse and Venus tables of Dresden reflect calculations, observations, and recording practices of the Classic period rather than later back-calculations. I think it is likely that 9.16.4.10.7 was a node passage

9.9.9.10.5
3 Chicchan 3 Ceh
(115 days before 9.9.9.16.0
1 Ahau 18 Kayab)

(17 × 584) + 1

Caracol St. 3

9.10.17.2.14
13 Ix 17 Muan
(148 days after
9.10.16.13.10
of fig. 5.1 from
Tortuguero Mon. 6)

(40 × 584)

Tortuguero Mon. 8   Tortuguero Mon. 6

(9.14.2.0.14)
12 Ix 17 Muan

(31 × 584) − 1

Altar de Sacrificios Sculptured Panel 4

9.16.12.5.17
6 Caban 10 Mol

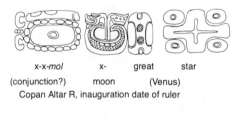

x-x-*mol*	x-	great	star
(conjunction?)		moon	(Venus)

Copan Altar R, inauguration date of ruler

9.10.3.17.0
4 Ahau 8 Muan

(67 × 584) + 5

Altar de Sacrificios Sculptured Panel 1 (no glyphic evidence of known astronomical import)

9.15.12.11.13
7 Ben 1 Pop

shell (?)
star, earplug
Tikal Temple 4, Lintel 2

(new verb?)

5.3. *Dates with apparent Venus interest, relationship to other tables unclear.*

(13.0.0.0.0)
4 Ahau 8 Cumku

Earth Star
Pot of the Seven Gods

9.7.10.16.8
9 Lamat 16 Ch'en   Caracol St. 3

9.8.3.16.0
1 Ahau 3 Xul   suggested base of 3 Xul table of Dresden
      15
9.10.15.1.10
10 Oc 3 Muan   9.10.15.1.1
                      11 Chuen 4 Muan

Tortuguero Mon. 6

                      9 Chuen 14 Zec
9.11.0.11.12   (9.10.0.11.11 or
10 Eb 15 Zec   9.16.6.1.10 of 3 Xul table)
                      or (9.13.13.6.11 or
                         9.18.18.14.11 of 13 Mac table)

                      Quirigua Altar L
                      star headdress
                      of ruler

9.10.11.9.6
13 Cimi 14 Zec

Tortuguero Mon. 6

9.16.4.1.1
7 Imix 14 Zec

Yaxchilan Lintel 41

9.15.12.2.2
11 Ik 15 Ch'en

Tikal Temple 4, Lintel 3

9.16.0.0.0
2 Ahau 13 Zec, believed dedicatory date of Tikal Temple 4, Lintel 3

Naranjo hieroglyphic stair

ruler of Tikal wearing
animal-skull-star headdress,
Tikal Temple 4, Lintel 3

5.4. *Miscellaneous monuments with star glyphs.*

date and would be inclined to guess that 9.9.18.16.3 7 Akbal 16 Muan was a helia-cal rising of Venus as morning star, but I think that there are too many alternate possibilities to be very sure of this. Our constantly improving understanding of the glyphs is already eliminating many previous anomalous interpretations.

Acknowledgments

Much of the alignment of dates in this paper was greatly facilitated by a computer program written by K. Ann Kerr and supported by the Canada Council, to whom I am greatly indebted. I also owe thanks to many of my colleagues in Mayan studies for access to unpublished drawings and photographs, in particular to Ian Graham and Berthold Riese for materials from Tortuguero, to Linton Satterthwaite and Wil-liam Coe for a drawing of Caracol Stela 3, to the Denver Museum of Natural His-tory for access to that monument to examine some glyphs more carefully, and to Peter Mathews for copying and recopying glyphs at various stages of work. The relevance of some of the material was first drawn to my attention by Michael Closs, who also saved me from a couple of careless slips. I also owe thanks to the Ameri-can Philosophical Society, which supported my preliminary work on this subject.

6

Current Astronomical Practices among the Maya

Judith A. Remington

Introduction

The importance of divinatory time-counting in ancient Mesoamerica has long been recognized (Thompson 1950, pp. 66–103). The fact that ten of the seventeen relatively complete surviving pre-Hispanic codices are calendrical astronomical (Peterson 1959, pp. 237–239) indicates that the cultural importance of this and associated concepts may not have been sufficiently stressed by modern investigators. Indeed, a world view based on a set of calendrical-astrological-astronomical premises seems indicated for Mesoamerica. Spanish chroniclers at the time of the conquest, such as Sahagun (1938) and Landa (Tozzer 1941), can be used to help explain these premises, but only if the assumptions upon which they were based are known.

At present the data are inadequate to deduce the basic assumptions of the astronomical approaches of the ancient Mesoamericans. Without this information, it is difficult to determine whether or not seemingly related events are, in fact, co-incidences. Thus, individuals presently studying the astronomical-calendrical implications of the codices, the artifacts, the architecture, and even the social organization of the ancient Mesoamericans are severely handicapped.

Few systematic efforts to recover astronomical data from the descendants of the ancients have been made. In an attempt to discover if survivals of non-Western cosmological assumptions, practices, and beliefs could be found, I spent three months during the late spring and early summer of 1974 in highland Guatemala among Cakchiquel and Quiche speakers. My particular point of departure was cosmology, but in Mesoamerican culture this is an extremely inclusive term. It includes astronomy, astrology, spirits, the gods, animals, humans, and the works of all of these. I had intended to limit myself to astronomy, but I found that the interest implied a form of shamanism; this required that it all be taken as a whole.

My approach was essentially exploratory. Preliminary work had exhausted the available sources written soon after the conquest; ethnohistoric sources written much later than A.D. 1600 were found to be inconsistent, bad copies of earlier misconceptions. The alternative was to go ask somebody.

Several considerations led to the choice of the Quiche language group as the focus. In the first place, Guatemala has placed less emphasis than Mexico on absorbing the Indians into Western culture; this seemed to increase the possibility of finding non-Western concepts. In the second place, the Cakchiquel and Quiche written histories demonstrated their membership in the high culture. Their histories state that they were participants in the Early Postclassic migrations; this in turn suggests that they may be the inheritors of Classic ideas. Third, there are a great many Quiche speakers; this increases the probability of preserving a cultural heritage. Finally, the Cakchiquel and Quiche towns near Lake Atitlan, Quezaltenango, and Antigua are relatively accessible.

The central highlands of Guatemala are populated by Maya speakers of Quiche, Cakchiquel, Tzutuhil, Rabinal, and Uspantec. As of 1961, a total of 537,434 Quichean speakers were in the midwest highlands (Whetten 1961, p. 23). Large numbers of Quiche and Cakchiquel speakers, as well as the total population of Rabinal and Uspantec speakers, are found to the east and north of this region. The two villages where I received most of my information were at the extremes of these areas. The Cakchiquel community, in the department of Guatemala, is at the northeasternmost extension of the region of Cakchiquel speakers. The Quiche community, in the department of Quezaltenango, is at the westernmost extension of the region of Quiche speakers.

Although I was looking for astronomical-astrological-cosmological data in both towns, the bulk of the astronomical-astrological data came from the Quiche community and the bulk of the astronomical-cosmological data came from the Cakchiquel community. The data presented in this paper are limited to those which fall into the Western cognitive category of astronomy.

Time

260-day Calendar

The 260-day calendar, *cholquih* according to Recinos and Goetz (1953, p. 28), is the *tzolkin* of the Yucatec Maya, the *tonalpohualli* of the Mexicans. A repeating sequence of twenty named days is combined with a repeating sequence of the numbers from one to thirteen. The calendar is used for divination. Only the Quiche informants gave information about the divining calendar. Although the names of the days are general information, the order of the days and the name of the current day are not. Specific knowledge of the calendar is the property of the shaman.

The days given correspond with one exception to those listed by Thompson for the Quiche (1950, p. 68), with two exceptions to those given by Recinos and Goetz for the Cakchiquel (1953, p. 29), and with four exceptions to those given by Caso for Quichean (1967, pp. 8–15). The meanings of the names of the days have been discussed by Thompson (1950, pp. 68–88) and Caso (1967, pp. 8–15) in great detail. Recinos and Goetz (1953, p. 29) give glosses which are close to what I was given. In most cases, however, the meaning of the name is not directly relevant to the divinatory meaning of the day even though it may have been in the past.

Each day has two divinatory meanings. The first meaning is more or less astrological, in that it refers to the characteristics of individuals born on that day. The second meaning is more properly divinatory, in that it refers to the kinds of things which are appropriate to that day.

365-day Calendar

Neither the Cakchiquel nor the Quiche informants gave any information about the old 365-day calendar (Yucatec *haab*) or the old 400-day calendar of the Quicheans. The Gregorian calendar is used exclusively.

Seasons

Maya winter (rainy season) changes to Maya summer (dry season) when the nights begin to be long and the days begin to be short. Conversely, Maya summer changes to Maya winter when the nights begin to be short and the days begin to be long. This is the reverse of the Western definition of winter and summer. The two times of the year when the sun is directly overhead are also important; this event is perceived as lasting a day and a night. The midpoint of the year is said to be August 20, the end of the general growing season.

Orientation in Space

Directions

The Cakchiquel informants gave the directions in Castellano (Latin American Spanish), but the Quiche informants had indigenous terms; south and north are both known as *k 'e lik* ('to the side'), east is called *axix* ('above'), and west is called *ikem* ('below').

Celestial Paths

Two maps (figs. 6.1 and 6.2) were traced from free-hand drawings made by a Cakchiquel informant; other informants checked the drawings and agreed to the accuracy. It can be seen that east is drawn as the base of the maps; astronomic north and south seem to be skewed toward the east.

Certain relationships were suggested by the figures and were confirmed in conversation. The ideal path of the sun and the moon intersect at the equinoxes. In this ideal picture, the moon should be to the south when the sun is to the north, and conversely.

Three classes of stellar paths are recognized. The first is the path of the northern circumpolar or near-circumpolar stars. These are seen as short arcs. Given the

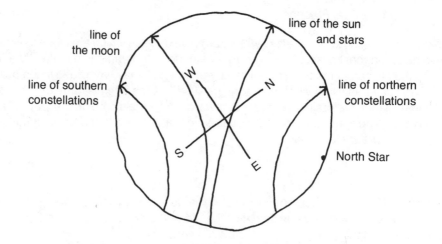

6.1. *Rainy-season celestial paths (March 22–September 22).*

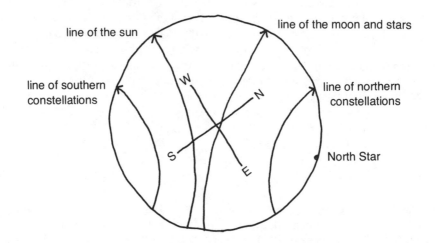

6.2. *Dry-season celestial paths (September 22–March 22).*

irregularity of the countryside, the low latitude, and the haziness of the countryside due to dust and smoke in the dry season and humidity in the rainy season, this is an understandable simplification. Into this category falls Ursa Major. The second category consists of stars which make short arcs to the south. The Southern Cross falls into this category. The third category consists of stars which pass overhead; these are perceived as those which make near half-circles or which are crossed by the paths of the sun and the moon. Orion falls into this category.

The sun was said to rise to the north when the nights are short (rainy season) and to the south when the nights are long (dry season). The length of the night seemed to be the basic reference point, as the length of the day was mentioned secondarily, if at all. I have reproduced the maps exactly as drawn, although the

statement that the sun rises to the north in the rainy season would seem to be con-
tradicted by them. The sun appears to rise to the southeast in both maps, although
it rises more to the north in the rainy season. Lacking further information, it therefore seems unwise to draw inferences, however tempting, from the maps.

When working with informants, I used traditional star maps and tables I had
worked out which gave the approximate time of day ($\pm$ one hour) and time of year
($\pm$ ten days) on which a given hour circle of right ascension was rising, culminating, or setting. One morning session, in order to determine whether or not the
informant and I were discussing the same star, I asked where it was now. The
question was vague, as I meant to ask where it would be when the sun set. The informant, however, thought for a moment, then pointed downward and eastward at
an angle of about thirty degrees. He then pointed upward to where it would be at
sunset: "Va por alla." My table checked, and thereafter, when I asked other informants similar questions, I received similar responses.

Astronomy

Eclipses

An eclipse of the sun or moon is described by a Cakchiquel phrase which glosses
as 'the sun (moon) carries sickness'. Cakchiquel women, according to the male
informants, are more frightened and say, "The sun (moon) is dying today (to-
night)." (For comparison, see Tozzer 1941, p. 138, n. 639.) Not only is the sun
(moon) sick itself, but in fact it "carries sickness." Children born near the time of an
eclipse will have impediments, such as blindness, muteness, or deafness. Women
who leave their houses must be thoroughly covered lest their future children be en-
dangered. In addition, machines will not function correctly. (For comparison, see
Thompson 1970, p. 243.)

For the Cakchiquel, a solar eclipse is much more dangerous than a lunar
eclipse because, in the event of a solar eclipse, evil spirits of all types come out of
the depths of the earth to seize the people. In both types of eclipses, however, the
danger to the people is shared by the eclipsed body. The first obligation of the
people (including the women who, although covered, are taking a serious risk) is
to help the sun or moon. This is done by going to the tops of the hills with every
form of noisemaker available, from drums to flutes to bowls beaten with sticks.
This noise helps the sun or moon to evade the sickness or death which threatens
it (see Thompson 1970, p. 235).

The Quiche use the phrase *skame k' x (k^x)*, or 'the sun (moon) died.' When an
eclipse is about to occur, the people are warned; the church bell may even be
rung. People close themselves in their houses and no one is allowed to leave. If it
is a solar eclipse, they are afraid that looking at the eclipsed sun will freeze their
eyes and cause blindness. Looking at an eclipse of the moon, however, brings all
kinds of sickness as with the Cakchiquel. The Quiche also use various kinds of
noisemakers. Once these are ready, the whole family kneels, uses the noisemakers, and laments the eclipse. In the case of the moon they say, "I hope she doesn't

die. I hope the moon goes on a straight path; perhaps she is in serious trouble because of what is happening." The people may cry in their grief. As one informant
said, "Half of the people here call the moon 'lady,' old moon (*mama k^x*). The moon
is a god; the sun is a god. He of the church who is god is only god of the earth."

Sun

The word for sun is also the word for day. The sun therefore not only defines the
day, it is the day. As mentioned above, the sun is a god; it is occasionally called
*ʔ x k'auma*ʔ by the Cakchiquel. As *auma*ʔ means 'grandfather' and *k'a* is a pos-
sessive prefix, the phrase glosses to 'the sun, our grandfather'. The sun is also the
point of reference for the stars. A star's position is given by the hour at which it is
in a certain place and by its position in front of (rising before) or behind (rising after)
the sun.

Moon

Three words are given for the moon: *ik^x* in both Quiche and Cakchiquel, *nan* ('old
woman') in Quiche, and *k'auti*ʔ ('our grandmother') in Cakchiquel. In general conversation the Quiche used the *ik^x* form. The Cakchiquel used *k'auti*ʔ generally; the
ik^x form was only used in formal phrases describing the phases of the moon. As
mentioned above, the moon is a god.
     The moon is described, beginning with new moon, by its appearance on the
first evening, the second evening, and so on. The new moon is called by phrases
which gloss to 'night of the moon' and 'the moon is born'. The second evening is
described by phrases which gloss to 'now the moon is seen' and 'first day of the
moon'. From the third evening to first quarter, the gloss is 'second (third, etc.) day
of the moon'. At first quarter, two glosses are used, 'the moon is filling' and 'half
time of the moon'. From then until full moon, the evening count continues.
     At full moon, the descriptions change to 'first evening of the full moon' and
'round moon'. From then until last quarter, waning, the gloss becomes 'the moon
rises at seven (eight, etc.)'. The waning quarter moon is known again as 'half time
of the moon' or 'midnight moon'. The count of rising time continues until the last
night before new moon, known as 'the end of the moon (month) today'. The word
ik^x is used here in the sense of month. This was also noted by Lothrop (Recinos
and Goetz 1953, p. 28).
     The phases of the moon are categorized in yet another way. It is tender while
it is waxing, seasoned while it is waning. The moon is dangerously tender, however, when it is new (from 12 to 72 hours, depending on the informant) and when
it is full (for 12 hours). When the moon is dangerously tender, there are many pro-
hibitions. If one chops wood, one cuts oneself. If one succeeds in cutting the wood,
it cannot be seasoned properly; it twists and bends. If one makes charcoal, it will
not burn. If one plants, there will be much growth but no harvest. If one harvests,
the crop rots. If one picks fruit, the fruit is juicy but bitter. If one cuts oneself, one
bleeds excessively. People are lethargic and work poorly. They are particularly

susceptible to sickness. During the rainy season, it rains more when the moon is tender than it does when the moon is seasoned.

The Quiche plant by the calendar, but harvest by the moon. They do not distinguish between dangerously tender and tender for harvesting. They harvest only after the full moon, when the moon is seasoned. This rule is vigorously applied only to milpa crops, specifically corn and dry beans, which are planted around 20 March "to await the rains." Crops planted on irrigated lands and late crops, such as greens, sown between September and December, may be harvested when ready.

The Cakchiquel both plant and harvest by the moon. Their harvesting rules are the same as those of the Quiche. Planting, however, is bound to both the calendar and the moon. The third day of the moon (fourth from new), when the moon is on "this side," is the ideal day for planting. Crops sown on this day grow more rapidly and mature earlier. I was told that a lime tree planted on the third day matures in seven years, but that eleven years are required if it is planted on any other day. Crops can be sown from the third day waxing to the quarter moon waning, at which time the moon is too seasoned and crops will not grow.

The middle of April, during the allowable lunar phases, is the ideal planting time in the Cakchiquel village. During this period, anything can be grown. August is the second best month; 20 August, the middle of the year, marks the end of the general growing season. After this date, beans are the only milpa crop which can be sown, from the eighth to the twenty-ninth of September, when the moon is favorable. In late December and early January, when the three stars of Orion's belt are on the eastern horizon at sunset, chayote can be sown. Ideally, the sowing takes place on 6 January, the Day of the Kings in Roman Catholicism. The three stars of the belt are commonly known as Tres Reyes (Three Kings). Lunar age also takes precedence in this case.

The moon is considered to be yellow. It is inhabited by a rabbit, *umul*. I asked for a drawing of the moon and received two (fig. 6.3). When the moon is rising, the mouth is down (*boca abajo*).

Planets

Venus is the planet of most importance. The Cakchiquel call it *locera macamil* from Castellano *lucero* or 'morning star' and Cakchiquel *macamil* or 'very bright star'. The Quiche call Venus "Santiago" when it is the morning star and *raskap*, 'thing of night' or 'something late', when it is the evening star.

According to the Quiche informants, Venus passed from behind the sun (when it was called *raskap*) to in front of the sun (when it was called "Santiago") in January of 1974. In February 1974, Santiago rose at 4:30 A.M. July is the month of Santiago; 3:00 A.M. is the hour of Santiago in the month of July. The informants said that Venus would not appear again as the evening star until January of 1975. All this is accurate. I was unable to determine if the positions of Venus were calculated over eight-year intervals (as in the Dresden Codex) or if only running observations were kept.

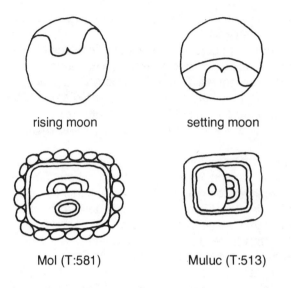

| rising moon | setting moon |

| Mol (T:581) | Muluc (T:513) |

6.3. *Informant's moon drawings with comparison glyphs.*

The Cakchiquel informants gave very little information about Venus. They did, however, mention a "comet" which appeared at 5:00 A.M. in February of 1974, together with the *macamil*. This may have been a reference to Comet Kohoutek or it may have referred to the appearance of Jupiter as a morning star, approximately a month after the heliacal rising of Venus. Incidentally, this was taken as a sign that the world would end in the year 2000.

I was unable to elicit specific information about planets other than Venus. The Cakchiquel informants did say that there were four *macamil*: *locera macamil*, *macamil*, *macamil gʔvn* ('yellow'), and *macamil kvku* ('red'); these seem to correspond to Venus, Jupiter, Saturn, and Mars. This is tentative, however, as the Cakchiquel used *macamil* freely when speaking of any bright star.

Meteors

Meteors are known as "excrement of the stars." No other information was given.

Stars

The stars, *camil* or *c'mil* in Cakchiquel and *c'umil* in Quiche, are used primarily to tell the time of night or to herald the time of year. I have attempted to identify them on the basis of the information given by the informants. Unfortunately, by the time I had learned enough to elicit the kind of information available, the rainy season had begun and viewing was bad to terrible.

The first groups of stars mentioned (and often the only group known) by Maya speakers in Guatemala is the Pleiades. The name *moʔots* (occasionally *muʔuts*) is general, from Chuj to Quiche. In Chuj the name is said to mean 'those who travel together'. In Quiche it is said to mean 'a handful'. The Cakchiquel say it is the name of the Seven Kids, Siete Cabritos in Castellano. In late June, *mo?ots* is said to rise at 3:00 A.M. It goes from behind the sun to in front of the sun when the rains begin. This occurs roughly in mid-May. Finally, it is considered the sign of the month of November, when it is called *Fetal akap*, 'signal of night', because it rises at sunset. It is said to be visible from 7:00 at night until 6:00 in the morning.

Only the Cakchiquel informants mentioned the constellation of the Wedding Party (Los Casorios), *a?akola?*. This is the head of Taurus, in which Aldebaran is the godfather, ϵ Taurus is the godmother, θ and δ are the couple, and γ is the priest or the onlookers. The fact that the terms used come from Catholicism suggests that this constellation may be post-Hispanic. The possibility of pre-Hispanic origin should not be ignored, however, as the group is visualized as a spiral, somewhat similar to that of the conch spiral (fig. 6.4).

Los Casorios

univalve shell
(T:210)

6.4. *Visualization of Maya constellation Los Casorios in Taurus with comparison glyph.*

The second most frequently mentioned constellation is that of Orion's Belt and Sword (fig. 6.5). It is known by the Cakchiquel informants as the Three Kings (Tres Reyes) and was mentioned above in connection with the January planting of chayote. A child born at this time is given the name of one of the kings. It is known in Cakchiquel as *ausi? camil*, 'three stars'. The one Chuj informant gave its name as *os t'ilan*, 'three in line'. To the Quiche it is the Three Marys (Tres Marias); in Quiche it is *c'ok*, 'the right angle', and comprises both the belt and the sword. For the Quiche the constellation is the sign of the month of December, when it is also called *retal akap*, 'signal of night', because it rises at sunset. It is said to be visible from 7:00 P.M. to 6:00 A.M.

The Milky Way is called the Course of Santiago (Corrida Santiago) by the Cakchiquel; my informants did not know of a Cakchiquel name. It is used to predict the coming of the dry season. The Quiche informants called it *raskap*, 'thing of

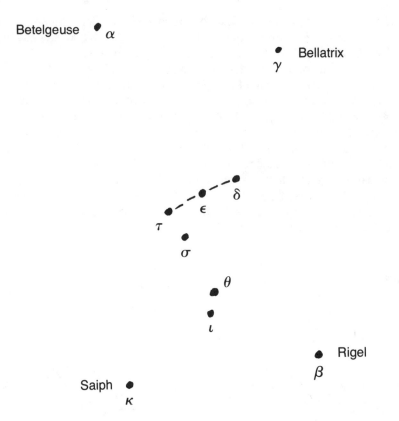

6.5. *Visualization of Maya constellation Tres Reyes or Tres Marias in Orion.*

night' or 'something late', the same term which was used for Venus as evening star. It rises in the evening around Christmas and is used to predict the coming of cold weather.

Only the Quiche informants mentioned the Gemini, known as *kiep c'umil*, 'two stars'. They are described as two stars which go together, the first of which is "half cloudy" and the second of which is a very large star which follows by about half an hour. There exists the possibility that the two stars referred to are Procyon and β Canis Minor but ethnohistoric sources indicate that Gemini formed a pre-Hispanic constellation (Tozzer 1941, pp. 131, 192 n. 1015, 220). The constellation is the sign of the month of January, when it rises at sunset. It is said to be visible from 7:00 at night until 6:00 in the morning.

The star Regulus is known by the Quiche as *hun c'umil*, 'one star'. It is the sign of the month of February. It rises at sunset and is visible from 7:00 in the evening until 6:00 in the morning. The Cakchiquel informants mentioned a star called *la gran lucero* or *macamil* (both of which mean 'bright star') which rises at 6:00 in the afternoon on February 9. This is probably Regulus, as 6:00 or 7:00 in the evening (or morning) seems to refer to sunset (or sunrise) rather than to the precise hour. If this is the case, the Cakchiquel use the appearance of Regulus as a signal to begin preparing their milpas. This star is then used as an alarm clock until the middle of April when it sets at about 3:00 A.M.

Another large star is of importance in the months of January and February. It is known to the Quiche as *sk^xek'ap*, 'dark' or 'giving notice of the night.' It is the opposite of Venus, which announces the day. It is in the "middle of the sky" shortly before sunset in November and disappears in the west at sunset in the latter part of January. Its disappearance means that the dry season (Maya summer) is drawing to an end. It seems likely that *sk^xek'ap* is Altair.

The next group of interest is the Thieves' Dagger or Cross to the Cakchiquel, the Thieves' Cross to the Quiche. The Cakchiquel call it *krus alo?oma?*; the Quiche call it *ki krusil elo?omap*, 'thieves' cross' in both cases. I have had considerable difficulty in identifying this consellation because it seems that there are at least three similar constellations with the same name. One Cakchiquel informant specifically stated that in mid-May there are three thieves' daggers; all are seen in the south, one at midnight, one at 2 to 3 A.M. and one at 4 to 5 A.M. In early June, one was said to be at its midpoint at 6:00 A.M. (or sunrise). Figure 6.6 gives copies of informants' drawings of the constellations without regard to orientation. The second cross, in time, is said to be more to the north than the third. Under the assumption that culmination times were given in all three cases, the best estimates of the positions thus seemed to be Right Ascension 21–22^h, 18–19^h, and 16–17^h. Further discussion elicited the fact that there are very many stars in the region of the first two crosses to appear. Even though this identification was verified only with the star maps, the second cross appears to be a group in Sagittarius, consisting of σ, ϕ, δ, and γ horizontally, and λ, δ, ϵ, and η vertically (fig. 6.7).

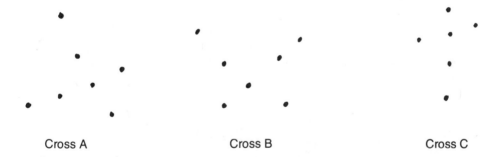

Cross A   Cross B   Cross C

6.6. *Copies of drawings of Thieves' Dagger constellations, in order of time but without regard to orientation.*

The first cross, in time, is probably located in Scorpio, as it seems that there was a pre-Hispanic constellation in or near Scorpio (Tozzer 1941, p. 193). Also, when doing linguistic work with Valley Zapotec informants, I was told of a cross consisting of many stars which was found in the Alacran (scorpion). This seemed more likely to be in the Milky Way (therefore Sagittarius?) than in Scorpio, however.

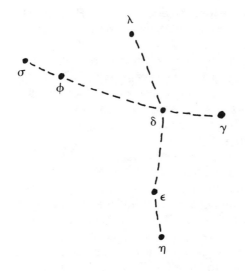

6.7. *Possible visualization of Cross B in Sagittarius.*

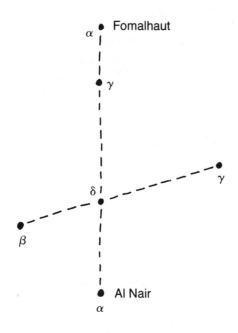

6.8. *Possible visualization of Cross C, with Fomalhaut and stars in Grus.*

The third cross, in time, seems to fall in Piscis Austrinus and Grus, although this is also speculative. A possible construction which is consistent with figure 6.6, Cross C, consists of Fomalhaut, α, β, and γ Grus, plus small connecting stars (fig. 6.8).

The Quiche informants also spoke of a Thieves' Cross which could be seen above from midnight to 3 A.M. in mid-June. This implies culmination at approximately 1:30 A.M. and tends to verify the identification of the Sagittarius cross. One informant said that the cross was not straight but rather was inclined to its left. This informant also mentioned a cross which could be seen from January through March, in March at midnight. The Southern Cross fits this description. Obviously a great deal more work needs to be done with these constellations.

A Cakchiquel informant told me of a custom followed by the people of Chinautla. There people receive a "secret" from the Thieves' Dagger. When this constellation culminates at 4 A.M., the boys of six or seven years of age are sent out with sticks of cane to stage a mock battle in defense of these stars. This is done so that the boys will use the machete well when they are adult.

The Quiche informants have a different use for the constellation. It is believed that these stars watch over thieves, who also walk at night. Before committing a crime, specifically robbery, it is necessary to get their protection; it brings luck. A potential thief must obtain two large, fully ripe bananas as offerings. Thus, when someone walks past a house at night carrying two bananas, one knows he is considering robbery. The putative thief goes out in the country at midnight, offers the bananas, and makes a speech to the constellation. He uses magical words which attract money to him. This can also be done with *c'ok* when it is visible at midnight.

The last constellation mentioned by the informants was the Big Dipper. The Cakchiquel call it *carro k'o reh*, 'car with a tail', and the Quiche call it the Siete Cabreras, 'the seven goatherds'. No Quiche name was given. The only information given was that the constellation could not now be seen (because of the rainy season?).

I was told by the Cakchiquel informants that at all times, during all seasons of the year, four large southern stars (star groups?) can be seen in the course of the night. In the middle to end of May, one rises at 4:00 P.M., one rises at sunset, one rises at 2:00 A.M., and one rises at 5:00 A.M. If one makes the assumption that they culminate 3–4 hours after rising because they are far to the south, we have Right Ascension 12, 14, 22, and 1. This suggests α, β Crux, α, β Centaurus, Fomalhaut, and Achernar. The latter star may also have been mentioned by the Chuj informant, who noted a star called *yecl pasco*, 'sign of Christmas', which he said was culminating at sunset on Christmas day.

One final note seems indicated. When I was working with the Quiche, I heard that there had been a flying-saucer incident two years before. I asked the shaman who was helping me that day about it. He thought it was most probable the objects were experimental craft of either the Russians or the Americans. I suggested that the technology seemed rather more advanced. He replied that any people capable of putting men on the moon could also develop advanced aircraft. He seemed a little indignant at my lack of faith in technology.

Conclusions

The three preceding sections have presented current data which indicate that present-day Maya cosmology contains many elements which seem to be survivals of pre-Hispanic times. Among these elements are the 260-day calendar, a non-European spatial orientation, and the names of several stars and constellations. It seems probable that some of the beliefs relating to solar and lunar eclipses, as well as some of the planting and harvesting practices, are also of pre-Hispanic origin.

The purpose of the study from which these data were obtained was to determine if pre-Hispanic cosmological survivals indeed existed, and, if so, if such survivals existed in sufficient quantity to warrant further investigation. I believe that the pilot study showed that both questions can be answered with an unqualified affirmative.

If we can establish a good body of pre-Hispanic data, many of the problems currently facing investigators in associated fields of study, from archaeology to iconography, will disappear. At worst, the variables with which we all must deal will be better defined. It is my hope that more investigators will find the problem of survivals as challenging and that some of us will be meeting again soon, in the field.

Acknowledgment

I am indebted to Anthony G. Ketterling for drawing the figures.

7

The Date-Reaching Mechanism in the Venus Table of the Dresden Codex

Michael P. Closs

Pages 24 and 46–50 of the Dresden Codex were first associated with the planet Venus by Ernst Forstemann (1906, p. 182). Despite the pagination, it is known that, in the original layout of the codex, page 24 immediately preceded pages 46–50. In fact, page 24 is the introductory page to the Venus table, which follows on pages 46–50. The structure and meaning of the Venus pages have been investigated by many students. A basic exposition of these pages is available in the writings of John E. Teeple (1930, pp. 94–98) and J. Eric S. Thompson (1971, pp. 221–227; 1972, pp. 62–70).

The whole-day mean of the synodic revolution of Venus is 584 days. This interval, known as the Venus round, or briefly VR, can be obtained by forming the mean of any 5 successive Venus revolutions. The Venus table consists of 13 rows, each row containing 5 Venus rounds. Since 5 Venus rounds are equivalent to 8 Vague Years of 365 days, the $13 \times 5 = 65$ Venus rounds in the table comprise $13 \times 8 = 104$ Vague Years or 2 Calendar Rounds. Each Venus round is subdivided into smaller periods of 236, 90, 250, and 8 days, associated, respectively, with the divisions of a Venus revolution into periods of visibility as morning star, invisibility at superior conjunction, visibility as evening star, and invisibility at inferior conjunction.

The Venus round is not sufficiently accurate for keeping track of the astronomical position of Venus over a long period of time. This can be seen by considering a more precise figure for a mean Venus period of 583.92 days. The mean Venus period of 583.92 days, or briefly VP, is 0.08 days shorter than a Venus round. Thus, one has the basic relation $VR = VP + 0.08$ days. Since the Venus table contains 65 Venus rounds and $65VR = 65 (VP + 0.08$days$) = 65VP + 5.2$days, the mean Venus position at the end of the Venus table is about 5 days later than at the beginning. It follows that, if the Venus table is to be used repeatedly, it will require some mechanism to preserve its astronomical integrity. Teeple (1930, pp. 95–96) discovered that such a mechanism could be constructed from the data in the intro-

7.1. *Page 24 of the Dresden Codex.*

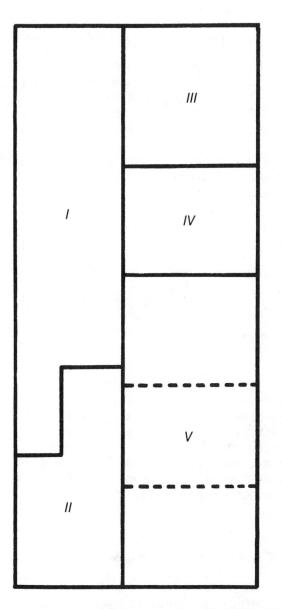

7.2. *The structural arrangement of Dresden 24.*

ductory page to the Venus table. His basic mechanism was later elaborated and extended by Thompson (1971, pp. 224–226).

The introductory page to the Venus table is illustrated in figure 7.1. The information on the page is structurally arranged in five distinct regions. These are indicated in figure 7.2 and are denoted Regions I, II, III, IV, and V. Region I contains a hieroglyphic text for which Thompson (1972, p. 64) proposed a partial translation. Its content does not seem pertinent to this study and will not be discussed here. Regions II to V contain chronological and arithmetical data which will be discussed.

Region II contains a Ring Number 6.2.0, and a Long Reckoning, 9.9.16.0.0, leading to the Initial Series 9.9.9.16.0. The base date of the Initial Series, 4 Ahau 8 Cumku, and the date reached by it, 1 Ahau 18 Kayab, are both recorded. In addition, the Calendar Round date 1 Ahau 18 Uo also appears. It should be stressed that 1 Ahau is the day name for the Venus god and is the lub (base) in the Sacred Round for Venus calculations.

Region III contains multiples of 65 Venus rounds, each followed by the lub day 1 Ahau. These are listed in table 7.1 together with their relationship to the Venus round, the Calendar Round, or briefly CR, and the mean Venus period of 583.92 days.

Table 7.1.
The Calendar Round Multiples in Region III of Dresden Codex page 24

(1).(1).1.14.0	=	260VR	=	8CR	=	260VP + 20.8days
(15).(16).6.0	=	195VR	=	6CR	=	195VP + 15.6days
(10).(10).16.0	=	130VR	=	4CR	=	130VP + 10.4days
(5).(5).8.0	=	65VR	=	2CR	=	65VP + 5.2days

Region IV contains four chronological counts which are not multiples of the Venus round. However, and importantly, they are multiples of the Sacred Round and so will preserve the Sacred Round date in any calculation. These counts are also followed by the lub day 1 Ahau. They have been referred to as "correction" factors but it is perhaps more appropriate to simply call them "calculation" factors. They are listed in table 7.2 together with their relationship to the Venus round, the Sacred Round, or briefly SR, and the mean Venus period of 583.92 days.

Table 7.2.
The Calculation Factors in Region IV of Dresden Codex page 24

1.5.14.4.0	=	317VR −	8d.	=	712SR	=	317VP + 17.4days
9.11.7.0	=	118VR −	12d.	=	265SR	=	118VP − 2.6days
4.12.8.0	=	57VR −	8d.	=	128SR	=	57VP − 3.4days
1. 5.5.0	=	15VR +	340d.	=	35SR	=	15VP + 341.2days

Region V contains a table of multiples of 5 Venus rounds exhibited in three successive rows. The multiples decrease from 4.17.6.0 (= 60VR) at the upper left, by regular intervals of 5 Venus rounds, to 8.2.0 (= 5VR) at the lower right. Following each multiple is the Sacred Round date which is reached when the given multiple is added to the lub 1 Ahau. The smallest multiple is assigned an erroneous Sacred Round date. Since 1 Ahau + 8.2.0 = 9 Ahau, one would expect to see 9

Ahau in this position. However, the Maya scribe has written this result as 8 Ahau. This is an interesting error because the number 8 has a very important role in generating the successive day numbers on repeated addition of 5 Venus rounds. For example, one has (modulo 13)

1 Ahau + 8.2.0 = (1 + 8) Ahau =   9 Ahau
9 Ahau + 8.2.0 = (9 + 8) Ahau =   4 Ahau
4 Ahau + 8.2.0 = (4 + 8) Ahau = 12 Ahau

and so on. In this fashion the Sacred Round positions recorded in the table are easily obtained. Thus, the scribal error may have resulted from the use of this procedure in constructing the table and the importance of the number 8 in it.

The Venus table on pages 46–50 of the Dresden Codex includes three sets of month positions which have 1 Ahau 13 Mac, 1 Ahau 18 Kayab, and 1 Ahau 3 Xul, respectively, as base dates in the Calendar Round. Teeple discovered that two of the factors in Region IV of page 24 could be used to unite these bases and at the same time maintain the astronomical usefulness of the table. He subtracted the third calculation factor in table 7.2 from the second and obtained the chronological count 4.18.17.0 (= 61VR − 4days = 61VP + 0.9days). With this calculation factor and the third factor in table 7.2, Teeple succeeded in constructing a mechanism for shifting between bases of the Venus table.

To explain the operation of Teeple's mechanism, suppose that 1 Ahau 18 Uo is taken as a base date for the Venus table. Counting 4.18.17.0 from this base, one reaches 1 Ahau 13 Mac. Since 4.18.17.0 = 61VR − 4days, this date is located 4 days before the end of the sixty-first Venus round in the Venus table. Because 4.18.17.0 = 61VP + 0.9days, the 1 Ahau 13 Mac date has a mean Venus position only one day later than that of the 1 Ahau 18 Uo base. Consequently, one can return to the beginning of the table and reuse it with a new base at 1 Ahau 13 Mac. Such a shift in bases will help to preserve the astronomical alignment of the Venus table. In contrast, if one continued to use the 1 Ahau 18 Uo base through 65 Venus rounds (the maximum extent of the table) and then reused the table with the same base, one would find that the mean astronomical position of Venus is 5 days later than it should be according to the data in the table.

It is clear that after several base shifts of the above type the 1-day difference in the astronomical position of successive bases will accumulate to several days. Teeple has suggested that, when the 1 Ahau 18 Kayab base was being used, such an accumulated deviation had already been built up. Thus, with this base, he proposed that the calculation factor 4.12.8.0 was to be used. This would lead to a new base at 1 Ahau 18 Uo. Since 4.12.8.0 = 57VR − 8days, the base shift would be made 8 days before the end of the fifty-seventh Venus round. Because 4.12.8.0 = 57VP − 3.4days, the mean position of Venus will then be 3.4 days earlier than its mean position at 1 Ahau 18 Kayab. This would then compensate for the accumulated deviation arising from four earlier base shifts of the type described previously.

Teeple has noted that the largest calculation factor, 1.5.14.4.0, equals 8CR +

4.12.8.0. He combined this result with the notion that the 1 Ahau 18 Kayab base would be used for a chronological count of 4.12.8.0 before shifting to a new base and argued that the astronomical base of the Venus table might have Long Count position 9.9.9.16.0 + 8CR, that is 10.10.11.12.0 1 Ahau 18 Kayab.

The various steps in Teeple's suggested mechanism are combined in table 7.3. The numbers in brackets measure the deviation, in days, of the mean Venus position of the bases from the assumed astronomical base of the table. It should be pointed out that, though Teeple proposed that the astronomical base might be at 10.10.11.12.0 1 Ahau 18 Kayab, it is inherent in his description of the base-shifting mechanism that 10.15.4.2.0 1 Ahau 18 Uo occupied the zero position for his base dates.

Table 7.3.
Teeple's Base-Shifting Mechanism

		Mean Venus position as calculated from an astronomical base at 1 Ahau 18 Uo
9. 9. 9.16. 0	1 Ahau 18 Kayab	(−17.4)
1. 1. 1.14. 0	8CR = 260 VP + 20.8days	
10.10.11.12. 0	1 Ahau 18 Kayab	(3.4)
4.12. 8. 0	57VR − 8days = 57VP − 3.4days	
10.15. 4. 2. 0	1 Ahau 18 Uo	(0)
4.18.17. 0	61VR − 4days = 61VP + 0.9days	
11. 0. 3. 1. 0	1 Ahau 13 Mac	(0.9)
4.18.17. 0	61VR − 4days = 61VP + 0.9days	
11. 5. 2. 0. 0	1 Ahau 3 Xul	(1.8)

Thompson (1971, pp. 225–226) accepted Teeple's system but made one addition to it. He took the smallest calculation factor in table 7.2, added a Sacred Round of 260 days to it, and obtained the revised factor 1.6.0.0 = 16VR + 16days = 16VP + 17.2days. The addition of this factor to the primary base at 9.9.9.16.0 1 Ahau 18 Kayab leads to a secondary base at 9.10.15.16.0 1 Ahau 8 Zac, which has the same mean Venus position as the later 10.15.4.2.0 1 Ahau 18 Uo. With this additional information, Thompson presented a somewhat more elaborate version of Teeple's system, which is exhibited in table 7.4.

It seems likely that a base-changing system similar to that constructed by Teeple and expanded by Thompson would have been known to the Maya. However, there are objections to the view that such a mechanism is built into the Venus pages of the Dresden Codex. Indeed, of all the bases appearing in table 7.4, only those at 1 Ahau 18 Kayab, 1 Ahau 13 Mac, and 1 Ahau 3 Xul actually appear as base dates in the Venus table. It is also notable that Thompson's most commonly

Table 7.4.
Thompson's Base-Shifting Mechanism

		Mean Venus position as calculated from an astronomical base at 1 Ahau 18 Uo
9. 9. 9.16. 0	1 Ahau 18 Kayab	(−17.4)
1. 6. 0. 0	16VR + 16days = 16VP + 17.2days	
9.10.15.16. 0	1 Ahau 8 Zac	(−0.2)
4.18.17. 0	61VR − 4days = 61VP + 0.9days	
9.15.14.15. 0	1 Ahau 8 Zip	(0.7)
4.18.17. 0	61VR − 4days = 61VP + 0.9days	
10. 0.13.14. 0	1 Ahau 13 Kankin	(1.6)
4.18.17. 0	61VR − 4days = 61VP + 0.9days	
10. 5.12.13. 0	1 Ahau 3 Yaxkin	(2.5)
4.18.17. 0	61VR − 4days = 61VP + 0.9days	
10.10.11.12. 0	1 Ahau 18 Kayab	(3.4)
4.12. 8. 0	57VR − 8days = 57VP − 3.4days	
10.15. 4. 2. 0	1 Ahau 18 Uo	(0)
4.18.17. 0	61VR − 4days = 61VP + 0.9days	
11. 0. 3. 1. 0	1 Ahau 13 Mac	(0.9)
4.18.17. 0	61VR − 4days = 61VP + 0.9days	
11. 5. 2. 0. 0	1 Ahau 3 Xul	(1.8)

used calculation factor, 4.18.17.0, does not explicitly appear in the introductory page but must be derived from the calculation factors which do appear. On the other hand, the calculation factor 9.11.7.0, which is recorded in the introductory page, does not explicitly appear in Thompson's mechanism, though it may be derived from the factors which do appear there. In addition, the calculation factor 1.5.5.0, also recorded in the introductory page, is assumed by Thompson to be erroneous.

A consideration of the nature of the Dresden Codex also raises doubts as to the validity of a base-shifting mechanism in the Venus pages. Thompson (1972, p. 111) writes:

> Codex Dresden is a book of divination. Except for a few almanacs in the nature of hymns of praise and recitations of offerings to the divine powers, the whole book consists of elaborate mechanisms for ascertaining the good or bad luck of periods of time, usually of particular days, but sometimes of longer periods. . . . In addition, the chapters which recount the heliacal risings of the planet Venus and of the solar eclipses . . . fall into the same group as the above for they, too, are divinatory. Both phenomena were greatly feared by the Maya;

these chapters recount the varying misfortunes to befall man according to the particular day on which these natural events should fall.

It is probable that the Dresden Codex is essentially a manual written to assist the
priest in the field in making his prognostications. Bishop Landa (Tozzer 1941, p.
27) writes that the high priest and his assistants "provided priests for the towns
when they were needed, examining them in the sciences and ceremonies, and
committed to them the duties of their office, and the good example to people and
provided them with books and sent them forth." The type of books provided were
likely akin to the Dresden Codex. Landa continues and notes that in the sacerdotal
college itself, the priests "employed themselves in the duties of the temples and in
teaching their sciences as well as in writing books about them." It would be here in
the intellectual atmosphere of the college that mathematical and astronomical
knowledge would be developed, written down, and taught. However, the Dresden
Codex is clearly not a scientific work in the above sense. Rather, it is a field manual
for the secular priest containing applications of Maya science to the practice of the
priestly profession. It should not be forgotten that it is precisely to these practical
applications that Maya science was directed. In keeping with the view that the
Venus pages would be used by a local priest away from the major centers of learning for the purpose of divination, one should expect that its arithmetical demands
would be kept to a minimum. Even the tables of multiples included in the Dresden
Codex can be interpreted to demonstrate that the original editor of the codex
sought to reduce the need of arithmetical computation in utilizing the augural material. In this context, the construction of a base-shifting mechanism, as proposed
by Teeple and Thompson, not strictly compatible with the direct use of the calculation factors provided, is difficult to justify.

It may also be noted that the Venus table contains month positions associated with two successive bases, namely, 1 Ahau 13 Mac and 1 Ahau 3 Xul. This
gives the table an effective life of almost 200 years, ensuring that when it was first
written it would not suffer rapid obsolescence. In fact, the life of the Venus table
may have been considered to be greater than the life of the codex, which could be
expected to suffer physical deterioration as the years went by. Surely, the Maya
priests envisioned that, with time passing, new editions of the Venus table would
be necessary and these, when prepared, would carry updated month positions
calculated from new bases. Such a practice on the part of the Maya would imply
that a base-shifting mechanism in the Venus pages is unnecessary. However, one
would require some device whereby the priest could reach the appropriate base
for a more-or-less current Long Count position and then enter the Venus table in
order to determine the approximate time of arrival of coming heliacal risings and to
acquaint himself with the associated auguries. This suggests that the data on page
24 may be intended to provide for a "date-reaching mechanism" rather than a
"base-shifting mechanism."

Because the three bases of the Venus table occur at the end of the 8-day period of invisibility associated with inferior conjunction, they are generally taken as
base dates referring to the heliacal rising of Venus as morning star. Table 7.4
shows that the mean position of Venus at the primary base, 9.9.9.16.0 1 Ahau 18

Kayab, is about 17 days earlier than the mean position at the later bases. When the calculation factor 1.5.14.4.0 = 317VR + 17.4days is added to 9.9.9.16.0, one reaches a secondary base at 10.15.4.2.0 1 Ahau 18 Uo. This base appears in Region II of page 24 next to the primary base. The mean position of Venus at this secondary base is about the same as for the later bases of the Venus table. These results suggest that 1 Ahau 18 Uo is recorded next to the primary base in order to engage the Long Count at an astronomical base for heliacal risings as morning star. The reason a nonastronomical primary base at 9.9.9.16.0 was selected is not clear, but it may be connected with the associated Ring Number calculation and the arithmetical properties of the Long Reckoning (Thompson 1971, p. 226; 1972, p. 62).

If one accepts that 9.9.9.16.0 is some 17 days before a heliacal rising of Venus as morning star, it is possible to explain the smallest calculation factor, 1.5.5.0. Adding 1.5.5.0 = 15VP + 341.2days = 15 VP + 17days + 324.2days to 9.9.9.16.0 1 Ahau 18 Kayab leads to 9.10.15.3.0 1 Ahau 13 Pax at a Venus position 324 days after heliacal rising as morning star. The 324 days approximate the Dresden interval of 326 days between a heliacal rising as morning star and a heliacal rising as evening star. However, the 324-day interval would be of considerable ceremonial interest, since exactly 260 days, or 1 Sacred Round, later one will reach a heliacal rising as morning star. Thus, successive heliacal risings as evening star and morning star would be assigned the same day of the Sacred Round. In a ritualistic sense, the day of heliacal rising is associated with the day of birth of Venus (the name day of Venus). Because the evening and morning stars are the same planet, the Maya would find it very fitting that they should have the same birth day. It follows that when the calculation factor 1.5.5.0 is added to 9.9.9.16.0 it leads to an astronomical base at a heliacal rising of evening star having the lub day 1 Ahau.

The two methods described above for engaging the Long Count at an astronomical base are summarized in table 7.5. Calculation A leads to heliacal rising as morning star and calculation B leads to heliacal rising as evening star. It should be

Table 7.5.
Astronomical Bases of the Venus Table

			Mean Venus position as calculated from an astronomical base at 1 Ahau 18 Uo
A.	9. 9. 9.16. 0	1 Ahau 18 Kayab	(−17.4)
	1. 5.14. 4. 0	317VR − 8days = 317VP + 17.4days	
	10.15. 4. 2. 0	1 Ahau 18 Uo	(0)
B.	9. 9. 9.16. 0	1 Ahau 18 Kayab	(−17.4)
	1. 5. 5. 0	15VR + 340days = 15VP + 341.2days	
	9.10.15. 3. 0	1 Ahau 13 Pax	(323.8)

pointed out that the latter astronomical base is influenced by ritual considerations and is only "approximate," a more realistic interval between heliacal risings of morning star and evening star being about 312 days.

A simple mechanism can be constructed to reach bases in the Venus table using only those calculation factors which are available on page 24. Such a mechanism is illustrated in table 7.6.

The system of calculations shown in tables 7.5 and 7.6 fit the available data very well. In each case the calculations proceed from the primary base at 9.9.9.16.0. Each of the calculation factors in table 7.2 is used exactly once. Two of the Calendar Round multiples in table 7.1 are used in the base-reaching mechanism of table 7.6. No other factors are introduced in the calculations. All the bases reached except that in table 7.5B appear in the Venus pages.

When the Long Count positions of the bases of the Venus table have been fixed, as below, one may then use the table of multiples in Region V of page 24 to place a given date in the Venus table. Suppose, for example, that one wishes to determine the approximate position of 11.3.3.0.0 1 Ahau 18 Muan in the Venus cycle. One may proceed as shown in table 7.7.

The mechanisms described in tables 7.5, 7.6, and 7.7 draw on the insights first developed by Teeple. However, the proposed scheme is not as far-reaching

Table 7.6.
A Base-Reaching Mechanism for the Venus Table

		Mean Venus position as calculated from an astronomical base at 1 Ahau 18 Uo
A.		
9. 9. 9.16.0	1 Ahau 18 Kayab	(−17.4)
1. 1. 1.14.0	8CR = 260VP + 20.8days	
10.10.11.12.0	1 Ahau 18 Kayab	(3.4)
9.11. 7.0	118VR − 12days = 118VP − 2.6days	
11. 0. 3. 1.0	1 Ahau 13 Mac	(0.8)
B.		
9. 9. 9.16.0	1 Ahau 18 Kayab	(−17.4)
1. 5.14. 4.0	317VR − 8days = 317VP + 17.4days	
10.15. 4. 2.0	1 Ahau 18 Uo	(0)
4.12. 8.0	57VR − 8days = 57VP − 3.4days	
10.19.16.10.0	1 Ahau 3 Xul	(−3.4)
5. 5. 8.0	2CR = 65VP + 5.2days	
11. 5. 2. 0.0	1 Ahau 3 Xul	(1.8)

as the base-shifting mechanism advocated by Teeple and is more closely tied to the Maya data and the probable use of the Venus table.

The results which have been derived are intrinsic to the structure of the Venus pages and are independent of any correlation. The interpretation of the available data places 9.9.9.16.0 1 Ahau 18 Kayab about 17 days before a mean heliacal rising of Venus as morning star. According to Thompson (1972, p. 63), his 11.16.0.0.0 correlation places 9.9.9.16.0 about 16 days before a heliacal rising of Venus as morning star.

Table 7.7.
A Date-Reaching Mechanism for the Venus Table

11. 3. 3. 0. 0	1 Ahau 18 Muan
− 11. 0. 3. 1. 0	Long Count position of the 1 Ahau 13 Mac base
2.19.17. 0	distance of 1 Ahau 18 Muan from the beginning of the Venus table
−2.16.14. 0	the largest multiple of 5VR which is less than 2.19.17.0; it is the seventh entry from the end in the table of multiples in Region V
3. 3. 0	distance of 1 Ahau 18 Muan from the beginning of the eighth row of the Venus table
−1.11. 4	1VR
1. 9.16	distance of 1 Ahau 18 Muan from the beginning of the eighth row on the second page of the Venus table
− 11.16	period of visibility as morning star
16. 0	
− 4.10	period of invisibility at superior conjunction
11.10	distance of 1 Ahau 18 Muan from heliacal rising as evening star; 1 Ahau 18 Muan is 20 days before heliacal setting and so is 28 days before heliacal rising as morning star which arrives at 3 Lamat 6 Kayab

8.1. *Copan Altar Q (block of stone 56 inches square and 30 inches high with 36 well-preserved hieroglyphs on top).*
(a) West side: four "astronomers" are seen facing the Calendar Round date 6 Caban 10 Mol (Maudslay 1889–1902, 1:plate 90).

8

Copan Altar Q: The Maya Astronomical Congress of A.D. 763?

John B. Carlson

"The Maya temple complexes, with their step pyramids, housed some astronomers, and we have portraits of a group of them on a large altar stone that has survived. The altar commemorates an ancient astronomical congress that met in the year A.D. 776. Sixteen mathematicians came here to the famous center of Maya science, the sacred city of Copan in Central America. . . . When the great conference met at Copan, the Maya priest astronomers had run into difficulty. . . . The congress was called to resolve an arithmetical problem of computation that perpetually troubled the Maya guardians of the calendar. They kept two calendars, one sacred and one profane, which were never in step for long; and they spent their ingenuity trying to stop the drift between them. . . . That was all that was done in A.D. 776 when the delegates proudly posed for their portraits" (Bronowski 1973, pp. 188–190) (see fig. 8.1).

Jacob Bronowski's 1973 description of events surrounding Copan Altar Q is a recent example of the perpetuation of the myth of a Maya astronomical convention at Copan. This uncritical repetition of an old hypothesis initiated a reinvestigation of the historical basis and evidence for this idea, in conjunction with an attempt to determine the actual significance and function of Altar Q and related monuments at Copan.

The specific claim is made that a group of Maya astronomers met on the day 9.16.12.5.17 6 Caban 10 Mol to (*a*) establish the length of the tropical year (365.2422 days) and (*b*) realign their 365-day *haab* with the tropical year. The *haab* gains about one day each four tropical years (i.e., it takes approximately 1,508 *haabs* for the 0 Pop [New Year's day] to again align with the same day in the tropical year). This day corresponds to 1 July 763 in the Goodman-Martinez-Thompson (GMT) correlation with the Christian calendar and 2 September 503 in the Spinden correlation. The question of which correlation is the correct one is crucial to the validity of the argument for an astronomical congress.

West
12   11   1   2

South
3   4   5   6

8.1 *(b) Drawings of the four sides with "astronomers" numbered 1–16 (ibid., plate 92).*

East

7 8 9 10

North

16 15 14 13

The key monument at Copan for this hypothesis is not Altar Q but Altar U, which possesses two *haab* New Year's (0 Pop) dates as well as the all important 6 Caban 10 Mol date. The suggestion is that 6 Caban 10 Mol is a so-called determinant[1] date relative to the two 0 Pop dates; that is, it is a date of significance in the Maya calculations to compensate for the slippage of their *haab* relative to the tropical year. Altar Q itself shows the four "astronomers" on the west side (see fig. 8.1) facing the 6 Caban 10 Mol "convention" date, but the last date on the monument (9.17.5.0.0 6 Ahau 13 Kayab), the "dedication" date, is suggested to be a hotun anniversary of the convention 12½ years later (A.D. 776) when the "astronomers" returned to Copan and "posed for their portraits."

The earliest reference to the ill-fated determinant calculations and Altar U goes back to Charles Bowditch (1910). According to Morley (1920, pp. 306–307): "Bowditch . . . was the first to point out that this inscription has two New Year's days in it, although in the writer's opinion he reads both incorrectly. . . . On the

Table 8.1.
Summary of the Derived Long Count Dates on Copan Convention Monuments with the Convention Date 9.16.12.5.17 6 Caban 10 Mol or Katun Anniversaries

Altar U	Altar Q	Altar R	Altar V
9.14.19. 5. 0			
9.15. 0. 0. 0			
	9.15. 6.16.17		
	9.15. 6.17. 0		
	9.15. 7. 6.13		
9.15. 8.10.12			
9.15. 9. 0. 2			
9.15. 9.10.17			
		9.15. 9.13. 0	
9.15.12. 5. 0			
9.15.12. 5. 7			
9.15.12. 5.17			
			9.16. 5. 3. 6
9.16.12. 5.17	9.16.12. 5.17	9.16.12. 5.17	9.16.12. 5.17
	9.17. 0. 0. 0		
	9.17. 5. 0. 0		
	9.17. 5. 3. 4		

After Morley 1920, p. 344.

basis of his readings he sees here an ingenious intercalary count—no less than the number of days necessary at 10.1.7.3.17 2 Caban 0 Pop to bring the calendar and the true solar year into harmony. Unfortunately, the three dates upon which this reading rests are probably incorrectly deciphered as used, and, moreover, 10.1.7.3.17 is too late to be historically probable at Copan."

Sylvanus G. Morley, in his monumental "Inscriptions at Copan" (1920), provided the data base and analysis of calendric material on the monuments of Copan necessary for all subsequent work. Much of his analysis centers on the most frequent date at Copan, the convention date 6 Caban 10 Mol which appears eight times on seven monuments, with several katun anniversaries. The relevant monuments and their derived Long Count dates are given in table 8.1. Five of these monuments are so-called altars, three of which (Altars Q, T, and V) show men or anthropomorphic creatures seated on "pillow" or "cushion" glyphs. Temple 11 contains the convention date twice, and the carved steps on the inner doorway show

Temple II	Altar T	Stela 8	Fragment E'
9.14.15. 0. 0			
9.16.12. 5.17	9.16.12. 5.17	9.16.12. 5.17	
(twice)		9.17. 0. 0. 0	
	9.17.12. 5.17	9.17.12. 5.17	9.17.12. 5.17
		9.17.12. 6. 2	
		10. 0. 0. 0. 0	
		(prophetic)	

twenty "astronomers" seated on cushion glyphs. Altar L possesses a similar scene with two "astronomers" but without the convention date. It does, however, have a direct relationship to the event which occurred on that date. I will call "convention monuments" at Copan those which possess the 6 Caban 10 Mol convention date or its katun anniversary or which depict the "astronomers." Morley (p. 345) concludes: "We may never know the exact nature of the event which took place at Copan on 9.16.12.5.17 6 Caban 10 Mol (whether it is historical or astronomical) but its paramount importance cannot be doubted any the less on that account, since it was either the starting-point or terminal date of so many important monuments."

The real "astronomical congress" originates with Herbert Spinden (1924) in "The Reduction of Maya Dates." Spinden used Morley's Copan data to back up the calendar correlation which bears his name and to establish his Maya astronomical and agricultural ("sacred and profane") calendars. It appears now that much of what he discovered in this context was fortuitous and incorrect.

The logic of Spinden's arguments can best be followed in six steps. First, he claims the existence of two Maya 365-day years—an astronomical year with the month of Pop beginning on December 22 (the winter solstice) and an agricultural year with Yaxkin beginning on April 21. The agricultural year is derived from the time of burning the milpa, the start of the rainy season, and dubious etymologies of Maya month names.

Second, Spinden (p. 130) notes the famous passages in the books of Chilam Balam of Tizimin and Chumayel (postconquest Maya chronicles) that in "Katun 13 Ahau; Pop was counted in order." According to Spinden's correlation, Katun 13 Ahau corresponds to the 7,200-day period ending on 9.17.0.0.0 13 Ahau 18 Cumku or 27 March 511. Spinden interprets the "counting of Pop in order" to mean a mathematical adjustment of the *haab* to realign it with the tropical year. David Kelley (personal communication) suggests the "counting of Pop in order" merely meant that the Maya had noted the *haab* had come into step with the tropical year again at the completion of the 1508 *haab* cycle.

Third, Spinden notes that there are two New Year's days on Copan Altar U (9.15.8.10.12 2 Eb 0 Pop [9 April 480] and 9.15.9.10.17 3 Caban 0 Pop [9 April 481]) and that the convention day (9.16.12.5.17 6 Caban 10 Mol [2 September 503]) lies in Katun 13 Ahau when Pop was "set in order" (p. 131).

These dates indicated that Pop was recorded as having been "counted in order" when in its slow movement through the seasons it came to the point decided upon by the Mayas as the first day of their agricultural year (April 9?). This day was not far distant from the earlier position of Yaxkin according to the internal evidence of month names and signs. These conclusions are purely speculative.

The fourth point in the argument concerns the "Copan astronomical baseline" —an alignment of two stelae 7 km apart on opposite sides of the Copan Valley. From Morley's (1925, p. 277) data (8°51 ′ N of W), it appears that, if one stands at Stela 12 in the east, sunset is observed on April 9 and September 2 behind Stela 10 in the west. These are the same days of the year found on Altar U and the validity of the Spinden correlation rests heavily on this coincidence. To quote Spinden (p. 131): "These dates, April 9 and September 2, are extremely important and furnish, in the opinion of the writer, decisive proof of the correctness of the present

correlation." Anthony Aveni (1975) has recently remeasured the Copan baseline
and found it to be 9°00' N of W and he finds that the sun sets over Stela 10 on
April 12 and September 1 as viewed from Stela 12. This type of information, more
accurate than that of Morley, detracts from the acceptability of the "astronomical
baseline" and calls into question the "decisive proof of the correctness" of the
Spinden correlation.

A fifth and more speculative suggestion of Spinden is that the Copan baseline
was moved by the Maya from a previous slightly more east-west alignment to its
present position. This deduction is based on dates on Stelae 10, 12, 2, and A and
Altar U. In an involved argument, he claims that the former sunset alignment pair,
April 5 and September 6, were physically shifted to April 9 and September 2. Spinden (p. 135) suggests: "The first set of these dates probably would mean that the
baseline was originally nearer to the east and west line of the equinoxes, and that
one or the other of the markers was shifted in a redetermination. This conclusion
is reinforced by the fact that the resetting was consummated at a time when 0 Pop
had passed April 9 and reached April 5." This hypothesis has virtually no supporting evidence.

In his sixth and final argument, Spinden (p. 140) suggests that the rows of
men seated on the cushion glyphs of the convention monuments constitute "more
or less formalized pictures of an astronomical congress held in 503 A.D." He discusses the sixteen men on Altar Q and twenty men in Temple 11 but does not deal
convincingly with the nonhuman "astronomers" on Altar T, suggesting that they
may "represent constituent tribes in the Mayan nation."

All of Spinden's arguments, including his correlation, appear to be unfounded
or highly speculative in light of current evidence. The question of the astronomical
convention now rests on two major supports: (*a*) determinant theory and (*b*) Spinden's constellation of arguments which relate to the Spinden correlation.

The basis for the Spinden correlation is almost nonexistent, and most scholars, though not all, accept the GMT correlation.[2] The late Sir Eric Thompson
(1931*a*, pp. 743–744) had in 1931 heartily endorsed the astronomical congress
though denying the Spinden correlation. He accepted it on the basis of John
Teeple's (1930) determinant theory. In 1975 he stated, "I would not now accept
that a session of astronomers is portrayed on Altar Q. I accept that date
9.16.12.5.17 commemorated a civil event, but conceivably was picked for astrological reasons [determinants]" (Thompson, personal communication).

According to most current opinion (Kelley, personal communication), determinant theory has fallen into disrepute. The results are consistent with those obtained for the calculation of intervals between a random sample of Maya dates.
This has not been conclusively established, but seemingly significant determinant
dates are probably the result of chance. Thus, it is quite probable that there is no
basis for the astronomical congress hypothesis.

If not a congress of astronomers, what did happen at Copan on 9.16.12.5.17?
I would agree with Clancy (personal communication) that "altar" in the classic definition of a place of offerings and sacrifices is probably not correct for Copan altars.
Throne, pedestal, seat, or dais would probably be more suitable hypotheses. The
personages of high rank ("astronomers") are shown seated on large cushion

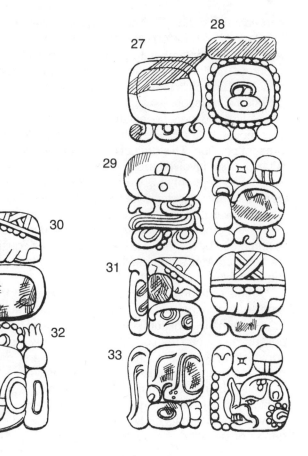

a

b

8.2. Copan.
(a) From top of Altar Q, E3–F4 (Maudslay 1889–1902, 1:plate 93).
(b) From west side of Altar U, A1–B4 (ibid., plate 98).
Interpretation (a) (after Kelley 1962, p. 329):

E3	F3	E4	F4
U Cab-?	Yax	Caan	Title?
	"Sun-at-Horizon"	Sky	Name?

Interpretation (b) (after Proskouriakoff 1960, p. 467):

A1	B1	A2	B2	A3	B3	A4	B4
6 Caban	10 Mol	Inaugural cluster		New Sun-at-Horizon	Sky	?	Copan Emblem Glyph

glyphs. I would submit that the altars were seats, probably cushioned with mats, for the Copanec royalty in direct analogy to the cushion glyphs.

The meanings of most of the cushion glyphs on Altar Q cannot be read with certainty. Some may be emblem glyphs; name glyphs of persons, families, places, societies, and so on; or a continuous inscription as suggested by Kelley (personal communication). Cushion #16 on Altar Q (fig. 8.1) is identified by Michael Coe (1973, p. 83) as the anthropomorphic Insect God A, God #30 on the Vase of the Thirty-one Gods. Gary Pahl (1970) identifies cushion glyph #6 as "Two-Legged Sky," a ruler of Quirigua, and #4 as "Eighteen Rodent," a ruler of Copan. Most of the cushion glyphs on Altar Q and the other monuments remain undeciphered.

Tatiana Proskouriakoff (1960) was the first to demonstrate the existence of a dynastic sequence at Piedras Negras, which has led to a reappraisal of the nature of the Classic Maya inscriptions. She determined that Thompson's "toothache" glyph (T684) functions as an inaugural or accession motif. She concluded (p. 468) that 9.16.12.5.17 6 Caban 10 Mol was probably an inaugural date and shows that it appears with the inaugural glyph or inaugural cluster on Altars U and V and Temple 11 (see fig. 8.2b).

Kelley (1962) explored the dynastic sequence at Quirigua and showed that there were close ties with rulers at Copan. He suggests that the family name of the rulers of Copan and Quirigua was "Caan," or 'sky'. In particular, Kelley shows that the glyph name of a Copanec ruler, "New-Sun-at-Horizon Sky," is associated with the date 9.16.12.5.17 on several convention monuments in the context of the toothache glyph (or inaugural cluster) or the *u-cab* phrase, an appelative glyph group (see fig. 8.2). The "astronomer" on the right front of convention Altar L is seated on the cushion glyph name "New-Sun-at-Horizon." The suggestion is that this very important date at Copan, 9.16.12.5.17, is associated with the inaugural or accession event of the important ruler "New-Sun-at-Horizon" of the "Sky" dynasty. This conclusion is in agreement with the work of Pahl (1970, 1974, 1975, personal communication) on the dynastic sequence at Copan.

We must still echo the sentiment of Morley that "we may never know the exact nature of the event that took place at Copan on 9.16.12.5.17," but if the members of the "Sky" family were astronomer-priests, it may still have been an "astronomical convention."

Notes

1. Determinant theory was first enunciated by John Teeple (1930, pp. 70–85). A good summary and discussion of the theory is available in Thompson (1971, pp. 317–320) in his Appendix V.

2. A new line of reasoning in corroboration of the GMT correlation from Closs (1976) uses evidence from three of the Maya books of Chilam Balam and Spanish historical materials: ". . . the new information, derived from Maya chronicles and controlled by Spanish sources, exhibits a weakness in (the Spinden) correlation in the very area where it has been assumed to be strongest. . . . insofar as the data of the Maya chronicles is concerned, some of the 'high ground' previously occupied by the Morley-Spinden correlation has been taken over by the Goodman-Martinez-Thompson correlation."

9

Ancient Maya Architecture and Planning: Possibilities and Limitations for Astronomical Studies

Horst Hartung

Contrary to the reluctance characteristic of the forties, fifties, and sixties, in the seventies scholars of Mesoamerican cultures generally accept the idea that there existed a consideration of astronomical events in pre-Columbian architecture and planning.

Architecture in Archaeology

It is important to consider some aspects of architecture in archaeology before explaining the role of architecture in archaeoastronomy. Sometimes the archaeologist discovers walls, structures, and buildings, all of which should be classified as architecture. Usually he goes ahead with the conservation of these architectural elements, getting involved in work which requires a specialist. A real problem arises when the archaeologist attempts reconstruction without consulting qualified experts. Such unadvised restoration often occurs in Mesoamerica.[1]

The decisive point in the conservation or restoration process is that there exists generally only one chance to do it correctly: when excavating the structures or shortly afterward when all possible data are at hand. Considerations and decisions made at this precise moment may save or deform a monument, often of incalculable value or even uniqueness. It is extremely important to recognize, while excavating a structure, whether there exists a probable astronomical relation in order to detect the corresponding alignment or visual lines with the best possible accuracy. It is not appropriate to discuss here how far and in what way the conservation or restoration of any newly discovered or existing old architecture has to be done. The "International Charter of Venice" (1964) is quite clear in this respect.[2]

Architecture in archaeology must be interpreted in terms of architecture, more precisely, in terms of the history of architecture. This may be the work of the art historian as one part of his or her research or of the architect specializing in historic interpretations. I favor the latter position, but not only from its theoretical side. The work of a practicing architect consists not only in the creative imagination of spatial conception, but also in the consequent evolution and logical application of the building process.

Antecedents

In "A Scheme of Probable Astronomical Projections in Mesoamerican Architecture," a contribution to the symposium Archaeoastronomy in Pre-Columbian America at Mexico City in June 1973 (Hartung, in Aveni, ed., 1975, pp. 191–204), some logical archaeological-architectural bases for recognizing items of astronomical interest in archaeological remains were established and points and constructions which may have served for astronomical observations were defined. The following schemes were analyzed:

1. The lasting form in which ancient astronomers marked important directions
2. Points of observation which can be linked with points of reference (sculptural and architectural elements and also artificial or natural elements in the landscape) in defining astronomical directions
3. Possible places of observation, preferably from the doorway of a temple
4. Structures facing and/or aligning with an astronomical direction
5. Lines of astronomical origin between buildings of different orientation
The contribution concluded with a warning not to confuse this class of lines and relationships with those arising from a visual-functional composition.

With these ideas in mind, in this paper certain architectural and planning aspects of the ceremonial center of Tikal will be analyzed. Although these are only in part connected to astronomical phenomena, they will explain some architectural considerations for the scholars in archaeoastronomy, in order that they may recognize similar dispositions at other archaeological sites.

Particular Aspects of Architecture and Planning at Tikal

Anyone who has studied with care the Tikal map of Carr and Hazard (1961) wonders about a possible conscious organization of the placement of structures. Several possible interpretations will be discussed, although a detailed astronomical investigation has yet to be realized (fig. 9.1).

In a 1965 study I could trace different systems of rectangular forms which connected decisive points on the map of Tikal. These ideas were presented in a paper only as a suggestion for further studies. At that time no support from other disciplines existed and the argument taken by itself was not completely convincing. However, two details were important: first, the existence of exact east-west lines and, second, the existence of exact 90-degree angles. An east-west visual line was recognized which leads over two (or three) "points" (characteristic architectural marks) to the distant horizon, quite adequate for an equinoctial observation (Hartung 1968, p. 123). In the map of a later publication (Hartung 1971, fig.

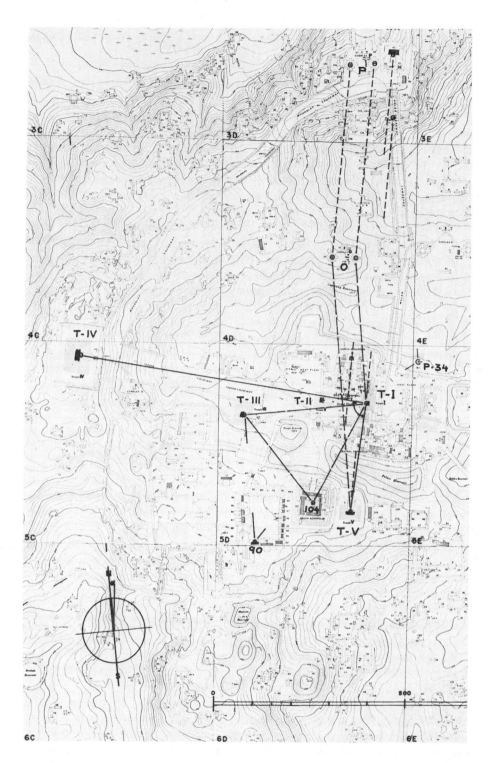

9.1. *Map of Tikal (Carr & Hazard 1961) including the relation lines which are discussed in the text.*

31-C) a distinctive east-west direction was preferred, namely the "interline" between the doorways of Temple I and Temple III, which face each other though they are separated by a large distance and do not lie on parallel lines (fig. 9.1). In January 1975 a measurement by Aveni, using a surveyor's transit and astronomical fix, revealed that this line deviates from east-west by only 6' of arc. Unless we assume a hole existed in the back wall of one or both of the buildings, no equinoctial observation on this east-west line could be made after the construction was finished. Evidently no such hole existed. Temple III was built in Late Classic times and a construction date of A.D. 810 has been suggested; this would be about 100 years later than Temple I.[3]

It surely was no problem for the Maya to define the exact line to the west from Temple I before starting the construction of the pyramid of Temple III (fig. 9.2). As the last platform of the pyramid is approximately at the height of the horizon, a rectification could easily have been realized and the doorway could have been located with precision. It is important to repeat here that the façades of Temple I and Temple III have different orientations: Temple I, approximately 9° east of north, and Temple III, approximately 18° east of north (Tozzer 1911, p. 106). It is open to speculation and investigation whether the different alignment of Temple III (as a late structure) implies a foreign influence.

The interdoorway relation at Tikal definitely supports the idea of the importance of the doorways as points of reference in Maya ceremonial center and city planning. In 1906 Zelia Nuttall suggested that doorways can be considered parts of astronomically oriented façades or may define observation lines from the interiors of temples.[4] To these long-forgotten suggestions can be added the recognition of the center of the doorway as the point of departure of visual and astronomical lines not parallel to the axis of the temple. (For details see Hartung, in Aveni, ed., 1975, p. 198, fig. 5.)

Exactly south of the doorway of Temple III a line leads to the center of a lateral building on the south side of the Plaza of the Seven Temples (fig. 9.1). It would not be worthwhile to mention this fact were it not that this building, Structure 5D-90, is at the same distance from the doorway of Temple III as is the doorway of Temple I from Temple III. That this disposition could have been arranged consciously by the Maya is supported by more obvious examples in other Maya ceremonial centers (Hartung 1971, p. 81).

A January 1975 measurement by Aveni from the doorway of Temple I to the doorway of Temple IV and to the doorway of Temple V gave a result surprisingly close to a right angle: 89°57' (figs. 9.1, 9.2, and 9.3). The deviation of both lines about 14 degrees from the cardinal points is not frequently found in the orientation of buildings at Tikal. No system formed by constructions with these orientations could be recognized in the overall planning of the ceremonial center. No extraordinary astronomical reference can be attributed to either of the lines of this right angle at Temple I. Perhaps glyphic and iconographic interpretations may help to identify the ritual, functional, or symbolic relation of these great temples. The published investigations place Temple I and Temple V as approximately contemporaneous (about A.D. 700), but Temple IV nearly half a century later (W. R. Coe 1967, p. 37).[5]

9.2. *The reconstructed Temple II limits the Great Plaza on the west side, here as seen from the doorway of Temple I. Temple III is visible to the left. Farther behind and to the right, the highest of the great temples at Tikal, Temple IV, projects out of the jungle at the horizon.*

How do we explain the right angle? It probably formed an essential part of the geometric knowledge of the Maya, a wide field still to be explored.[6] The layout of their ceremonial centers constituted for the Maya an excellent opportunity for the application of geometry on a large scale. The great temples of Tikal seem to demonstrate this with the precise east-west line from Temple I to Temple III and the right angle at Temple I subtended by reference points in the doorways of the distant Temples IV and V. These recent results are at odds with Eric Thompson's insistence that "the Maya . . . seem to have been incapable of making a true right angle" (1974, p. 94).

The doorways of Temples I and V also can be considered as departure points of two south-north lines, which connect to the Twin Pyramids of Complex O. The construction of these pyramids was accomplished shortly after the two great temples (A.D. 731). From the pyramids of Complex O two parallel lines lead northward to the Twin Pyramids of Complex P, which were erected one katun later (A.D. 751). These lines are not south-north but have approximately the same direction as the main axis of the North Acropolis, the dominant orientation of the central part of Tikal.[7]

In 1968 George Guillemin analyzed the development and function of the Tikal ceremonial center. Although he wrote that from the monumental temples and palaces to the modest little house platforms the buildings appear to be oriented, "psychologically reassuring to be aligned with the solar trajectory," and that the North Acropolis, "the most ancient and sacral focal point of the ceremonial center, is arranged to face the cardinal points," he apparently believed that "the orientation was applied as a matter of belief and principle, in a symbolic manner, and visibly without intention of mathematical exactness." He concluded that "a specific study undoubtedly would produce some coincidence, but . . . is likely to offer little probability of producing conclusive results" and "the orientation would be a more religious concept than an urbanistic norm" (pp. 1–5).

In 1969 Robert Fuson, a geographer, published an article about the orientation of Maya ceremonial centers, wherein he studied Chichen Itza, Uxmal, and Copan, drawing the solstice and equinox lines on rather schematic maps of these sites. As these lines do not refer to precise architectural features, they do not constitute any proof of astronomical orientations, though it is worthwhile to emphasize his suggestion of a possible orientation toward magnetic north.

In an unpublished study a similar kind of analysis was applied by Arthur Sanford (1974) to the maps of Chichen Itza, Uaxactun, and Tikal. His essay covers relationships between structures that satisfy solstice and equinox sun rise/set, extreme moon rise/set, and north-south alignments. The astronomical directions for Tikal drawn by Sanford at the scales of 1:2,000 and 1:4,000 (based on the Carr-Hazard maps) raise many doubts. An exact north-south visual line from a high pyramid (Str. 3D-43) to a stela (P-34) standing at a lower level and at a distance of 800 meters may be acceptable; but a sun line (marked as certain) from a small mound (Str. 6B-25) crossing over a higher elevation and through the central part of the ceremonial center and down to the same stela (P-34) over more than double that distance has meaning only on the drawing board. At the same time the doorway of a temple was taken in various cases as a reference point for a line directed

9.3. *View southward from the doorway of Temple I at Tikal, with the Central Acropolis in the foreground and Temple V behind. To the right extends the unexcavated South Acropolis, covered with high trees.*

to sun and moon over insignificant buildings at large distances. In other instances the point of reference of or to the structure was marked only by a circle. Such an indication must be explained in more detail. Which architectural feature is referred to? Is direct visibility implied? These questions are important since many of Sanford's lines impinge obliquely on the back or side wall of a building. Years ago it was demonstrated with Structure A-XVIII at Uaxactun that a north-south line leading to its back wall has a sensible explanation (Hartung 1972, pp. 20–25).

More importance can be attributed to Sanford's geometric observations than to his astronomical ones. He noted five right triangles and five isosceles triangles, although they are not all of the same quality; in three of them the Preclassic pyramid Structure 5C-54 never permitted a visual relation. He noted the right angle formed by lines from Temple V to Temple I to Temple IV to be 89°52' from measurements made on the map, a result which is quite close to the *in situ* measurements of Aveni, but between the center of the corresponding doorways. The map measurement may have referred to the central point of the upper platform of Temple I. This does not seem logical in the corresponding construction process, as Temple IV was not built at the same time and this reference point could not be defined later in order to trace the line at 90° to Temple IV.

The most interesting contribution by Sanford is his recognition of the existence of an isosceles triangle in an important position. The point of departure is the doorway of Structure 5D-104 inside the South Acropolis. The distance from there to Temple I and to Temple III is practically the same, 282 meters and 283 meters (map measurements). A logical hypothesis is that Temple 5D-104 and Temple I already existed. Then an east-west line was drawn from the doorway of Temple I, and the doorway of Temple III was placed at the point where a line from the doorway of Temple 5D-104 intersected the east-west line, so as to form an isosceles triangle with the base line from Temple I to Temple III.

After analyzing several interpretations about Tikal, it should be clear that in this paper the emphasis is on the architectural and planning data, their interrelations and interpretations, which may or may not be based on astronomical considerations. The archaeoastronomer can easily measure the alignments of the buildings and also limited visual lines in the restored central part of Tikal, but more distant views are possible only from the high temples and between them. It is generally recommended that the investigator begin with the map interpretation in order to study all possible astronomical lines. It would even be desirable to put the map data into a computer and revise the results. The final decisions should go through the hands of different specialists, and field measurements must confirm the proposed results.

Limitations in Astronomical Directions

The orientation of buildings to heavenly bodies implies a certain limitation in their possible position, without considering here the correspondent placement at a right angle. These orientations refer in importance first to the sun, second to the moon, and third to the planet Venus, the next most brillant celestial object. Then follow in importance other stars (or groups of stars) and, possibly, comets. In the latitude of the Maya zone the sun's rising and setting positions move during the year to an extreme of about 25° on either side of the east-west line. The extreme points of Venus and the moon are a few degrees farther to the north and to the south of these lines. Except for the rising and setting of a few bright stars, few events of astronomical significance occur within approximately 60° of the astronomical north and south directions. If we take the rise and set points during the year of all possible heavenly bodies, almost any orientation can be justified. The selection and limitation of astronomical objects must proceed logically according to their importance and visibility. Extreme positions and special events, such as the zenith passage of the sun, heliacal risings, and comets, deserve our particular attention.[8]

Alignments of Ancient Maya Structures

Both the pole-and-thatch house on its platform and the most complicated ceremonial center are part of the same concept of Maya architecture: the former being a simple and ingenious construction, the latter a developed and sophisticated building. The houses often followed the orientation adopted by the residential unit, probably corresponding to a clan grouping as has been suggested for Tikal (Haviland 1968).[9] Frequently the major ceremonial buildings display a special orientation, based on a careful layout, for their particular ritual assignation. We can assume that the importance of a particular structure determined the accuracy of its astronomical orientation. The layout of a platform for a present house has to be considered in terms of ability of its builder, in contrast to an outstanding ceremonial complex which deserves measurements with extraordinary care.

Generally the lower parts of the façades of structures (preferably between the extreme points) are the most accurate for defining an alignment, although often the basements were not traced with the same care as the buildings themselves. The transverse axis might be different from a perpendicular to the façade and the sides of the structure are not always at right angles. For field work it is recommended that the investigator make detailed notes and sketches of how the alignments were taken, measuring the walls at different heights, reckoning decisive points in various ways, tracing diagonal lines on platforms with the corresponding angles, and giving special consideration to retaining walls, which usually have given away and are no longer in their original position. A comprehensive knowledge of ancient architecture is indispensable in finding the convenient points of reference to be measured.

Extreme care in the measurement of probable astronomical alignments is necessary in cases where the building has been reconstructed or only partly restored. A detailed study of the excavation reports is highly recommended. Ideally, the archaeologist should immediately measure the alignment of an exposed structure: he or she can judge best how the original direction probably was traced. As early as 1928, Oliver Ricketson recommended that all investigators take accurate and copious bearings when exploring new sites, in case there arises the faintest suspicion that the "building or structural feature may have been designed in accordance with astronomical direction" (1928a, p. 225).

Visual Lines in the Ceremonial Centers and Their Surroundings

Stelae, altars, platforms, and other monuments or parts thereof may have served as reference points for visual lines, sometimes between these elements. More frequently, visual lines start from a temple doorway. Also, they may lead to the doorway of another building, where the visual line is of a different direction from the orientation of either of the reference structures. The case of the great temples at Tikal is a demonstration of the last-mentioned example. The rather large distances between the temples represent a guarantee for precision. The exact east-west line from Temple I to Temple III is nearly 320 meters long; the side lines of the 90-degree angle at Temple I to Temple V measure about 270 meters and to Temple IV almost 750 meters.

It is convenient to mention here a contrary opinion regarding accuracy in Maya architecture: "At Tikal, greatest Maya site, orientations of front walls of the five great pyramid temples (rear-wall readings differ by up to 1°37′) read 7°1′, 9°3′, 9°5′, 10°46′ and 18°16′ (Tozzer 1911, p. 115). One suspects that in the first four cases the Maya sought uniform orientation, and so variation arises from sloppiness, for such variability occurs all over the Maya area and is a warning against crediting the Maya with intentions and precision for every significant orientation noted" (Thompson 1974, p. 94).

Greater accuracy can be supposed if the distances between reference points are located in the landscape. Such a case is exhibited in the relation of the Palace of the Governor at Uxmal to the main pyramid at Nohpat, already well known (Hartung 1971; Aveni 1975).

An early published example of a long-distance line between stelae is the "Copan astronomical baseline" (figs. 9.4 and 9.5), which can be traced from the eastern side of the Copan river valley, halfway up a mountain (Stela 12), to the ridge on the western side (Stela 10), 6.6 km distance (see also the contribution by Aveni, these proceedings). Stelae 10 and 12 seem to have formed part of a system of at least six stelae which were erected at relatively large distances in the Valley of Copan about the same, rather early time: 9.11.0.0.0 = A.D. 652 (GMT correlation). These six stelae (3, 10, 12, 13, 19, and 23), as also Stela 2 and possibly Stelae 1 and 6, can be assigned to Ruler II, as was suggested by Pahl (personal communication 1974). More stelae and/or reference points probably existed in the valley in former times.

On the other side of Mesoamerica, at Teotihuacan, it has been shown that two of the so-called astronomical circles form a line exactly perpendicular to the main axis of the city (Millon 1968, p. 113). Recent investigations indicate that these circles may be part of an astronomical system similar to that at Copan, which extends over the wide Valley of Teotihuacan (Gaitan et al. 1974).

The Maya made long-distance constructions with their *sacbeob* (raised arti-

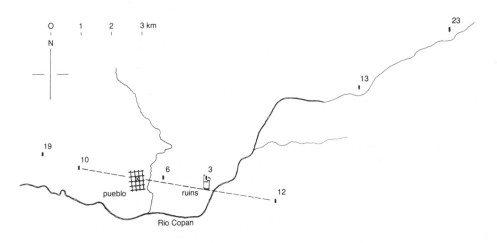

9.4. *Sketch map of the locations of Stelae 10 and 12 in the Valley of Copan. The so-called baseline between them is marked by a broken line. No elevations are indicated; visibility between stelae is not always possible.*

9.5. *View from Stela 10 looking eastward over the Valley of Copan to Stela 12, whose approximate location is marked by a circle. Copan buildings are visible below the circle. For the view in the opposite direction, see Aveni's paper, this volume, fig. 1.4.*

ficial roads), executed generally in straight lines. The largest of these still-existing causeways runs a distance of about 100 km from Coba to Yaxuna in northern Yucatan.

The foregoing evidence suggests that the ancient cultures of Mesoamerica were able to work with extreme accuracy in their observations and their tracings, which were manifested in planning, architecture, and monuments.

Reference Points in Mass and Open Space

Markers, mostly stelae and chiseled or pecked circles, situated in the landscape permitted precise reference points for rechecking and future observations. This is not the case when we are concerned with structural mass and delineated open space in ceremonial centers.

By the twenties there was already speculation that the crossing points of the rectangular ground plans of pyramids and the centerpoints of open space (plazas and patios) had a significance in the layout of ceremonial centers and may have served as reference points (Marquina 1928). The former are visible only *before* construction (only if traced on the ground) and afterward only if a corresponding marker was placed on top of the pyramid. The latter are visible only *after* constructing the space-defining buildings, and then visible only if fixed by a monument. Consequently, both of these reference points are valid only in case of an existing marker. If none exists, the central point of an open and usually quite irregular space cannot be accepted as part of the planning concept; as such it is intangible. It should also be emphasized that a monument may have no relation as a "central point of space" in the conceptual sense.

The famous tomb inside the Temple of Inscriptions at Palenque constituted an invisible focus for the placement of later buildings, a conscious magical-religious relation to a most-honored person. The central doorway of the large temple, exactly above the entrance to the crypt, in part served as a visible reference point (Hartung 1971, 1972).

In this consideration of open space and architectural mass (or occasionally volume), the small platforms in front of the temple doorways and the masonry blocks (sometimes called altars) in the stairways may be considered as parts of either aspect. The platform in front of the entrance to Temple 22 at Copan, delimited by sculptural elements, emphasizes the spatial aspect; the clear-cut masonry block situated in the stairway on the north side of Temple 11 at the same site refers to the aspect of mass. The precise placement of both seems to conform to a planning principle at Copan: a line between them runs parallel to the transverse axis of the Ballcourt and to a line between Stela M and Altar O (figs. 9.6 and 9.7). Both are at the same distance from the masonry block and represent important monuments in the Court of the Hieroglyphic Stairway (Hartung 1971, p. 100). One is inclined to propose a visual line from the doorway of Temple 22 to the masonry block (or vice-versa), but a careful measurement revealed that the references are the central points of the area in front of the doorway and the central point of the masonry block (Hohmann, personal communication 1972). These places may have served "as a

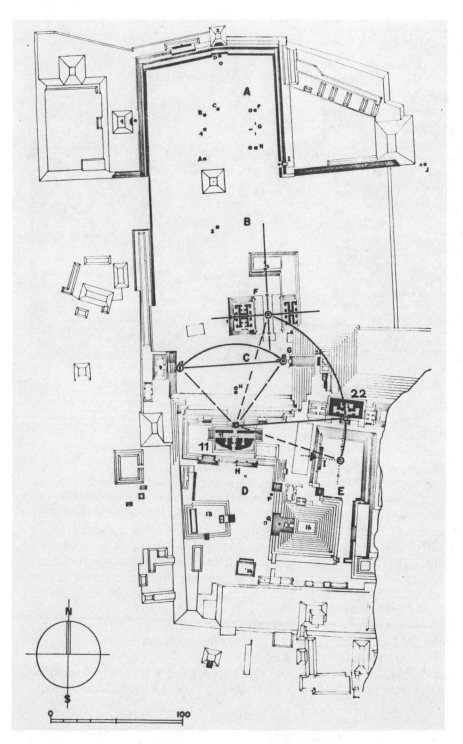

9.6. *Map of Copan with some of the important relation lines. The arcs were drawn to indicate same distances from the masonry block in the northern stairway of Temple II. (Redrawn after Morley 1920 and with data after Hartung 1971.)*

9.7. *The Ballcourt at Copan represents one of the most impressive compositions of exterior space in Maya planning.*

sort of reviewing stand" as was speculated for a similar block in front of the temple building of Temple II at Tikal (W. R. Coe 1967, p. 37).

The distance from the masonry block in the north stairway of Temple 11 to the front of the doorway of Temple 22 at Copan is the same as the distance to the central marker in the Ballcourt and is also the same as the distance to the central of three markers in the East Court of the Acropolis. The first of the markers forms an integral part of the bi-axial symmetry of the Ballcourt, "the most eloquent of all forms in displaying the Mesoamerican concern for space design among edifices" (Kubler 1958, p. 519). It is limited by constructions on both longitudinal sides and open, though only partly to the north, on the short sides. The sculptured slabs in the floor of the East Court, a slightly irregular plaza formed by high stairways with a small access at floor level in the south, are placed in a line pointing to the impressive doorway of Temple 22. The central marker lies along the axis connecting the Jaguar Stairway with the Altar of Venus.

The placement of markers in open space is very suggestive for astronomical interpretations and seems to be at least partly due to geometric considerations.

Geometry and Geomancy

The knowledge of the Maya in mathematics is well known and documented, particularly in the astronomical calculations of the Dresden Codex. Can one also suppose they had an interest in geometry? The placement of structures on archaeological site maps reveals for a trained observer the possible existence of geometric forms, systems, and even networks which are not always casual.

The Maya conception of the four world directions strongly implies the notion of a right angle. This is indicated not only by the logical application in construction (walls connected at 90 degrees, the most common way to form a building worldwide and for all time), but also by the distribution in space of the structures and monuments, though this need not necessarily produce a rectangular or grid pattern.

Different examples of right angles can be detected by map interpretation and in part confirmed by topographic measurements. A precise (in-front-of-the-building) relation—that is, at 90 degrees to the façade—has been proved, and furthermore astronomically, in the case of the Palace of the Governor at Uxmal (Hartung 1971; Aveni 1975).

Map interpretation has revealed isosceles triangles along with the existence of a 30-degree angle in several triangles. An example of the latter is a 30-degree subdivision to related structures at Yaxchilan (Hartung 1971). Of course, this does not exclude the use of other units of angles under different conditions.

In a 1968 paper I noted that the distances from the Caracol to the centerpoints of the most important ballcourts at Chichen Itza are the same. In a later publication these centerpoints were shown to be connected by an arc which passed over other reference points (Hartung 1971). It was not observed at that time that the angle was a radian, in other words an arc of the same length as the radius (Flores and Delaye, personal communication 1974).

On a more sophisticated level we can imagine a system or network, rectangular or of another form, which fits the layout of the ceremonial center. Such a network may have been visible in ancient times only to those who were initiated, as was suggested in 1966 (Hartung 1968). One may even ask whether "there was, between AD 600 and 900, an overall organization of the entire Maya Lowlands that was strongly influenced by the Maya's quadripartite view of the universe and that featured four regional capitals" and that "around these capitals developed the familiar hexagonal lattices of secondary centers" with "tertiary hexagons developed around these secondary centers" (Marcus 1973, p. 911).

The examples of geometry in Maya planning must have their origin and reason in Maya cosmology and religion, in the most profound area of Maya thought, perhaps even in the unconscious. The basis of Maya geometry seems to lie in geomancy, a wide field still unexplored and uninvestigated in Mesoamerica. Geomancy was applied especially in ancient China and in prehistoric Britain, where it continued until the end of the Middle Ages and left excellent material for a comparative study. Two indications in the literature suggest geomancy in Maya architecture; both refer to the famous Group E at Uaxactun, considered to be an astronomical observatory.[10]

Since geomancy defines the centers of energy inherent in the landscape, one may speculate that the magnetic declination was detected by the Maya and may have been used for the orientation of their structures. Ruppert and Denison (1943) referred to a certain preference for the 7°40′ east-of-north orientation of Maya structures. This coincides with the 7½-degree easterly magnetic declination considered as a good average for the Maya zone in 1965 by Fuson (1969).

The Role of Light and Shadow

Two days in ancient Mesoamerica were noted by the annual passage of the sun exactly through the zenith. At this time a vertical pole casts no shadow at noon and architecture presents a very special aspect. Also the equinoctial days seem to have been considered important for shadow casting, as is the case with the Castillo at Chichen Itza. Local people have noticed that on both equinoctial days of the year, about one hour before sunset, an undulating line is produced by the shadow of the northwest corner of the building on the western side of the north stairway, which has a serpent head on the lower end of its balustrade (Rivard 1970). The implied visibility of the image of the serpent (an undulating line with the serpent's head at its end) only on the equinoctial days underlines the importance of these days for the Maya and suggests an examination of this relation in more detail.

In April 1966 while standing in the doorway of Temple II at Tikal, I noticed that the temple cast its shadow exactly on the stairway of Temple I (fig. 9.8). Might the original form of the roof comb have projected its shadow on a fixed day at the height of the doorway of Temple I? It may be rewarding to look for similar situations in Maya architecture, as they could be numerous and significant.

Final Remarks

Astronomy should be considered an inseparable part of ancient Maya culture; in other words, any observation and result must be regarded in terms of its significance in Maya cosmology and religion. We should try to understand the meaning and consequence for the Maya, for the priest as well as for the people. Our progressing knowledge of the ancient Maya clarifies more and more the apparently disorderly placement of the structures in the ceremonial centers. Buildings were time related; they were planned for and served a specific use, which we are attempting to reveal. Generally, the buildings were altered later as opinions changed about rituals or religion, or even by personal decisions of a ruler.

In these studies new ideas from one discipline may considerably advance the programs of another. Interdisciplinary work is decisive. We must enlarge the field of information to more than the traditional sciences. The often-rejected influence of astrology should be revised for positive contribution. Investigations on geomancy are practically nonexistent and it is precisely this "ancient science" which may have contributed to the choice of placement of not only buildings but also entire centers. Geometry in planning may be the consequence of geomancy and/or extraordinarily well developed mathematics. As the sun and the moon produce shadows, it is logical that the Maya paid attention to this phenomenon. The elusiveness of the shadow represents a fascinating aspect. All the aforementioned

9.8. *The shadow of Temple II, produced by the setting sun, is marked on the stairway of Temple I at Tikal. Did there exist here and at other places a conscious consideration of the cast shadow?*

fields are closely related to astronomy as well as to architecture and planning; they deserve further conscientious study.

It is remarkable that the first scientific explorers of the Maya ruins were pre-occupied with measuring exact orientations of buildings. In 1913 Alfred Tozzer included a chapter on orientation in his publication on Nakum.[11] Astronomical investigations were realized in the Maya zone in the 1920's and 1930's, with Group E at Uaxactun and the Caracol at Chichen Itza as the most relevant examples. These results constituted the data which were accepted as definitive for a long time. From the 1940's through the 1960's there seemed to have been an indifference to further studies in the field of building orientations. It is only since about 1970 that a steadily growing interest has developed in the new science of archaeoastronomy in Mesoamerica.

Acknowledgments

To Anthony Aveni and Sharon Gibbs, I am indebted for helpful criticism of this paper. My participation in the Colgate symposium was in part supported by CONACYT grant No. 805.

Notes

1. "Adapting himself to the criteria of authenticity, style, aesthetics, and structural technique, subject to the material employed, the archaeologist proceeds to restore a building, once the necessary data is in his possession" (Roman Pina Chan, an archaeologist, in Gendrop 1974, p. 4).

In his recent publication "La restauracion arquitectonica de edificios arqueologicos," Augusto Molina, an architect, remarks in the conclusion, ". . . I have tried to demonstrate that we are lagging behind both in the theoretical approach to, and in the practice of, restoration of the prehispanic buildings of Mesoamerica." He continues, ". . . conceptually, at least, there has been a backward trend in this important activity." After commenting on "the low quality of present archaeological restoration in Mexico" (as related to architectural remains), Molina rejects the arguments generally presented by those who often reconstruct ruins: ". . . none of the reasons, be they of didactic, touristic, economic or nationalistic character, that are generally adduced to justify the (reconstruction) work that has been done on our prehispanic buildings, is valid; this kind of work largely destroys the historical character of the buildings" (1974, pp. 74, 75; his translation).

2. "Article 15. . . . ALL RECONSTRUCTION WORK SHOULD HOWEVER BE RULED OUT 'A PRIORI'; ONLY ANASTILOSIS, THAT IS TO SAY, THE RE-ASSEMBLING OF EXISTING BUT DISMEMBERED PARTS CAN BE PERMITTED" (ibid., p. 28; his translation).

3. The suggestion is based on the fragmentary text of Stela 24 at the base of its stairway (W. R. Coe 1967, p. 76). It seems probable that this date may refer to a time when the construction was already finished.

4. ". . . the ancient astronomers observed certain stars from the dark

cell or chamber through the open doorway of their temples, which were invariably situated on an elevation" (Nuttall 1906, p. 291).

5. Hieroglyphic inscriptions on wooden lintels indicate that the temple was built at about 9.15.10.0.0 or A.D. 741 (GMT correlation), confirmed by the radiocarbon dates of the beams with an average age of A.D. 720 ± 60 (W. R. Coe 1967, p. 81).

6. It is interesting that the modern Quiche use the concept of the right angle. Remington notes in "Current Astronomical Practices among the Maya" (these proceedings): "The second most frequently mentioned constellation is that of Orion's Belt and Sword. . . . To the Quiche it is the Three Marys (Tres Marias); in Quiche it is *c'ok*, 'the right angle', and comprises both the belt and the sword." In the original tape recording of her lecture the statement is even more explicit.

7. Temple V and Structure 3D-43 (the main pyramid of the North Group) can be connected by a line in this same direction. Parallel to this is a visual line from Temple I to the large Rock Sculpture in the Maler Causeway, the access road to the North Group.

8. It has been suggested that pre-Columbian buildings were oriented to the directions of the rising and setting sun on certain days of the year (Sartor 1974; Tichy 1974). These may be the days of festivities related to a specifically oriented temple. Tichy interprets information by Duran (1971, p. 78) to imply that to every god there corresponded a definite direction of the rising sun in the Mexican highlands during Aztec times.

9. "The Teotihuacan grid is boldly imposed on the landscape. It overrides topographical differences and imposes the Teotihuacan conception of order on its surroundings" (Millon 1968, p. 112). Thus, even the inhabitants of the far outlying barrios (residential units) felt themselves related to the great city and center. Of course there was no such grid at Tikal or other Maya cities, but a similar kind of identification may have existed.

10. Group E at Uaxactun and the similar assemblages at twelve or more neighboring sites have been considered by Kubler as "geomantic groups" (1958, p. 518). The excavator of Group E, Oliver Ricketson, concluded the chapter "Astronomic Features of Group E" with the observation (referring to the temples) "that their erection is to be more clearly associated with geomancy than with observational astronomy" (1937, p. 109).

11. "The buildings all face roughly one of the cardinal points. Unfortunately it was impossible to find the front wall of a single building in a position so that a careful orientation could be determined. The only wall which was available for a careful survey was the back wall of the inner room of Temple A. Merwin found that this was 3°42'20" east of north, referred to the true meridian. . . . Professor Robert Willson, who has been much interested in the question of the orientation of pre-historic buildings, has suggested to me the possibility that the true line of sight was neither the front walls of the buildings nor the inside wall at the back, but rather a line running at right angles from the inner back wall of the building to the front of the structure directly in the middle of the main doorway. This is an important subject of investigation and one which should not be neglected by future explorers in Central America" (Tozzer 1913, p. 155).

Native Astronomy and the Plains Caddoans

Waldo R. Wedel

Introduction

Among most historic tribes of the North American Great Plains, there appears to have been relatively little concern with astronomical phenomena as compared, for example, with the neighboring Southwest or Pueblo area. All Plains Indians were surely aware of such obvious and regularly recurring events as day and night; the rising and setting of the sun, moon, and stars; the seasonal shifting of the sun from its overhead midday course in summer to one low over the southern horizon in winter with concomitant environmental changes; the varying positions of the stars and consellations; and the fixed position of the north star at all times. Short-lived but exceptional or spectacular phenomena—for example, the appearance of a comet, an eclipse, or a meteor shower—seem as clearly to have briefly disturbed the Indians and were often regarded by them as omens of misfortune. But, if one may judge from the published record, the reactions of most Indians to these matters seem not to have been extensively integrated into their everyday life, their religious thinking, or their surviving art and mythology. In large part, the same can be said of the archaeological record as this has been recorded and interpreted to date, with a few notable exceptions.

The Pawnee and their more southerly kindred, the Wichita and the Caddo, are among the few exceptions to the foregoing generalizations. Until 1876 the most populous and influential native people of Nebraska, the Pawnee, consisted of four bands totaling at most perhaps eight to twelve thousand individuals in early historic times. Residing in a group of permanent earth-lodge villages on the Loup and Platte rivers of east-central Nebraska more than 100 miles west of the Missouri River (Wedel 1936) and maintaining a certain aloofness from the fur traders, they were more successful than most of their contemporaries in resisting the debilitating effects of white contact with its alcohol, new diseases, and other disruptive influences. Although the tribe was known to Euro-Americans since the mid-sixteenth century, most extant information on Pawnee religion and cosmogony was collected after its uprooting and removal to Oklahoma, some 400 miles south of its Nebraska homeland, in 1875, by which time the population had dwindled to about 1,440 persons.

The Wichita, at the time of their discovery by the Spanish in the mid-sixteenth century, seem to have occupied a more-or-less similar prestigious position some 200 miles south of the Pawnee on the Arkansas River (Wedel 1959). From here they moved farther south in the late seventeenth and eighteenth centuries, eventually to the general vicinity of the Wichita Mountains and the Red River drainage in western Oklahoma and adjacent Texas. Here, too, most of the detailed ethnographic data we have were gathered in the late nineteenth and early twentieth centuries and thus may vary, but in ways we can no longer assess, from the native lifeway of the first century or two after their discovery. As one consequence of this, correlation of the archaeological record with the ethnographic is made much more difficult and uncertain.

The Ethnographic Record

The ethnographic data relating to the southern Plains Caddoan-speaking tribes and their views on astronomical phenomena must be reviewed here briefly because they form a sort of bridge to the archaeological past toward which we are proceeding. This is not to imply that inferred parallels between ethnography and archaeology necessarily mean identical procedures and practices on the part of the human populations involved. But, because we are here dealing with a comparatively restricted geographical area occupied by linguistically related peoples sharing a basically similar way of life, I believe there is legitimacy in the proposition that we may be concerned with the same basic concepts expressed in somewhat different ways and media.

The Pawnee knowledge of astronomy was characterized as "very limited" by J. B. Dunbar (1882, p. 743), the son of a Presbyterian missionary who labored at the Plum Creek mission near the Pawnee villages during the first four or five years (ca. 1842–1846) of J. B.'s life. These villages were then variously located along the Loup River in present Nance County and on the Platte River in Monroe County, Nebraska. One wishes that the elder Dunbar, during his twelve years of service to the tribe (ca. 1834–1846), had taken closer note of the local Indian beliefs and practices of that turbulent period in Pawnee history. As far as I can find in the published letters (Dunbar 1918, p. 605), the only remark regarding celestial events refers to an eclipse of the sun on 30 November 1834. From this, some of the Pawnees inferred that "many of their wives and children would die after this event, and that it would be very cold." Dunbar reassured them with an explanation of the spectacle. His co-worker, Samuel Allis, writing of the many "superstitions" he had witnessed among the Skidi Pawnee, included the belief (1918, p. 707) that "when the starrhs [sic] fall, the enemy is comeing [sic] to make war with them." Some of the Oklahoma Pawnee today recall the belief that "when the stars fly around [meteor showers], great leaders will die."

In the literature on the Pawnee, I have found no references to their reactions to other celestial phenomena, such as the appearance of a comet. In 1858, Donati's comet created much unrest among the Mandans, Hidatsa, and nearby Sioux around Fort Atkinson on the Middle Missouri River (Boller 1868, pp. 143, 154), being regarded by them as a portent of disaster. A search through Indian agent reports for that year turned up no information concerning the attitudes of the Pawnee.

By contrast with the sketchy missionary reports noted above, trained observers many years afterward found that Pawnee religion and ritual were heavily interlaced with traditional, mythological, and anecdotal material which is perhaps more accurately termed star lore. The principal deities (Dorsey 1904*b*, p. xix) were identified as Morning Star and Evening Star, respectively male and female, and the former associated also with war. Next in rank were the gods of the four world quarters, standing in the semicardinal positions and supporting the heavens. Sun and Moon were of much less importance in the Pawnee pantheon. According to Weltfish (1965, p. 80), the gods of the four cardinal directions were created first, with Evening Star in the west and Moon as her helper, Morning Star in the east with Sun as his helper, North Star ("It which doesn't move"), and South Star (Canopus). Gods of the semicardinal directions are enumerated by the same observer as Black Star in the northeast, Yellow Star in the northwest, White Star in the southwest, and Red Star in the southeast. Their correlation with specific stars in today's sky remains uncertain.

Several constellations were recognized and named by the Pawnee, who were aware of the variations in their rising and setting. Corona Borealis was believed to represent a circle of chiefs, who were the patrons of the chief's society on earth (Fletcher 1904, p. 234); and according to Dorsey (1904*b*, p. xix), the North Star presided over the doings of this celestial assemblage. Dunbar (1882, p. 743) said that the Pleiades were associated with cold weather; the Milky Way represented the line where the "two hollow hemispheres" that formed the sky came together; the Great Dipper bore the same name among the Pawnee; and a part of the constellation Cassiopeia was known as "turkey's foot" from some fancied resemblance to that member. Unpublished field notes by Fletcher (NAA:MS 4558 [93]) differ in some details: for example, the Milky Way was the path followed by the spirits of the dead as they traveled southward to their permanent abode, the Great Dipper represented four people carrying a sick person, and so forth.

A Pawnee sky map at the Field Museum of Natural History, painted on buckskin and kept in a sacred bundle, has been cited by Buckstaff (1927) as evidence of a rather advanced knowledge of the night skies before the coming of white men. Stars of several magnitudes are indicated by simple crosses of varying sizes. A band of tiny stars denotes the Milky Way, with the winter heavens shown at the left and the summer heavens on the right. Constellations include the Pleiades, Lyra, Corona Borealis, Ursa Major, Ursa Minor, Coma Berenices, and Andromeda, all depicted much as we recognize them today. As further evidence of the high quality of the Pawnee observations, two double stars are recorded—one pair in Ursa Major, the other between Lyra and Corona Borealis near the Milky Way.

The author attributes to Dr. Ralph Linton, then of the Field Museum staff, the information that "this map is at least 300 years old." The basis for this estimate is nowhere set forth, and the figure given is surely excessive. It would imply that the map dates back to an early historic seventeenth-century manifestation of Pawnee culture known to archaeologists as the Lower Loup Phase (Dunlevy 1936; Grange 1968; Wedel 1938) and has been handed down through ten generations or more of caretakers, withstanding in the process frequent bundle renewals and other adversities. I view with skepticism both the age estimate and the author's observation that the age "would bar any white influence" on the map and its depictions.

Passage of the year was reckoned by the Pawnee in moons or months, alternately twelve and thirteen in number, but "there was much confusion in the system" (Dunbar 1882, p. 744). The regular months were grouped by threes, with the first three (December to February) regarded as winter and successive triads as spring, summer, and autumn. When appropriate, the thirteenth month was intercalated at the close of the summer quarter. Two seasons, one cold and one warm, were also recognized. There was no system of calendric notation, and past years, if referred to at all, were tied to some outstanding event, such as an epidemic, a poor crop, a bad hunt, and so forth.

The permanent villages of the Skidi Pawnee, at least, were traditionally arranged in a ritually prescribed order. Four major villages formed a central group, placed as if at the corners of a great square. At the west end of an imaginary line through the center of the square was a fifth village, whose shrine derived from the star of the west, that is, the evening star. At the opposite end was the village with the shrine of the star of the east, or morning star. Around this basic grouping were placed the other seven villages of the Skidi, so that the arrangement of the villages on the Nebraska landscape mirrored the pattern formed by the patron stars in the sky (Dorsey 1904b, p. xx; Fletcher 1902, p. 731, and NAA:MS 4558[93]). The stars of the six leading villages, as above enumerated, were paired, the northeast (male) with the southwest (female), the southeast (male) with the northwest (female), and the evening star (female) with the morning star (male). As these linkages indicate, the heavens were thus divided into two segments—the east, which was male, and the west, which was female (fig. 10.1).

The ceremonial year began about the time of the spring equinox, specifically with the First Thunder ceremony. According to Fletcher (1902), the shrine of the star of the west led off the annual ceremonial circuit on this occasion. The shrines of the other four main villages rotated the leadership thereafter, each village leading for one year and then giving way to its successor. The shrines of the four main villages pertained to the secular tribal affairs: hunting, planting, conferring of honors upon warriors, and so forth. The evening and morning star shrines, on the other hand, dealt with cosmic forces and man's dependence on the supernatural for life, food, and happiness.

The ritual for which the Pawnee were probably most widely known was the oft-described Morning Star ceremony. This was a summertime event, staged whenever a warrior or chief dreamed appropriately; it was to ensure soil fertility and successful crops. It involved the scaffold killing of a young female captive in what has been compared to certain Mexican sacrificial rites (Dorsey 1907a; Linton

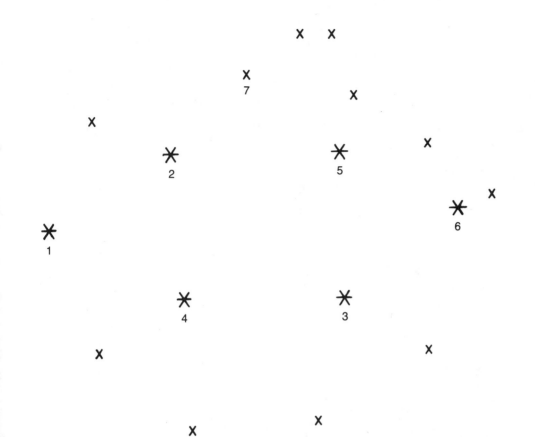

10.1. *Villages of the Skidi Pawnee and their star associations. 1, Star of the West (Evening Star); 2–5, four leading stars (not identified); 6, Morning Star; 7, North Star. Unnumbered crosses indicate other villages. (After Fletcher 1902 and n.d.)*

1926; Wissler and Spinden 1916). According to Wissler and Spinden (p. 49), the ritual tended to coincide with the period during which Mars was the morning star. Murie (Fletcher NAA:MS 4558[93]) reportedly thought the red star of morning was Jupiter, and that the proper time for the Morning Star ceremony was when Jupiter comes up in the east. The Skidi were the only Pawnee band that practiced the ritual in historic times. It is noteworthy that Dorsey (1907a, p. 67) suggested this may once have been a solstice ceremony, since a watered-down version without the human victim was staged at the time of the winter solstice.

The star cult was also reflected in the plan and construction of the Pawnee earth lodge, which was the usual type of habitation at their permanent villages. The circular floor, from 20 to 50 feet in diameter, symbolized the earth; its domed roof-wall superstructure, the overarching sky (Fletcher 1902, p. 735). Around the un-lined central firepit, which held a small bit of the sun, the superstructure was supported by four large posts set more or less in the semicardinal directions so as to approximate a square or at least a rectangle; these four posts represented the

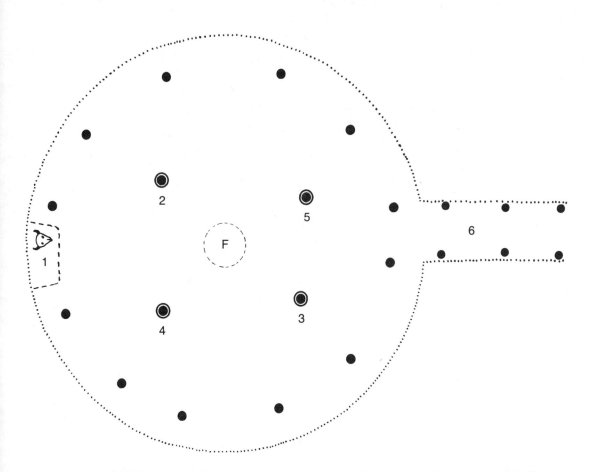

10.2. *Floor plan of Pawnee earth lodge ca. A.D. 1600. 1, platform shrine with bison skull; 2–5, center posts; 6, entrance; F, fireplace. (After Strong 1935.)*

star-gods of the four leading villages. They were sometimes painted, in colors coded to the semicardinal directions (fig. 10.2). The tunnellike doorway opened toward the east, so that the rising sun could shine directly upon the household altar, a low platform situated at the west side of the floor and holding a bison skull and perhaps other sacred objects. Above the altar, a sacred medicine bundle was hung from the lodge frame to symbolize the household god. This contained various articles: bird skins, animal skulls, perhaps an ear of corn, a pipe and stem, and so forth, all believed to help ensure good fortune for the owner and his household, provided the bundle was not dishonored by irreverent handling and was renewed each year at the proper time and with appropriate ritual. According to Weltfish (1965, p. 79), the doorway and the smokehole directly above the fireplace sometimes served the priests within as a convenient place from which to observe the positions of the stars and constellations by which their ceremonies were guided.

The considerable importance attached to the semicardinal positions and directions should be noted here. This point is frequently mentioned by Weltfish (1965a, passim), and it appears to have some archaeological relevance for the re-

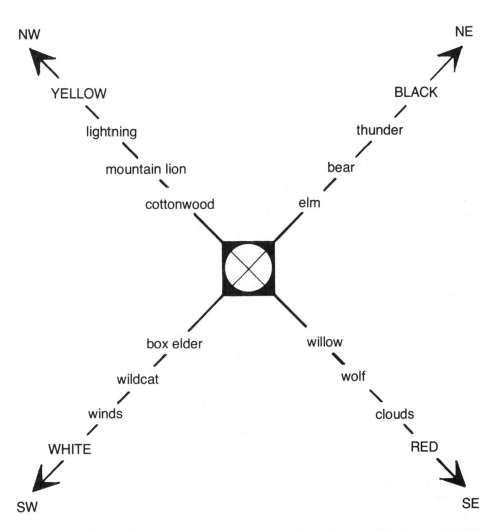

NW

NE

YELLOW

BLACK

lightning

thunder

mountain lion

bear

cottonwood

elm

box elder

willow

wildcat

wolf

winds

clouds

WHITE

RED

SW

SE

10.3. *Association of colors, natural forces, animals, and trees with the semicardinal directions among the Pawnee. (After Weltfish 1965.)*

gion as well, as will be indicated below. A color was associated with each of the semicardinal directions (fig. 10.3). The shrine or bundle for each of these four villages included an ear of corn of a color to match its directional position. In classifying the varieties of corn among the Pawnee by color, one of Weltfish's informants followed a northeast-southwest-northwest-southeast sequence, from which she noted (Weltfish, p. 122) that "this diagonal succession forms a simple cross, the Pawnee symbol for a star" (see also Dunbar 1882, p. 745). Animals, trees, and other elements in nature were likewise associated with the semicardinal directions (Weltfish, p. 112).

For the Wichita, there is much less ethnographic information than for the Pawnee and other more northerly Plains tribes, and most of it is from a single source (Dorsey 1904*b*). First met by Europeans in central Kansas in 1541, the Wichita

experienced drastic cultural and populational changes after ca. 1750. Their numbers, estimated at perhaps four to six thousand in the eighteenth century, had
fallen by 1868 to an "official" 572 persons. Later, during the period 1875–1900, the
formal political organization under which the Wichita and the closely related Waco,
Tawakoni, and Kechai lived fell apart; thereafter, very little remained of the old way
of life (war parties, most ceremonies, bison hunting, and grass-house villages)
except as fading memories among the older people. It has been remarked that the
1850–1875 period is "the oldest date for which Wichita culture can be reliably reconstructed" (Schmitt and Schmitt 1952, p. 64); this is more than two centuries
after the date of the archaeological remains in central Kansas (Wedel 1959, p.
571) which are believed to represent the Wichita, or at least a very substantial
portion of them, as they first emerge into documentary history.

According to Dorsey (1904b, p. 18), the "religious system of the Wichita, like
that of the Pawnee, though to a less extent, may be characterized as a star cult."
Chief of the gods and creator of the universe was "Man-never-known-on-earth,"
not specifically identified by Dorsey with a celestial body. Of successively lesser
rank were the Sun; then Morning Star, who kept the stars in their proper order and
ushered in the daylight; South Star, protector of warriors and chiefs; North or Pole
Star, who showed people the way north and was also guardian and patron of the
medicine men; the stars of the Great Bear, associated with war parties; and, finally, Moon, special guardian of women and associated with increase of life among
animals, birds, and plants. Dorsey (1904b, p. 16) noted further that "the extended
and beautiful rituals, so characteristic of the Skidi and other bands of Pawnee,"
were lacking among the Wichita. His observation that Wichita religious ceremonies
"began many years ago to decline . . . due largely to the fact that the Wichita were
largely concerned with acts of war" seems open to question. Except for Dorsey, I
have found no details on the star cult among the Wichita nor do there appear to be
any data on the astronomic aspects of their religion and theology prior to ca. 1750,
while the native culture was still flourishing. This is particularly unfortunate because archaeology suggests some interesting possibilities that will be touched
on elsewhere.

Some symbolism was attached to certain features of the Wichita grass house,
though to a lesser degree than is recorded for the Pawnee earth lodge. Doorways
opened both east and west to admit the sun, and in former times, there was also
a door to the south so that "the god of the south wind may look in at noon" (Dorsey
1904b, pp. 4–5). At the top of the domed structure, four poles pointed in as many
directions to the cardinal points. These represented the four world quarters, or
gods; the peak above was symbolic of the creator in Wichita mythology. Whatever
other orientations existed with respect to habitations, villages, or other aboriginal
features and constructions is apparently not recorded in the ethnographic and historic literature now available for the Wichita.

Among the Arikara, northernmost linguistic kindred of the Pawnee and Wichita, there seem to have been no notable evidences of the complex star lore possessed and exercised by the Skidi and other Pawnee. In the south, for the Caddo,
Swanton (1942, p. 238) tersely observes that "their connection with the Pawnee
and Wichita appears in strong traces of a star cult."

The Archaeological Evidence

Since so much of the Pawnee concern with the stars and other celestial matters involved ritual and ceremonialism rather than material culture, it is not to be expected that there will be much direct relevant archaeological evidence. At present, where only tentative band identifications are possible for most known Pawnee archaeological sites and in-depth analyses exist only for the pottery remains (Grange 1968), there is no way of correlating, even very roughly, the traditional distribution of Skidi villages with mirrored star patterns in the heavens. Indeed, in historic times the numerous Skidi ("Panimaha," etc.) villages indicated on earlier maps had for all practical purposes been supplanted by one or two large villages, as seen by American explorers in the early nineteenth century. In the last Nebraska earth-lodge settlement of the Pawnee at Genoa, the Skidi occupied the northwest end of the community. Possibly this and other large band villages of historic times consisted actually of tight little clusters or groups of houses, "held together by a common name" (Dorsey 1907b, p. 71) but not necessarily joined to one another to form a single large town, with each cluster representing a once separate and independent village. Or the traditions as recorded may tell it like it never really was, an idealized pattern which did not exist at any point in the actual history of the Skidi.

Historically, the Pawnee earth lodge was a familiar and well-known feature of the Indian landscape in east-central Nebraska. Shared with many other semisedentary village Indian tribes of the eastern Plains, it has been described by a number of travelers and contemporary observers. From these descriptions, together with the results of archaeological excavation of several scores of these structures, it appears that in the nineteenth century the native builders often departed in certain particulars from the traditional east-facing lodge with four central supporting posts (Wedel 1936, p. 43; 1938). In the latter respect, the number of posts varied from four to as many as ten or twelve, but in any case an even number so as to produce a bilaterally symmetrical structure centering, ideally, on an east-west line from the entrance through the fireplace and across the altar platform on the west side. The parallel between this arrangement of basic lodge features and the celestial pattern of stars representing the four, five, or six main villages of the Skidi (figs. 10.1 and 10.2) is noteworthy, as Fletcher (1902, pp. 734–735) pointed out long ago.

Another departure from tradition involves orientation of the door. This did not always open toward the east but seems to have been customarily in the southeast quarter of the lodge, primarily, one supposes, to face away from the cold northwest winds and prevailing storms rather than to satisfy some idealized ceremonial requirements. The traditional stipulation that the lodge be so oriented that the sun's first rays could fall on the shrine at the west side thus was not fulfilled by many of the historic structures. It must be noted that many of the later historic lodges were of considerable size—up to 40 or 50 feet in diameter, or more, so that procurement of the large trees required by a four-post central support may have been a serious problem on some occasions. If the ceremonial four-post number was ever seriously observed, it would probably have been in the smaller lodges of earlier times.

Later, as houses were built larger to accommodate more occupants, more center posts were added or a secondary circle of posts was placed between the four center ones and the outermost series of roof-wall supports (cf. Dunlevy 1936, p. 164 and fig. 6). Analysis of the extant archaeological data, with particular reference to orientation of house floors and alignment of the basic structural features, ought to provide some clues to changing concepts and practices among the Pawnee through time.

Archaeologically, we still know almost nothing regarding the usual type of habitation used by the Wichita while they lived in central Kansas and at the time of their first contacts with white men. Other aspects of their material culture, stone-working, pottery-making, bonework, and so forth, are rather better known (Wedel 1959, pp. 210, 571), though our information is still far short of that available for the Nebraska Pawnee. In one particular, however, it appears that Wichita archaeology is unique and without known parallel in the Plains region or elsewhere. I refer to the so-called council circles.

Council circles are the principal surface features apparent today at five Indian village sites in central Kansas. On the surface, where not defaced by modern civilization, a typical council circle consists of a low central mound, 20 to 30 yards in diameter, surrounded by a shallow ditch or a series of oblong depressions running end to end around the mound in a roughly circular, subcircular, or elliptical pattern. In at least two instances there seem to have been two ditches or discontinuous depressed zones around the central mound. The rough measurements possible from surface traces and aerial photographs indicate that the outside diameter of these configurations ranged from approximately 30 to nearly 70 yards. Maximum relief is 18–36 inches. Other than surface contours, there was little to distinguish these features prior to excavation, except that tips of sandstone boulders were visible here and there at two of the circles. Artifacts and trash were to be seen only where rodents or vandals had burrowed or the surface was otherwise broken. Their designation as council circles by local historians nearly a half-century ago (Jones 1928, p. 541) was not because of any sound indication as to their function but rather for want of a better term.

Excavations have been made in three of the circles, all in Rice County (Wedel 1959, p. 215; 1967; 1968). The most extensive work was at the Tobias site (14RC8) nine miles northeast of Lyons. Before excavation, this consisted of an elliptical arrangement of six shallow oblong depressions, varying considerably in size, form, and depth but clearly visible from the air by their dark-green grass cover. This ellipse measured about 40 yards in length; its long axis was directed eastnortheast-westsouthwest and very close to 30° from east-west. Excavation revealed a series of four oblong or curving dug basins, forming a roughly quadrilateral pattern *inside* the ellipse and only very roughly paralleling the surface depressions. There was no overlapping of dug basins by surface depressions, and there is no reason to believe that the concentric pattern was not planned.

The dug basins were positioned in the semicardinal directions—northwest, northeast, southeast, southwest with respect to the central mound. They varied in length from 30 to nearly 60 feet, in depth from 32 to 36 inches, and in width from 10 to 12 feet. The southeast and southwest basins were much longer than the two in the north half of the circle. In the center of the court formed by the four basins was an unworked sandstone slab about one foot underground, beneath which were four tabular bone beads. In the general vicinity were large amounts of ashes suggesting hearth cleanings.

In each basin, the fill between 12 and 24 inches beneath ground level included many sandstone slabs and boulders, mostly unworked and unshaped. These were in all sizes and shapes, ranging in weight up to 200 pounds; many would have required the efforts of two or more persons to bring them to the spot from the creekside sandstone ledges 100 yards or more to the east. Beneath this layer, the lower 6–12 inches of basin fill included masses of burned earth, some bearing pole and grass impressions and associated with charred pole and post fragments, twigs, and other debris. Under this material, inferentially the remains of burned-out lodge structures, the floor exhibited a row of ash-filled fireplaces running down the midline; in the longer basins, a line of postholes or charred post stumps similarly followed the midline, these posts alternating at about 7–8-foot intervals with the firepits. Fragmentary pottery, broken and unbroken bone, stone, shell, and other artifacts littered the floor around the hearths. Charred basketry containing shelled corn, and other masses of corn, both shelled and on the cob, suggested the remains of baskets and bags of harvested grain which may have been hung from the ridgepole or stored among the rafters. Human bones, nearly always disarticulated and isolated and never as whole skeletons, were scattered in and above the burned zone and below the boulder-filled level in each of the basins.

It seems clear that the four basins represented the ruins of as many dugout houses, each built in or over an elongate excavated pit on a framework of poles supported by posts, thatched with grass, and then at least partly covered with earth or clay daub. The stone slabs were presumably laid or stacked against the exterior base of the thatched-house wall where it met the rim of the excavated basin, but whether as reinforcement, as fire guard, or for another purpose, we do not know. When the house burned and the superstructure collapsed, these boulders slid into the pit where we found them, not uncommonly in imbricate position.

About 800 yards east by south of the Tobias circle is the Paul Thompson circle (14RC12), smallest of the five. Incomplete excavations here in 1967 showed that there were again four oblong house basins situated, like those at the Tobias site, in the semicardinal positions around the slightly mounded center. Again they lay within the discontinuous circle formed by the surface pits. Two of the basins were cleared. Each had fireplaces scattered along the midline, small storage pits, and a few postholes. There were again many sandstone boulders in the fill along the walls. Less obvious was the evidence of burning here except in the form of several charred poles up to 4 inches in diameter, suggesting at least partial destruction by fire. Small ash-filled fireplaces were scattered about the court within the circle, perhaps indicating a work area for domestic activities, such as outdoor cooking. An unusually large fireplace, approximately 42 inches in diameter, was found a few inches beneath the ground surface at the approximate center of the court and below the highest part of the mound as we estimated it prior to excavation.

Our tentative conclusions were that this circle complex, like that at Tobias, had consisted of four thatched semisubterranean longhouses, arranged in the semicardinal positions around a mound; that these houses had been a scene of some domestic activities but their occupants alone were not numerous enough to account for all cultural materials scattered over the village site in which the council circle occurs; and that abandonment may well have been connected somehow with a conflagration.

A little more than a mile east by south of the Thompson circle, on the Hayes site (14RC13), is the third and largest of the Rice County circles. Although surface details have been badly obscured by several decades of plowing, the double circle arrangement of dug basins inside an outer ditch is again found here. According to the owner, whose father broke sod in about 1928 where the circle lies, there were once two concentric circles around the mound, at least one of them continuous and the other possibly quartered. Our excavations here in 1967 were severely limited by several circumstances. They strongly suggest, nevertheless, that there were again four dug basins, irregularly oblong and unevenly spaced in the semi-cardinal segments of the circle. In all four basins, we found disarticulated human bones, as at Tobias; but unlike the Tobias and Thompson circles, this one had no boulders in the fill, perhaps because the nearest stone outcrops lay much farther from the circle. A second circle(?) of dug basins, apparently coinciding with the surface depressions, included very little occupational debris in the fill, thus sharp-ly contrasting with the inner series. However, as at the Thompson circle, at or very near the center of the Hayes circle was an unusually large, well-defined, ash-filled fireplace about twelve inches underground, nearly four feet in diameter and con-taining a strongly layered ash and charcoal fill almost a foot deep.

The oblong basins we excavated or sampled inside the circles at these three sites are believed to represent in each case a planned house complex. The houses, semisubterranean, elongate and sometimes curving in ground plan, and presumably provided with a ridgepole and hip roof, were quite unlike the usual earth-covered lodges of the region and the grass lodges of the historic southern Plains. At the same time, the regular occurrence of small domestic fireplaces, to-gether with the close similarity of the included artifacts to those found elsewhere in the storage pits and refuse mounds at these and related nearby village sites, all support the view that these were indeed habitations. By whom they were inhab-ited, a village elite, a priestly class, or some other special group, we have no hint from any available ethnographic or historic records of Caddoan or other Plains In-dian groups.

The more-or-less central placement of each circle in its particular village com-plex further suggests a special-purpose structure. Yet nothing we found in the cir-cles sampled could be construed as clearly ceremonial furniture or paraphernalia unless it was the large ash-filled fireplaces centrally situated in the Hayes and Thompson circles. There is no evidence that any of these structures was palisaded or otherwise defensively arranged, though the ground plan of each calls to mind Trevino's description of the fortified Taovayas ("Wichita") town on Red River where the Indians repelled an attack by the Spaniards under Don Diego Ortiz Pa-rrilla in 1759 (Duffield 1965). We unfortunately know nothing archaeologically con-cerning the usual type of dwelling at these central Kansas sites. Where roads and ditches have been cut through the sites, nothing identifiable as a lodge floor has ever been recognized, as is commonly the case at other village sites where earth-lodge floors and house pits have been intersected. Since most central Kansas Wichita sites are much too extensive to be explained on the basis of the two or three score people who could have been accommodated by the pit houses in the circle complexes, we infer that most of the erstwhile villagers probably dwelt in less substantial grass-thatched surface houses, essentially like those described by the early Spanish and later American explorers and identified in later historic times with the Wichitas in Oklahoma and Texas.

One other circumstance appears to support the idea that the council circles were special-purpose structures. All but one are situated on ridge or bluff tops which, except for a few large trees, provide unobstructed views of the horizon. The Tobias, Thompson, and Hayes circles are aligned in such a manner that design rather than chance seems to be indicated. In native times, when these circles were in use and thatched lodges stood in each basin, with smaller, fewer, or no trees along the intervening creek banks, an observer standing some 70 yards south of the Tobias circle and looking east by 30° south would have had both the Thompson and the Hayes circle in his line of sight. At the winter solstice, this observer could also have seen the sun rise where his sight line intersected the horizon, for in this latitude (N38°5) the midwinter sunrise is at 30° south of east, according to U.S. Naval Observatory personnel (Wedel 1967, p. 63). Field observations on 21–22 December 1965 confirmed this sunrise alignment. Conversely, an observer standing by the large central fireplace at the Hayes circle and watching the midsummer sunset would have been looking just past the edge of the large central fireplace at Thompson, with the Tobias circle immediately to the right of his sight line under the setting sun. This, too, was confirmed by sighting on 21 June 1971. The Hayes circle, to judge from aerial photos made before recent deep plowing and heavy washing rains, may actually have been an ellipse whose long axis closely paralleled the solstice sight line just described (fig. 10.4).

In previous discussions of the Kansas council circles and their possible relevance to solstitial phenomena (Wedel 1967, 1968), I have suggested that the human skeletal material associated with at least two of the complexes may have figured somehow in sacrificial rites revolving around the solstices. We have no record of human sacrifice among the Wichita or among the Pawnee except by the Skidi band with its much publicized Morning Star ceremony. Winter solstice rites were of considerable importance to Pueblo Indians in the Southwest, with whose late prehistoric and early historic representatives along the upper Rio Grande the central Kansas Indians demonstrably had strong trade relationships. Conceivably, therefore, some of the southern Plains Caddoan groups may have acquired or elaborated through intertribal contacts certain solstitial practices or performances that required human victims.

On further reflection, certain considerations resulting from additional field work now seem to militate against this thesis. At the Hayes circle, where eighteen or more partial to nearly complete human skeletons and numerous dissociated bones were mass buried near one end of an unfinished(?) house pit, accompanying artifacts that almost certainly represented mortuary offerings were essentially identical with those found in cache pits, on and in trash heaps, and on the site surface generally. These artifacts, consisting of bone and stone projectile points, bone awls, glass and shell beads, turquoise, and other items, are acceptable evidence that the supposed sacrificial victims were probably honored members of the local community rather than captives who experienced ritual death. The clear indications of hasty interments, in large part disorderly and in a still unfinished house, suggest that these people were more likely victims of a community catastrophe, perhaps involving enemy action or an epidemic. It is possible that these individuals were victims of the smallpox epidemic that visited the Quapaw and their neighbors on the lower Arkansas and Mississippi rivers ca. 1698–99 or of some earlier visitation.

Eddy (n.d., p. 27) has correctly observed that, in an earlier discussion of the Kansas council circles, I "reported no distinctive marking at the proposed intersection point, which leaves the summer solstice [Tobias Circle] line highly conjectural. Moreover, he did not give the measured azimuths of any of the alignments and we do not know the uncertainties involved. A more detailed survey of the site positions is surely needed, to check Wedel's aerial survey and to investigate other possible interalignments of the three mounds."

With all of this I agree. I would also point out that precise instrument measurements will be difficult to get on structures that have been repeatedly plowed or partially excavated and whose exact boundaries and dimensions were set, not by masonry, adobe, stone, or brick walls, floors, columns, and the like, but by earthen walls subject to erosion and ready to collapse as soon as their builders ceased maintenance and repair operations. The apparent alignments with solstice lines in the case of the Rice County circles and with a moonrise azimuth at maximum northward declination in the Paint Creek circle (fig. 10.4, insert) may be entirely coincidental, though I find the idea of an astronomical basis rather more palatable. If the central fireplaces and other features in the circles can be accurately relocated, some of the uncertainties noted by Eddy may be amenable to correction through careful work with appropriate instruments.

Considering the fact that the builders of these structures were in an area whose historic inhabitants clearly possessed a well-developed star cult (e.g., the Pawnee), not far removed spatially from other people who demonstrably made use of topographically marked horizon points for agricultural purposes and their ceremonial calendars (Fewkes 1897, p. 269; 1898, pp. 67–68; Parsons 1936, 1939a, 1939b), it seems entirely possible that the early historic Wichita peoples of central Kansas would have devised similar time markers of their own construction by which to regulate their ceremonial system and their yearly round of economic and subsistence activities. Whether such structures as they might have erected in the absence of suitable horizon markers, perhaps sighted in with poles, fires, or other makeshift devices, would have been any more precise than were our eyeball sightings in 1965 and 1971, I cannot say. Absolute accuracy would probably not have been essential to the contemporary ritual leaders, any more than it was required in the construction of dwellings, altars, or other features.

In the literature on North American archaeology, there appears to be surprisingly little that bears on the subject at hand. At the great Middle Mississippi

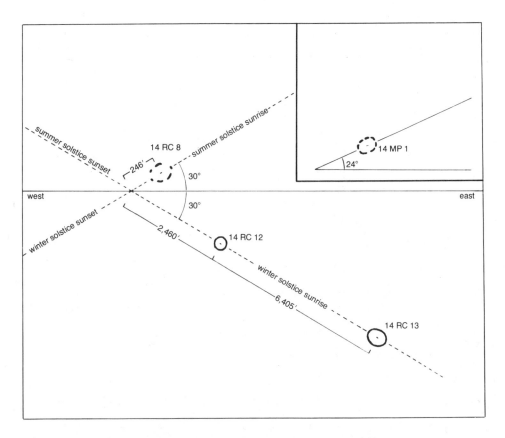

10.4. *Orientation and alignment of council circles in central Kansas.*

townsite of Cahokia, on the American Bottoms near St. Louis, Wittry (1964) has described several arcs of large postholes that appear to have been segments of four circles from around 240 to nearly 500 feet in diameter, which he suggests were much earlier in time than the Kansas council circles by half a millennium or more. In the northwestern plains of Wyoming, the Big Horn Medicine Wheel alignment has also been recently identified (Eddy 1974) as a device for marking summer solstice horizon points of the rising and setting sun and for certain star risings. This alignment appears to be rather more recent than the council circles, perhaps at ca. A.D. 1750 or thereabouts. Despite lingering skepticism about these and other correlations made through interdisciplinary studies, I suspect that continued investigation will turn up many more archaeological features with astronomical implications when the widely scattered and often fragmentary data collected, and still to be collected, will have been critically re-examined by competent scholars.

Acknowledgments

I gratefully acknowledge helpful observations and suggestions on the Pawnee from Garland Martha Blaine, Oklahoma City.

11

Medicine Wheels and Plains Indian Astronomy

John A. Eddy

Early Indians of the Plains

      It seems fair to say that we know less about the early inhabitants of the Great Plains than about any of their contemporaries on the continent, including their presumed relatives, the Mesoamericans. Both groups were here at the same time and for about the same length of time. Both are presumed to have descended from Asiatics who crossed the Bering Strait some 20,000 to 50,000 years ago. Both were briefly observed *in situ* by Europeans in the sixteenth century. But unlike the more colorful Mesoamericans, the Indians of the Plains left no written language and no well-developed art. Unlike their Anasazi neighbors to the south, the Plains Indians didn't build much. And unlike the case of the woodland tribes of our eastern seaboard, intensive observation of the Plains Indians did not begin until they had had more than 200 years to adjust to their first contacts with Spanish explorers. Between Coronado and Lewis and Clark the life of the Plains Indians was drastically changed, and we are often warned that the ways of the equestrian Sioux or Cheyenne may shed little light on the ways of their unknown, pedestrian ancestors. They were quick to adopt certain changes and, I think, to abandon earlier traditions. All these factors tend to hide much of the history of an already dim and indistinct people.

     I am surprised that we know anything at all about the early Plains Indians considering how few were here and over what a great area they ranged. It is generally held that when Columbus first set foot upon this continent there lived between the Mississippi and the Rocky Mountains about as many people as now reside in my home town of Boulder, Colorado. They were spread over an area of more than a million square miles and what are now fifteen western states and provinces. And most of them were constantly on the move, seldom if ever stopping to build anything lasting or substantive.

     These nomadic people did leave behind a great many stone circles, two to six meters in diameter which we now call tipi rings (Wedel 1961). They are simple circles, made of loaf-sized rocks, sprinkled over the plains and foothills from Texas to northern Canada. R. G. Forbis of the University of Calgary has estimated that in southern Alberta alone more than half a million were left (1970). We can assume that perhaps five or six million were built on all the Great Plains. By sheer number alone they must have been used for something ordinary and routine and most archaeologists now accept that they are stones which were used to hold down the hide covers of tipis—like tent stakes today—and left behind when camp was broken. Thus, they preserve a record of where the tipis were set, how they were arranged and what were their diameters.

The Plains inhabitants also left a number of large effigy figures traced out in field stone on the surface of the ground, linear stone alignments (some of which may have been associated with buffalo drives), and a number of enigmatic large wheel patterns which have come to be known as medicine wheels (Eddy 1974; Wedel 1961). An example, shown in fig. 11.1, is the medicine wheel near Sun

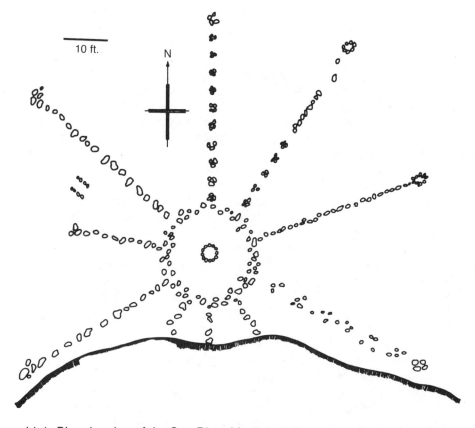

11.1. *Plan drawing of the Sun River Medicine Wheel, near Lowry, Montana, which is typical of one class of geometrical wheels. In 1975, erosion of the river bank, bottom of picture, had destroyed nearly half of the structure.*

River, Montana. Medicine wheels consist in general of a central circle or rock pile (the hub) from which lines of rock radiate like spokes. Often associated with the wheels are other piles of rock (or cairns) and occasionally one or more concentric circles. Medicine wheels are larger than tipi rings, ranging to a hundred meters in diameter; sometimes the central cairns are truly massive—ten meters or more across and several meters high.

The word *medicine* implies magic or supernatural and is an adjective probably applied for want of a better descriptor and without special significance. Medicine wheels have been something of a mystery in that most of them are old enough that their original function, if any, is long forgotten and the identity of their builders lost. The earliest Indian informants could offer little more about them than that these structures were there when they came (Grey 1963) and were often considered sacred. More recent informants have claimed that some of them were built to memorialize Indian leaders, and indeed this may explain some of the more modern (and usually smaller) examples (Dempsey 1956; Kehoe 1954; Kehoe and Kehoe 1959). As a class of archaeological features, medicine wheels and their cairns are hard to date since they are most often found on hilltops and mountaintops where soil is thin and stratigraphy is difficult. Some could be 100 years old, or 1,000, or maybe 10,000. Artifacts found in the few that have been professionally examined most often come from a late prehistoric culture, but this could sample only the latest stage of use—just as belongings found in a park are most likely left by the last picnickers. The most extensively excavated medicine-wheel cairn, at Majorville in Alberta, gave evidence of more-or-less continuous use from about 2500 B.C. (Forbis and Calder 1971). Thus, it is contemporaneous with the Egyptian pyramids and the early stages of Stonehenge. Other medicine wheels are probably a good deal more recent, but no one is sure of this.

The Big Horn Medicine Wheel

Surely the best known example, and the only one whose location is commonly known, is the Big Horn Medicine Wheel in north-central Wyoming, between Sheridan and Lovell, just south of the Montana border (Grey 1963). It lies at about 3,000-meters altitude near the summit of Medicine Mountain, one of the highest peaks in the Big Horn Mountains, near a steep precipice with clear horizons and a commanding view. It is probably the most elaborate and best protected of the known wheels and is now enclosed in a high fence under the care of the U.S. Forest Service.

The Big Horn wheel consists of a hollowed-out central cairn, about 4 meters in diameter, from which twenty-eight spokes radiate. The spokes, which average about 12 meters in length, terminate in a crude circle. Around the periphery of this rim are six smaller cairns, one of which, in the southwest, lies at the end of an extended spoke outside the main circle (fig. 11.2).

The Big Horn Mountains were considered special by a number of Plains tribes and the medicine wheel has been claimed by or for the Crow, Sioux, Cheyenne, Arapahoe, Shoshone, and probably others. In fact when it first came to the atten-

11.2. *An aerial view of the Big Horn Medicine Wheel between Sheridan and Lovell, Wyoming. The structure is atop Medicine Mountain at an altitude of 9,640 feet (2,940 m.) and since about 1925 has enjoyed protection by the U.S. Forest Service. (Forest Service photograph.)*

tion of archaeologists, in the early twentieth century, none of the local Indian informants claimed to know either its location or its use. A number of the early vague responses may have held unrecognized clues, for several associated it with the sun, and light, and, indirectly, the dawn. Early archaeologists recognized its similarity to one form of the Cheyenne Medicine Lodge, or Sun Dance Lodge, which had a central post and twenty-eight radiating rafters. In some versions of the Sun Dance Lodge there was an altar at the west, roughly where one of the peripheral cairns is placed. But other correspondences were imperfect and there was no known precedent for a two-dimensional stone facsimile of the Sun Dance Lodge; nor was there any generally accepted reason for its construction at a mountaintop site where there was little evidence of prolonged habitation.

It now seems likely that the structure was built for calendric purposes—specifically to mark the summer solstice sun and certain stars of midsummer dawn, and that it was last used for this purpose 200 to 700 years ago (Eddy 1974). A line through the center of the distinctive outlying cairn and the central cairn points to within ⅓° of the place of sunrise at summer solstice, and a similar line from another

11.3. *Sunrise at the Big Horn Medicine Wheel at time of summer solstice 1974. First flash of sun appears in line with cairn E (foreground) and central cairn O (see fig.11.4).*

of the outlying cairns points to sunset on the same day. The place of sunrise is easier to mark than sunset (for reasons of eye fatigue) but the fact that both are marked is interesting and probably significant. It says that were midsummer dawn beclouded, the users had another chance to mark the solstice sun the same day when it set. The summer solstice sunrise alignment is illustrated in figure 11.3, from on-site observation on solstice 1974. The alignments could have been the result of accidental placement, although the odds against chance alignment on sunrise and sunset to the measured accuracy are greater than 4,000:1.

Far less certain are alignments suggested for three of the remaining cairns, and the central cairn, on three prominent stars: Aldebaran in Taurus, Rigel in Orion, and brightest Sirius. These are three of the brightest stars in the sky at the latitude of the Big Horn Mountains and, more significantly, the only bright stars that rose near dawn in the few months of the year when the high-altitude site could be occupied. Their alignments are shown diagrammatically in figure 11.4. The first of these, Aldebaran, rose heliacally (just before dawn) at the site in roughly A.D. 1200 and could have been used for several centuries around that time for a precise check on summer solstice; today at summer solstice it rises un-

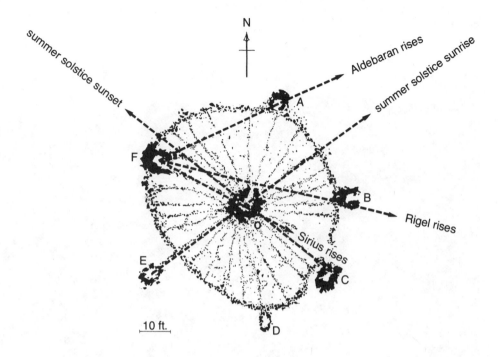

11.4. *Cairn alignments found at the Big Horn Medicine Wheel by Eddy (1974).
Aldebaran, Rigel, and Sirius are stars of summer dawn and thus form a consistent
set with the summer solstice sunrise.*

seen in the glare of dawn. The other stars whose alignments are indicated rose
heliacally at later intervals of about 28 days (roughly one "moon," and the number of spokes in the medicine wheel) after Aldebaran: first Rigel; then, near summer's end, bright Sirius. Thus, six of the seven cairns seem to fit a consistent and
practical plan; one, a smaller cairn near the south extremity of the wheel is unexplained, other than as a possible north-south marker, for which it is about 11°5 in
error.

The astronomical explanation of the Big Horn Medicine Wheel proposes that it
was built and used as a summer solstice marker, for calendar use, and probably
for ritual, since the important Sun Dance ceremony was held by some tribes at
the time of summer solstice, "when the Sun was highest and the growing power of
the world the strongest" (Neihardt 1932). A precise calendar would not be needed
for this purpose, although with the help of the heliacal rising of Aldebaran the medicine wheel could have given an accuracy of several days. Its secrets could have
been known but to a few, thus explaining in part why nineteenth-century informants could not offer any use for the structure. The significance of the summer
solstice to nomadic hunters could have its origins in an earlier era, when some of
the Plains peoples had a more agricultural existence.

By this astronomical explanation the cairns are the more important features of
the structure, and they may have been built and used first (perhaps originally just
two or three of them for the sun) and other cairns and the spokes and rim added

later as refinement or simply an embellishment. Recent archaeological investigation has confirmed that the central cairn is much older than the spokes of the wheel (Wilson 1975). As for its date of use, the Aldebaran alignment suggests possible use for a helical solstice marker in the twelfth to fourteenth centuries, although this could be the marks of but one set of users. The solar alignments at the Big Horn site would have been useful for millennia, since the change in the obliquity of the ecliptic is very slow.

If the Big Horn wheel was used for astronomy it throws new light on a little-known people and tells us what they were doing with their heads to complement the stone-tool evidence which speaks chiefly of the dexterity of their hands. It says that they were more knowledgeable about the sky than many would have thought and probably knew more about it than do their modern descendants. Neither of these revelations seems to me especially surprising since the Indians of the Plains lived chiefly out of doors and surely spent more time looking at the sky than most of us do today. Depositions from modern Plains Indians say little of astronomy, but the practical use of the sky and its changing patterns could well have been one of the traditions of the Plains people that was lost or diluted in the cultural revolution between Coronado and the nineteenth-century settlement of the West, or perhaps even earlier in their history.

The astronomical explanation would not seem strong if it rested on a single case and a single site. An obvious test is to apply it to other known medicine wheels, of which about half a hundred are known today. As we shall see, a number of these show probable alignment on the same celestial features as does the Big Horn site: the summer solstice sun and the same stars of midsummer dawn.

North American Medicine Wheels

The medicine-wheel sites in North America which are known to me are shown in figure 11.5. The map is surely incomplete, but it includes most of the professionally identified examples and a few which are definitely questionable. Medicine wheels are found along the broad swath of plains and foothills that bound the front range of the Rocky Mountains. Most of them, unlike the Big Horn wheel, are on rolling prairie, far from the mountains. Much of the land on which they lie was glaciated during the last (Wisconsin) ice advance: the high short-grass plains and foothills where there was abundant glacial till or other loose rock to pile.

Medicine wheels are a feature of cooler climates. Most of the forty or fifty known sites are in Canada, on the plains of Alberta and Saskatchewan. I know of but one small wheel in the Dakotas, only four in Montana, and three in Wyoming. There may be sites in Colorado. But the term "medicine wheel" has such a loose definition that these numbers and geographic distinctions are probably academic if not artificial and misleading. I know of no sites south of the Big Horns which resemble the medicine wheels north of there, and one suspects that true medicine wheels are indeed an artifact of the northern plains, built generally above about 45° latitude.

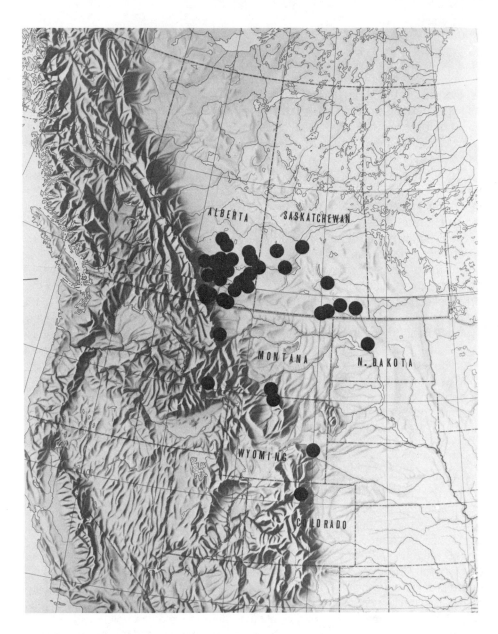

11.5. *Distribution of known North American medicine wheels. Most of them are found along the foothills and plains that bound the front range of the Rocky Mountains. Several types of structures are included in the broad definition "medicine wheel" and the majority do not seem to be astronomically associated.*

Two Sites in Colorado and Montana
of Possible Astronomical Significance

An interesting rock alignment which may be a primitive wheel is found in rugged mountains of northeastern Colorado, now within the Rocky Mountain National Park (Husted 1963). It is apparently old, judging by the sunken rocks and their lichen cover. The alignment consists of a small cairn on a hillock from which two lines, or spokes, of rocks meander about 30 meters in roughly opposite directions, ending in rough piles of stones. The alignment is unusual in that it lies on a windy crest above Trail Ridge Road, at about 3,500-meters altitude. Nearby is a reported Ute trail.

    A brief investigation of the site with transit in 1973 revealed that a line through the longer spoke to the central cairn as a foresight points to the rising point of the summer solstice sun (fig. 11.6). The structure is crude and alignment rough, and

11.6. *A rock alignment in Rocky Mountain National Park near Trail Ridge Road at an altitude of 11,400 ft. (3,500 m), which may be a rudimentary medicine wheel. The transit stands over a small central cairn from which two crude spokes radiate; one marks the direction of summer solstice sunrise.*

there is about a 1-in-20 chance that it could be accidental. If it was intentional, however, it raises an interesting question of motive. There are no tipi rings or other evidence of habitation in the area and, indeed, I cannot think that anyone would expect to find them there. Trail Ridge was reported to be a major Indian route across the Continental Divide, but I am surprised that anyone would have stopped along its cold and windy reaches to mark the solstice sunrise. Perhaps more than anything else it says we shouldn't always press for logical motives beyond joy, or personal satisfaction, or to demonstrate that it could be done.

Another rudimentary site which gives evidence of summer solstice alignment is the medicine wheel on the Crow reservation near Fort Smith, Montana (Brown 1963). The Fort Smith Medicine Wheel is mentioned in local Indian legends, although apparently it was not investigated by professional archaeologists until 1922. It rests on a grassy, rock-strewn knoll (elevation 945 m) with clear horizons, overlooking the flood plain of the Big Horn River. The Fort Smith wheel is about 60 km north of the Big Horn Medicine Wheel as the crow flies. The structure is a surface pattern of partially sunken stones, resembling a simple sun symbol. Six rays, or spokes, radiate from a central ring of about 1-meter diameter. The rays are irregular and unsymmetrically spaced and vary in length from about 10 to 20 meters. Four of them continue over the flat edge of the flat top of the knoll, giving the wheel a drooped appearance (fig. 11.7).

A survey with transit in 1973 showed that the longest of the six spokes is placed to mark sunrise at summer solstice, using the central circle as a foresight, in the same manner as the Big Horn wheel. This was confirmed by observation on the site at sunrise on summer solstice 1974 (fig. 11.8). The solstice sunrise spoke is not perfectly straight and the marking is therefore crude. Summer solstice sunset is not marked, and there is about a 5 percent chance that the sunrise line is accidental. On its own, the Fort Smith wheel is not impressive as an astronomical marker and I am not sure that it is. On examining it in 1973, however, I found an apparently unnoted feature which may give added evidence of sky association: between the spokes on the side opposite the solstice sunrise line is a small sun symbol, about 60 cm across and fashioned of lichen-covered stones which are well sunken into the ground. It looks like a miniature of the parent wheel: a tight central circle from which five short rays extend. In 1975 I found this same symbol at the end of a solar-aligned spoke at the Moose Mountain Medicine Wheel, and later it was found by the Kehoes at two other possible astronomical wheels in Saskatchewan. I have not found it at any of the obviously nonastronomical medicine-wheel sites, and it may be that it was a meaningful mark.

11.7. *An aerial view of a medicine wheel on the Crow Indian Reservation near Fort Smith, Montana (courtesy National Geographic Society). The simple wheel has six spokes, each from 30 to 60 feet (about 10 to 20 m) long. One spoke marks the direction of summer solstice sunrise.*

11.8. Sunrise at summer solstice 1974 at the Fort Smith Medicine Wheel, Montana (see fig. 11.7). A pole has been placed in the center of the hub of the wheel. The first flash of the sun appears nearly in line with one spoke, with the hub a foresight point.

Medicine Wheels and Cairns in Canada

By far the largest number of known medicine wheels are found in the prairie provinces of Canada: at least thirty are known in Alberta and ten in Saskatchewan. Many are not wheels but simply large cairns, some without spokes, rings, or other associated features. The nearest to the Big Horn or Fort Smith wheels is a month's walk to the north—a distance (600 or 700 km) almost as great as that which separates the Big Horn site from the clearly distinct Pueblo culture to the south of it. Although some of the Indians of the short-grass plains surely roamed from Wyoming to Canada, we should be cautious in assuming that the Big Horn and Canadian medicine wheels had common builders, purpose, or eras of use. Nevertheless, an examination of the Canadian cairns and wheels for astronomical association seems obviously necessary in light of the claims made for the Wyoming and Montana sites.

With the support of a grant from the National Geographic Society, I was able to examine almost half of the known wheels in Canada in the summer of 1975—the Alberta sites in collaboration with Professor R. G. Forbis, head of the Department of Archaeology of the University of Calgary, and a few Saskatchewan sites with A. B. and T. F. Kehoe, professional archaeologists who were in Saskatchewan under a National Museums of Canada grant. In this report I will summarize only the first findings from Alberta (Eddy and Forbis 1975), where we examined thirteen sites, and briefly describe one specific site in Saskatchewan which seems of particular interest.

Our survey of the Alberta sites resulted in a number of general conclusions:
1. Most of the Canadian sites are wholly unlike the Big Horn Medicine Wheel in that they are dominated by the central cairn. Some of these cairns are huge and contain up to 100 tons of rocks (as compared with perhaps 1,000 lb. in the central cairn of the Big Horn wheel). Some of the sites consist of nothing but the cairn. These large central cairns often have a ring or rings about them, 5 to 30 meters in diameter and roughly circular.
2. The number of spokes varies, and we found examples with almost any number, including one and none. The only other wheel which like the Big Horn site may have had 28 spokes is the Majorville Cairn in south-central Alberta (fig. 11.9), but it has been so badly rifled and rearranged that the number of original spokes is probably beyond recall. The central cairn contains an estimated 50 tons of rocks ranging in size from a few to several hundred pounds. Excavation by Forbis and Calder in 1971 found evidence of layered construction and possibly continuous use between about 4,500 and 500 years before the present (2500 B.C. to A.D. 1500).
3. Spokes point in almost all directions. They do not predominantly lie in the cardinal or the intercardinal directions, as is sometimes claimed on cursory examination (fig. 11.10). There is a slight preference for southwest-directed spokes and other features which could be summer solstice sunrise oriented, were the central cairn a foresight, as at the Big Horn site. More than half of the wheels examined have spokes or other directional features which point within 2° of the summer solstice sunrise. There is also a tendency for spokes or other features to lie in those directions from center which would point to the rising places of the same three stars which were apparently marked at the Big Horn wheel: the brightest stars of the summer dawn, Aldebaran, Rigel, and Sirius (fig. 11.11). But many of the sites examined do *not* show these or other possible sky associations and do not seem to be strong candidates for astronomical use.
4. All the sites which we examined lie on hilltops or high mesas and all have clear horizons. They are almost always on the highest hill around, and in cases where we had difficulty in locating one we could usually find it by picking out the highest hill and looking there. (This does not mean, of course, that every high hill in Canada has a medicine wheel or cairn on it.)
5. Almost all the sites we examined had tipi rings in the general vicinity, indicating that they were near places of semipermanent encampment. This is unlike the Big Horn wheel, which is at an unlikely place for lengthy dwelling, although there, too, tipi rings, believed to be of an earlier era, are about 1 km away. Several of the medicine wheels had tipi rings within them, either as a central circle or on or near the spokes.
6. In Canada none of the known medicine wheels is in mountains or foothills or

11.9. An aerial view of the Majorville Cairn in south-central Alberta (courtesy R. G. Forbis, University of Calgary). The wheel has been badly desecrated by vandalism but the outline of some of the original spokes remains. Overall diameter is about 100 feet (30 m). The large central cairn contains an estimated 50 tons of rock. Excavation by Forbis and Calder (1971) demonstrated that the central cairn had been gradually built up in about 4,000 years of presumably continuous use, beginning in about 2500 B.C.

even within sight of the mountains. They are most often a feature of the bald and treeless prairie and would make good landmarks.

7. Medicine-wheel patterns seem diverse and seldom if ever repeated from site to site. Symmetry is unusual. Spokes seldom extend from the center in diametrically opposed directions. There seems to be no preference for an odd or even number of spokes, or for the number 4, as one might expect were they meant to point to cardinal or intercardinal directions.

8. The ages of the structures are almost completely unknown, for several reasons. They lie on hilltops where the deposition of soil by wind is not a simple function of time and where dating by stratigraphy is difficult. Few have been investigated professionally; systematic archaeology of the plains of Canada only began a few tens of years ago. Finally, all the cairns have been rifled to some extent. Only two sites

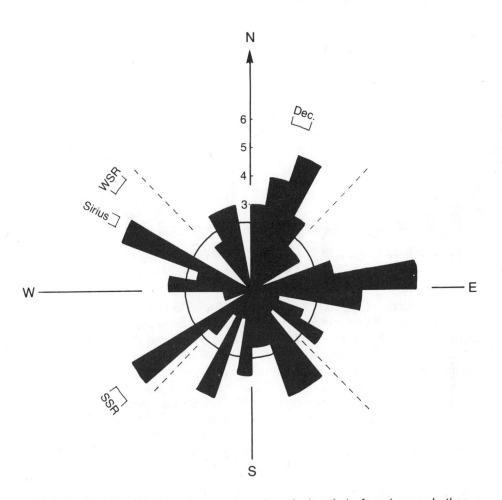

11.10 *Distribution of (true) compass directions (azimuths) of spokes and other directional features of twenty medicine-wheel sites as measured from center of each wheel, from a survey by Eddy and Forbis (1975). Circle at center is for random distribution. No significant grouping is found for the set of cardinal or intercardinal directions, with the exception of frequent east-directed features. Directions are shown which, using center of wheel as a foresight and end of spoke as a backsight, would mark summer solstice sunrise (SSR), winter solstice sunrise (WSR), the place of rise of Sirius, and the direction of magnetic north-south (Dec.) in the modern era.*

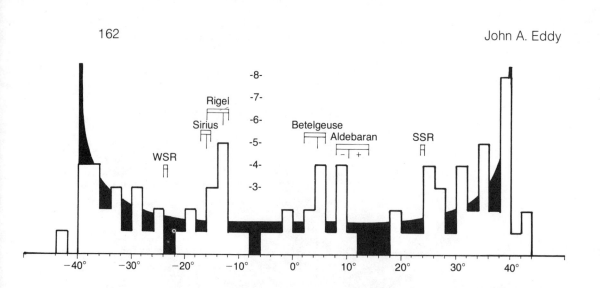

11.11. *Distribution of apparent sky directions (indicated celestial declinations) of spokes and other directional features of twenty medicine-wheel sites, from a survey by Eddy and Forbis (1975). The solid curve behind the histogram is for random distribution of azimuths to illustrate the nonlinear mapping of azimuth to celestial declination. Thus, the large number of apparent alignments near declination +40° is probably not significant. Declinations are marked for four stars of summer dawn, summer solstice sunrise (SSR), and winter solstice sunrise (WSR), each for a time span from about 500 B.C. (−) to A.D. 1000 (+), with A.D. 1 also marked in center of bar. Alignments on the rising places of Sirius, Rigel, Betelgeuse, Aldebaran, and the summer solstice sun seem significant.*

which we examined in Canada are protected by anything but isolation, and neither of these is protected as well as the fenced but unguarded Big Horn wheel.

The most general conclusions one can draw from a survey of the medicine wheels of Canada is that they are quite definitely a "mixed bag" of things classified incorrectly under one rather miscellaneous heading. They were very probably built by different peoples over a long period of time and for possibly different or evolving purposes. A few (generally the most elaborate) seem of probable astronomical association; some are very likely burial mounds or commemorative structures like those described by Kehoe and by Dempsey; some may be landmarks; and some of the smallest may be simply decorations. The fact that an appreciable number of them show astronomical alignment on the directions of rise of a restricted set of summer-sky objects (fig. 11.11) seems to me significant.

The Moose Mountain Medicine Wheel

Moose Mountain in southeastern Saskatchewan is not a mountain at all, but a low, timbered ridge that stretches across softly rolling farmland. From a distance it could look like the humped back of a moose, and this may explain its name. It rises only about 780 meters above sea level, or about 150 meters above the nearby plain. On a hilltop at one end of the ridge is a large but little-known medicine wheel, which is alluded to in Indian legends of that land.

Thomas Kehoe, curator at the Milwaukee Museum and former Provincial Archaeologist of Saskatchewan, located the Moose Mountain Medicine Wheel several years ago and became more interested in it in 1974 when he noticed some remarkable similarities between its pattern and that of the Big Horn wheel in Wyoming (fig. 11.12). The Moose Mountain wheel is about twice as large and like most Canadian wheels has a massive central cairn, about 6 meters in diameter, built of an estimated 60 tons of piled-up rock. An egg-shaped ring of stones encompasses it. From the central cairn five long spokes extend, each ending in a small and partly sunken cairn, one or two meters across. One of the spokes extends farther than the others and ends in a slightly larger cairn; it stretches toward the southwest like the distinctive sunrise spoke of the Big Horn Medicine Wheel. Positions of the other Moose Mountain cairns seem to match the relative positions of other Big Horn cairns. In fact, if the spokes and rim of the Big Horn wheel were erased (and we think they are later additions) the Moose Mountain and Big Horn wheels would look much like twins, although hundreds of miles apart and in vastly different terrain. The cairn positions seem close enough to have been positioned from the same set of plans, although adjusted in size—scaled down for Wyoming, or up for Saskatchewan.

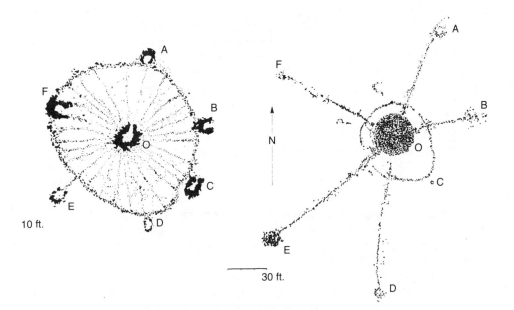

11.12. *Maps of Big Horn Medicine Wheel, Wyoming (left), and Moose Mountain Medicine Wheel, Saskatchewan, show similar patterns of cairns. The Moose Mountain wheel is about twice as large as the Big Horn wheel and apparently much older. (From Kehoe, Kehoe, and Eddy 1975.)*

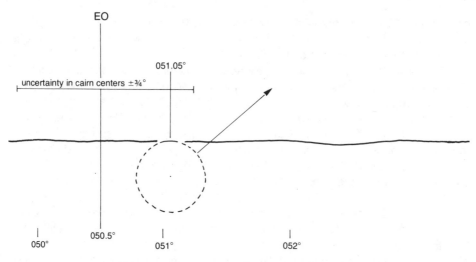

EO

051.05°

uncertainty in cairn centers ±¾°

050°   050.5°   051°   052°

11.13. *True azimuth of first flash of sunrise at summer solstice for Moose Mountain (051°05) and direction of line (EO) between cairn E and central cairn (O). Discrepancy of about 0°5 is less than uncertainty in fixing present centers of cairns E and O. (From Kehoe, Kehoe, and Eddy 1975.)*

Tom and Alice Kehoe and I carried out a careful survey of the site in June of 1975, during the time of summer solstice (Kehoe, Kehoe, and Eddy 1975). The eastern skies on the mornings around solstice were not very clear, but our transit measurements (fig. 11.13) established that a line from cairn E at the end of the long, southwestern spoke to the central cairn (line EO) marked the direction of sunrise at summer solstice to within our ability to specify the cairn centers (about ¾°). This was confirmed by observation through broken clouds at dawns on several mornings near summer solstice.

The other Moose Mountain cairns were in positions to mark, fairly closely, the rising points of the three Big Horn summer stars: Aldebaran (line FA), Rigel (FB), and Sirius (FO). There was no spoke or cairn to match the solstice sunset cairn C in Wyoming, but this may not be significant since sunset is a redundant mark which is harder to place than sunrise.

We found other surprises which made the case more interesting. At the end of the sunrise spoke was a little sun symbol—a central cluster of rocks from which short rays projected—fashioned of field stone set into the soil, much like the one that I had seen at Fort Smith, Montana. It made us wonder if it was a sign which read "this is the one." Later the Kehoes found the same symbol at other Saskatchewan wheels. But most intriguing at Moose Mountain were the specific placements of the outlying cairns which corresponded to the Big Horn stellar cairns.

Checking of the suspected stellar alignments is better done by calculation, since the positions of these stars have shifted appreciably with time. If we assume that the other Moose Mountain cairns were used for the same stars in the same manner as at the Big Horn wheel, and for the same era, we find that they are all a

few degrees off. This could mean that most of the similarity with the Big Horn Medicine Wheel is accidental, and that these cairns weren't placed to mark stars at all.
But the pattern of their close fit and the impressive alignment of the distinctive
spoke and cairn on summer solstice sunrise makes me reluctant to accept that
conclusion. It could also mean that these other cairns marked not Aldebaran,
Rigel, and Sirius, but different stars. That too seems unlikely, given the solstice
sun alignment—since no other stars as bright as these rise near dawn at the time
of summer solstice. It more probably means that we are using the wrong date.

The shifting declinations of these prominent stars are well known and easily
applied to such an analysis (Aveni 1972). Comparing them with present cairn positions offers a way, coincidentally, to assign an approximate date to an undated
and enigmatic structure. Hawkins (1968) has postulated that practitioners of astro-
archaeology should not attempt to determine construction dates from astronomical
alignments, since there are many bright stars and since over periods of many millennia their changing declinations will often define multiple sets of solutions. I think
this is a good warning but a bad rule. When there is other intelligence, or obvious
ways to restrict the set of solutions, or a strong, consistent rationale—such as the
apparent marking of the brightest stars in a tight region of the heavens with some
seasonal significance—then it seems safe to proceed with caution.

Aldebaran seemed to be the most practical star marked at the Big Horn wheel,
since during the late prehistoric and early historic periods it rose heliacally at summer solstice at the site. Of the three stars marked it is also the one whose stellar
declination changes most with time, due to its position on the precessional sphere.
It is therefore probably the best of the three for estimating a date of use based on
azimuth line. The cairn alignments at Moose Mountain fit Aldebaran best for about
150 B.C. to A.D. 150. The declination of Sirius changed little over the past two
millennia, and its alignment does not provide a very critical test; Sirius is well
marked at the site for the period between about 0 and A.D. 1000. Rigel is optimally
marked for the modern era and is the fly in the ointment of antiquity. It was the least
accurately aligned star at the Big Horn wheel, and at Moose Mountain the best fit
to past positions is still 2° in error. It may be that Rigel is an erroneous identification, but it is the only likely candidate among bright objects in the band of declination that is indicated.

Thus, the cairn alignments at Moose Mountain suggest an early date of use
for Aldebaran and Sirius and perhaps a later date for Rigel. Three other features
of the alignments support the earlier date. These are the direction of error in the
solstice sun alignment, the date of heliacal rising of Aldebaran at solstice, and a
likely use of the unexplained cairn D (see fig. 11.12). Each is explained briefly
below.

As indicated earlier, the solstice sunrise alignment at Moose Mountain is off
by about 0°.5, if it was first gleam that was marked and if it was marked in the way
we suppose. This error is probably not significant since we cannot specify the precise points of reference in the cairns (and particularly the large, amorphous central cairn) to define a line better than about ±¾°. If, however, we interpret the *direction* of the indicated error as a true indication of a systematic misalignment with
time (due to the slow change in the obliquity of the ecliptic) the sense of the slight

misalignment speaks for an earlier date. This, of course, is shaky evidence and should not be taken alone.

If Aldebaran were used because of its heliacal rising at solstice, then it offers probably the best date estimate, since in right ascension its change is appreciable with time and since its interpretation does not depend upon accurate reconstructions of cairn shapes or centers. A date estimate based on heliacal rising is independent of one derived from azimuth alignments, since the former depends chiefly upon the right ascension coordinate and the latter on declination. Latitude enters both; the same star will rise heliacally at solstice in different eras for different sites because of the latitude effect. Aldebaran, which was a good heliacal solstice star at the latitude of the Big Horns in the late prehistoric/early historic period was of no use at that time at Moose Mountain, which is 5° farther north in latitude. At Moose Mountain, Aldebaran rose heliacally at summer solstice in an earlier period, optimally in about A.D. 380 but useful between about A.D. 180 and 580. The earlier limit is consistent with other astronomical evidence cited above.

A final feature which suggests use of the Moose Mountain wheel 1,500 to 2,000 years ago is the cairn D which corresponds, roughly, to an unexplained cairn at the Big Horn wheel. A line from D to the center cairn on Moose Mountain points about 6° east of north, as compared with the Big Horn line which is 11°5 west of north. In each case they could represent attempts to mark the north, since we know that the cardinal directions were important in symbolism among some historic Plains tribes. (Some, like the Pawnee, preferred the intercardinal directions, NE, SE, SW, and NW, according to Weltfish [1965]). The approximate directions north, east, south, and west are easily identified, but without a compass they are uniformly difficult directions for precise astronomical horizon marks, particularly at high latitudes. The pole star is 45° above the horizon in the Big Horns and 50° high at Moose Mountain; it is not a simple thing to project its direction to the horizon plane. South is only a little simpler, and the sun gives us no easy way to mark east or west, since it races through these horizon points at the equinoxes.

Probably the easiest way to mark the north horizon point astronomically is to note the place where bright northern stars brush the horizon in their daily rotation about the pole. The handle of the Big Dipper, for example, swings across the horizon every day for many northern latitudes, and if any of its stars has declination equal to the colatitude of a site it will touch the horizon at lower culmination at precisely astronomical north. The problem with this scheme is that only the brightest stars can be used, since dimmer stars will never be seen at the horizon and since any higher point of culmination is difficult to identify. This makes the stars of Ursa Minor of little use in this regard and effectively limits the choices to a handful of the brightest stars in the sky, ideally of magnitude zero or brighter, and at any epoch at any place it is unlikely that one of these could be so used.

There are only five stars visible from Canada brighter than first magnitude, and one of them, Capella (magnitude 0.2), is in the far north sky. Its present declination (+46°) makes it circumpolar at latitudes north of Boise, Rapid City, and Toronto. Capella was once far enough south on the celestial sphere to rise and set at Moose Mountain, and there was a time when it was so nearly circumpolar that

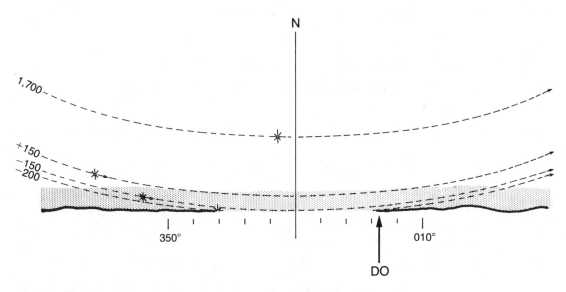

11.14. *Northern horizon at Moose Mountain, Saskatchewan, showing circumpolar path of Capella at lower culmination at dates from 200 B.C. to A.D. 1700
and direction indicated by cairn alignment DO of the Moose Mountain Medicine
Wheel. Capella may have been used as a north marker, using the place where
it appeared to brush the horizon. This use would have been limited to several
centuries around the start of the Christian era.*

it brushed the horizon there. During a period of perhaps several hundred years it
could have served as a nearly ideal marker for a north horizon point. Its magnitude
would have kept the star visible to within about 0°5 to 1° of the horizon (fig. 11.14).

The epoch when Capella was usable as a horizon north marker at Moose
Mountain coincides with the other astronomical evidence: a period around the time
of Christ. In about 150 B.C. it was in position to touch the horizon at its daily lower
culmination, but with corrections for refraction and extinction the usable dates
came sometime after: probably between about 100 B.C. and A.D. 200, after which
it would have become rapidly less useful. In the most usable era (about A.D. 100–
200) Capella would have disappeared into the haze near Moose Mountain horizon
a few degrees west of north and reappeared a short while later a few degrees east
of north. A sophisticated observer could have marked both points and interpolated
to find precise north, had he need or inclination to do it. This precision seems unlikely for any purposes we can now imagine, and it seems more probable that the
point of disappearance or, more consistently, *appearance* of the bright star would
have been taken as an acceptable north point. This could explain the Moose
Mountain alignment between cairn D and the central cairn, which was a line 6° east
of north. What is more, the only time of year when Capella reaches lower culmination at night is in early summer (between April and July) the season when the

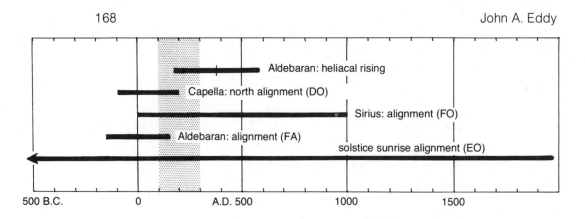

11.15. *Summary of possible astronomical alignments at the Moose Mountain Medicine Wheel, with respective dates of applicability. A most likely period of use of A.D. 100 to 300 is indicated.*

solstice-related markers at Moose Mountain would also have been used. This use of Capella as a near-north marker could explain the enigmatic cairn D at the Big Horn wheel as well (fig. 11.4).

The astronomically derived dates for Moose Mountain are collected in figure 11.15. Some are more restrictive than others and all are subject to error due to variable refraction and our limited knowledge of the precise reference points in each cairn. The consensus, however, seems strong for an early date of use, most probably about A.D. 100–300. This could be a date of construction, with a much longer period of use that followed, as in the case of the Majorville Cairn.

If the Moose Mountain astronomical dates are approximately right, then it appears to have been used a thousand years or more before the Big Horn Medicine Wheel and for identical purposes. This does not imply that the two structures were "built from the same set of plans"—only that they were built by people with the same sky traditions. The similarity of their pattern and proposed use suggests that a Plains sky calendar was in use for at least a thousand years and that the summer solstice and summer dawn stars were important parts of an abiding lore.

As far as I know ethnological research has found no evidence of this utilitarian astronomy among the northern Plains Indians. We may assume that by the time of the historical era on the Plains (the eighteenth or nineteenth centuries) much or all of the Indian's practical lore of the sky was gone. Its utter absence in the ethnographic record seems to me an interesting commentary on how easily traits are lost in any society and how fragile are learning and knowledge without the written word.

We can hope that conventional archaeology will be able to test the age of the Moose Mountain wheel. Modern concepts of early men in America leave little doubt that he lived on the Great Plains for millennia. That he built a stone pattern on Moose Mountain nearly two thousand years ago should come as no surprise. Nor should the suggestion that at the time of Christ the Indians of the American Plains were watching, and using, the sky.

Acknowledgments

Much of the work reviewed here was done jointly with Richard G. Forbis of the University of Calgary and with Thomas F. and Alice B. Kehoe of the Milwaukee Public Museum and Marquette University. I am indebted to the National Geographic Society for financial support through a research and exploration grant.

12

Rock Art Representations of the A.D. 1054 Supernova: A Progress Report

John C. Brandt
Ray A. Williamson

In a recent article (Brandt et al. 1975) a team of workers reported on several sites thought to contain records of the A.D. 1054 supernova. This work extended the investigation of Miller (1955) who found two examples of rock art in northern Arizona which could be records of the supernova event. Details of the astronomical circumstances on 5 July 1054 may be found in our earlier paper. There we also commented on the rarity of crescents among rock art design elements in the southwestern and western United States. We repeat our warning that the case for rock art representations of the supernova is entirely circumstantial in nature and subject to considerable uncertainty. Within the framework of this warning, however, we feel that the circumstantial case has been made stronger by the discovery or rediscovery of several new sites.

Before discussing the new sites we will describe two sites which were mentioned in our earlier paper but which we had not investigated. The first example is a petroglyph reported by Roberts (1932, pl. 62b) above the Village of the Great Kivas, New Mexico. This configuration of a bright object and a crescent is a typical example of the rock art motifs described in our earlier paper. As we explained, the petroglyph reproduces the view in the eastern sky on the morning of 5 July 1054 (Julian calendar). The crescent is not properly oriented, but as we have shown earlier (1975) this is not particularly significant. In addition to the main petroglyph, we found two representations of a crescent and a bright object on rock faces about 5 meters away. Since these examples display different distances between the crescent and the bright object, these petroglyphs could represent an attempt to show the changing appearance of the event due to the apparent motion of the moon with respect to the background stars; they are shown and described in figure 12.1. Tree-ring dates of logs used to construct the Village of the Great Kivas (Roberts 1932, p. 156) place the early construction phase of the pueblo in the early part of the eleventh century, so the site was certainly inhabited in 1054.

12.1. *Village of the Great Kivas petroglyphs: possible supernova representations about 5 meters east of the main pictograph published by Roberts (1932). The two crescents appear near the top of the photograph approximately 4 meters above the ground. Note the greater distance between crescent and star in the right-hand panel.*

12.2. *Scholle petroglyph. The crescent and star appear at the bottom of a rock panel that faces east. The pictograph was enhanced by an aluminum suspension in water (coating removed immediately afterward). The left-hand part of this photograph is shown in fig. 113 in Schaafsma's (1972) book.*

The second site is near Scholle, New Mexico (site no. LA4092). It is not as spectacular as the site near the Village of the Great Kivas, but once again it shows the form elements thought to represent the supernova event (fig. 12.2). It appears near the base of a larger rock art panel whose elements are stylistically part of the Abo division of the Rio Grande Style described by Schaafsma (1972, p. 131). This would indicate a date later than 1054 for the panel, but an unexcavated pueblo nearby may provide better dates than are possible by stylistic comparisons.

The following sites have come to our attention since June 1973 and are not mentioned in our earlier work. An interesting petroglyph is located at San Cristobal, New Mexico. This representation, shown in figure 12.3, reveals the same general elements, but the use of an outer larger circle to represent a bright object is unusual. The San Cristobal petroglyph lies nearly flat on the ground at present. There is some question about the probable date of this record. The earliest date for

12.3. San Cristobal petroglyph. The boulder which contains this petroglyph is lying on the ground. Several other stars and one other crescent are inscribed on the rock face.

the nearby San Cristobal pueblo is A.D. 1380. We have found no information on possible earlier habitation of the site.

We have found other sites through literature searches or through correspondence. One record is painted on a cave ceiling near Breckenridge, Texas, and appears in Kirkland and Newcomb (1967, pl. 121, no. 3). There is no positive dating information available from this site.

Another site discovered in Capitol Reef National Park, Utah, was reported to us by Dr. Klaus F. Wellman (1976). It consists of two crescents and a bright object or sun symbol incised on a canyon wall. This petroglyph is from the Fremont Culture region, and the nearby area was inhabited at the time of the supernova. We have no other information on this petroglyph.

We have a report of a pictograph in Baja California discovered by Crosby (1975). The pictograph is from the region termed the Great Mural heartland. According to Crosby, this art is characterized by "the rarity of abstract symbols of any sort" and a "propensity for depicting real objects such as men, animals, arrows and spears" (p. 167). Because Crosby considers this pictograph to depict a real event and because it comes from an area not thought to be culturally connected with the regions where other examples of the crescent–bright object conjunction are found, this example assumes a particular importance for our discussion of the Crab Nebula supernova. Of further interest is the fact that Crosby has found no other pictures which could be interpreted as depicting the sun, moon, or any other celestial object. Also, there are almost no examples of simple circles in the Great Murals. We agree with Crosby, therefore, that this is a picture of a real event, and that it is very likely a representation of an unusual one. The dating of the Great Murals is very uncertain, but the very sparse data available do not preclude a date of 1054 for this picture. Because conjunctions of the moon and bright planets are a common occurrence, we would expect to find more pictures of this kind if the painters of the Great Murals were given to routinely depicting astronomical events.

Also, we have received a photograph of a possible record at the Hueco Tanks site (near El Paso) from C. Grant (1975, private communication).

Finally, there are the rock art panels reported by Koenig (1975) and Mayer (1975) which include a crescent and starlike object. They make persuasive independent arguments that these are also representations of the 1054 event.

Representations of crescents have been considered to be rare in rock art, although the crescent motif was often used in pottery, shields, and ceremonial objects (Koenig 1975; Stephen 1936). Recently, many more crescents have been located (Mayer 1975), some associated with possible bright objects. Compared to other design elements, however, they remain rare. Because the close conjunction of a bright planet or star with the crescent moon is a striking appearance, we would expect pictorial representations of this occurrence to be more common than they are. The relative lack of rock art crescents and bright objects leads us to believe that most of the records we know of are representations of the Crab Nebula–moon conjunction.

An argument opposing our hypothesis has been put forth by Ellis (1975), who feels that these markings depict sun-watching stations. She further asserts that her informants assure her their ancestors would never have kept records of anything. We have no doubt that sun-watching stations were in use in Anasazi country at the time of the supernova. Two possible examples of these exist in Chaco Canyon, New Mexico (Williamson et al. 1975).

In particular, we agree that the Chaco Canyon pictograph site is a possible sun-watching station. The use of the site is indicated by the presence of a sun symbol on the vertical wall below the crescent/hand/star configuration (Brandt et al. 1975). There is a good view of the eastern horizon from the spot and it is near a major pueblo, Penasco Blanco. If it was a sun-watching station, however, there is no reason to believe that the Indians who used it would not record such an unusual event as the supernova-moon conjunction, particularly if it occurred near a socially significant event in the life of a pueblo. Unusual celestial events tend to be noticed and recorded if they seem to correspond with an earthly event of great importance, for example, the 1066 record of Halley's comet on the Bayeux Tapestry and Thucydides' frequent mention of solar and lunar eclipses in his *Peloponnesian War*. It may be correct to assert that record keeping is a rare event among the New Mexico–Arizona Pueblo Indians, but we are not convinced by Dr. Ellis's extrapolation to nine hundred years ago and to other cultural areas.

There is a further difficulty with Dr. Ellis's argument. Several of the sites we have reported on here and elsewhere are quite poor for sun watching. The Baja California, Fern Cave, and Breckenridge sites are caves. Neither sunrise nor sunset can be seen from the Symbol Bridge site. In New Mexico and Arizona most of the sites could have been used for sun watching, but only the Chaco Canyon and Village of the Great Kivas sites are especially suitable for the purpose.

Several writers (Ellis 1975; Koenig 1975) have suggested that the rock art records we have reported on may be representations of Venus and the crescent moon. While it is true that the morning and evening stars were, and still are, important deities in the Puebloan pantheon, it is not clear whether they were represented in rock art. There are certainly examples of such representations in the masks and ceremonial garb of the Hopi (Fewkes 1900, pl. 28) and Zuni (Stevenson 1904, pl. 28), but the only identified rock art example was at Zuni (Cushing 1941, p. 128). It is entirely possible that the more recent practice of associating the crescent moon and the morning or evening star is the remnant of a tradition which began with the supernova appearance. Although the morning star was absent from the sky when the supernova appeared, the two appearances may have become confused with one another.

The lack of accurate dates for rock art sites remains the greatest obstacle to establishing a one-to-one correspondence between the representations we have reported on and the supernova appearance in 1054. Except for the San Cristobal and Scholle petroglyphs for which there is some question of the dates of their execution, all the examples we have located to date are consistent with the 1054 date. Further evidence which would enable us to accept or reject these two sites and narrow the possibilities for the remaining sites is sorely needed. In addition, in order to test whether a significant percentage of these sites are likely to be sun watching stations, we need to understand more fully what may constitute that sort of solar observatory (Williamson et al. 1975).

In summary, our present tally of possible western records of the A.D. 1054 supernova now numbers more than fifteen and includes examples from Arizona, Baja California, New Mexico, Texas, and Utah. Thus, we feel that our circumstantial case is greatly strengthened.

An Examination of Miller's Hypothesis

Dorothy Mayer

Introduction

In the early 1950's British astronomer Fred Hoyle suggested that records of the 1054 supernova, and particularly of the initial waning crescent moon–supernova appulse, could appear in rock art of the southwestern United States (W. Miller 1955, p. 8). Hoyle's suggestion was taken up by Mount Wilson astronomer William C. Miller, who found two possible depictions of the supernova in northern Arizona. This paper deals with the supernova hypothesis as it is expressed in Miller's seminal 1955 paper, "Two Prehistoric Drawings of Possible Astronomical Significance."

The two possible supernova depictions found by Miller are severely plain. The Navaho Canyon petroglyph is a "waning" crescent with a large circle underneath; the White Mesa rock painting is a waxing crescent whose lower cusp is occulted by a large circle (figs. I3.1A and I3.1B). Both waning and waxing forms of the crescent have been allowed by Miller and subsequent investigators, although the supernova is supposed to have been in appulse with the waning moon, because contemporary people have been found to make errors in recording the direction of the cusps (Brandt et al. 1975, p. 52). Miller says that the factors which led him to regard these figures as possible supernova depictions were (*a*) their "unique character" and (*b*) the rarity of the crescent figure in northern Arizona rock paintings. In this paper I shall investigate the role of these factors, and of cusp direction, in the structure of the hypothesis. I will use fifteen previously unnoted examples of crescents in conjunction with circles or deep pits found in standard surveys of Nevada and California rock art.

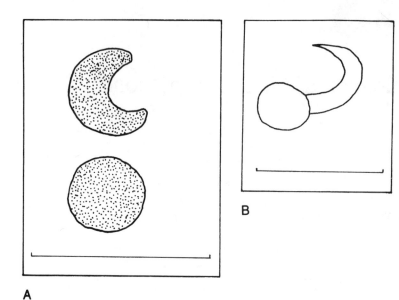

A

B

13.1. *The possible supernova depictions found by Miller. Miller's photographs appear in Brandt et al. 1975, p. 47.*
A: *the Navaho Canyon petroglyph.*
B: *the White Mesa rock painting.*

The Crescent Figure

Other investigators besides Miller have had the impression that the crescent figure is rare in southwestern rock art. In *Prehistoric Rock Art of Nevada and Eastern California* (hereafter PRA), Heizer and Baumhoff (1962) do not even list the crescent as an element, though they list as elements the "rain symbol" with two examples and the "lozenge chain" with five examples; subsequent supernova seekers also have noticed very few examples of crescents in this work. However, in looking fairly carefully at these illustrations, I have developed an incomplete list of over seventy petroglyphs containing crescents of varying degrees of amplitude. A preliminary survey of Heizer and Clewlow's (1973) *Prehistoric Rock Art of California* (hereafter CRA) has yielded a still-expanding list of over sixty petroglyphs containing crescents. Of course not all these crescents are lunar—after all, a crescent is a useful symbol for many purposes, as well as being the form of many interesting common objects—but I think I can show that some of them are lunar and that it may be worthwhile to consider whether others of them are also lunar.

A possible explanation for not seeing crescents in petroglyphs may lie in what is regarded as a "crescent": we have been conditioned to regard the cartoonist's depiction of the crescent moon as the "crescent figure," and when looking for crescents we may look only for this form. The lunar crescent, however, varying constantly in amplitude, only occasionally approximates this "cartoonist's moon."

Of course, finding a number of crescents in Nevada and California petroglyphs does not mean that Miller is incorrect in stating that the crescent figure is rare in northern Arizona, and no overall survey of the Arizona rock art sites is yet available.

Crescents near Circles and Pits

Perhaps the issue of the number of crescents in rock art is not really crucial to Miller's argument. After all, if Miller had been aware of a number of examples of crescents, he would probably still have been impressed by the White Mesa and Navaho Canyon depictions, because examples of crescents near a large circle or with a cusp occulted by a large circle occur much less frequently than simple crescents. However, in the petroglyph figures of PRA and CRA, I have found five examples of crescents with a circle eclipsing a cusp; four of these have the lower cusp eclipsed. These are as follows, together with a sketch of the relevant figures. (ARF refers to the Archaeological Research Facility, University of California, Berkeley.) They are fully illustrated in the figure numbers shown:

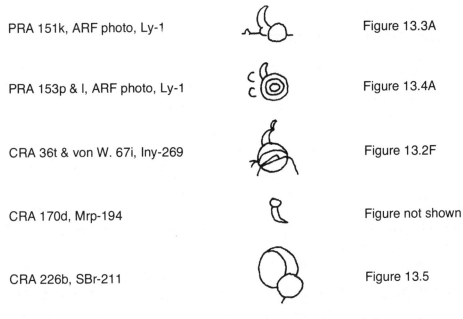

PRA 151k, ARF photo, Ly-1		Figure 13.3A
PRA 153p & l, ARF photo, Ly-1		Figure 13.4A
CRA 36t & von W. 67i, Iny-269		Figure 13.2F
CRA 170d, Mrp-194		Figure not shown
CRA 226b, SBr-211		Figure 13.5

There are also at least ten examples of crescents near large circles or pits, as follows:

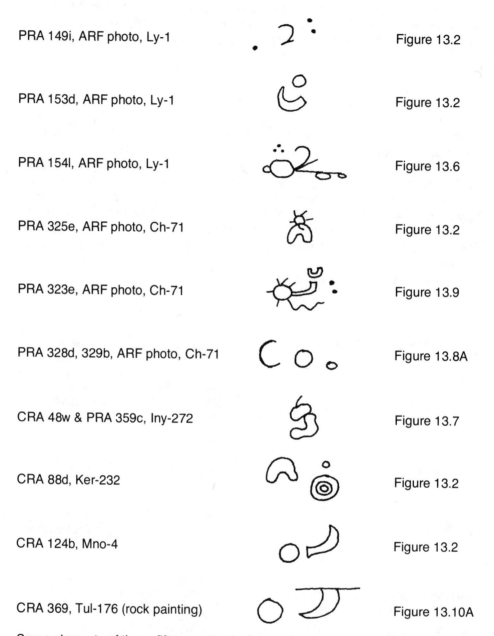

PRA 149i, ARF photo, Ly-1	Figure 13.2
PRA 153d, ARF photo, Ly-1	Figure 13.2
PRA 154l, ARF photo, Ly-1	Figure 13.6
PRA 325e, ARF photo, Ch-71	Figure 13.2
PRA 323e, ARF photo, Ch-71	Figure 13.9
PRA 328d, 329b, ARF photo, Ch-71	Figure 13.8A
CRA 48w & PRA 359c, Iny-272	Figure 13.7
CRA 88d, Ker-232	Figure 13.2
CRA 124b, Mno-4	Figure 13.2
CRA 369, Tul-176 (rock painting)	Figure 13.10A

Some elements of these fifteen petroglyphs can be compared in table 13.1. An X signifies that a particular element is recognizable in the petroglyph. Uncertainties are indicated by parentheses.

Since these examples have a similarity in character to Miller's Navaho Canyon and White Mesa examples, are they also possible depictions of the l054 supernova? And if some of these figures are not supernova depictions, what are the implications for Miller's hypothesis?

In investigating these questions I shall use only information contained within the form of the petroglyph itself, and I will adhere to the conditions for testing the astronomical content of petroglyphs stated in earlier papers (Mayer 1975, 1976). One of these conditions is to use only glyphs containing enough figures to provide a number of possible relationships of form and position, which must then correspond to the relationships found in the sky. Because of this condition I must release from consideration six of the examples, which occur either by themselves as Miller's examples do or which occur with very few other figures. Although these possible supernova depictions are "indeterminate" in terms of the test conditions for the astronomical hypothesis, they may become determinate as the hypothesis evolves. An example of an astronomical petroglyph of elegantly simple appearance which nevertheless contains enough relationships to work with is found in Wellman (1976). These indeterminate examples are shown together in figure 13.2. (The scale marker is one foot long in each case.)

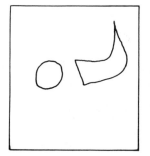

A. PRA 149i, ARF photo, Ly-1

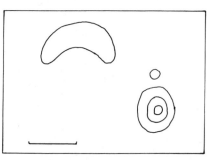

B. PRA 153d, ARF photo, Ly-1

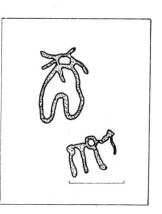

C. PRA 325e, ARF photo, Ch-71

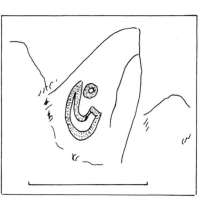

F. von Werlhof 1965, p. 67i, Iny-269

D. CRA 124b, Mno-4   E. CRA 88d, Ker-232, rock painting

13.2. *Examples of crescents in conjunction with circles or pits, which are indefinite lunar or supernova depictions in terms of the astronomical hypothesis.*

Table 13.1.
Statistics of Crescent Petroglyphs in California and Nevada

Site	Petroglyph		Fig.	Horizon orientation of crescent
Nevada				
Ly-1	PRA 151k, ARF photo		13.3	E
Ly-1	PRA 153p & I, ARF photo		13.4	E
Ly-1 0	PRA 149i, ARF photo		13.2	W
Ly-1 0	PRA 153d, ARF photo		13.2	E
Ly-1	PRA 154l, ARF photo		13.6	(W)
Ch-71 0	PRA 325e, ARF photo		13.2	
Ch-71	PRA 323e, ARF photo		13.9	E
Ch-71	PRA 328d, 329b, ARF photo		13.8	E
California				
Iny-272	CRA 48w & PRA 359c		13.7	W
Iny-269 0	CRA 36t & von W 67i		13.2	E
Mno-4 0	CRA 124b		13.2	W
Ker-232 0	CRA 88d		13.2	
Mrp-194	CRA 170d			E
SBr-211	CRA 226b		13.5	E,W
Tul-176	CRA 369		13.10	W

Horizon orientation of other asterisms	Other crescents	Concentric circles	Flanged circles	"Sun" sign	1054 Supernova
N			X		X
	X	X	(X)		(X)
			(X)		0
					0
W			X		
				X	0
E			X	X	(X)
E			X		X
W					
	X		X		0
					0
		X			0
E	X	X	(X)	X	0
E	X	X	X		
W	X	X	(X)	X	

Another example (CRA 170d) occurs within a sufficiently complex panel, but this panel occurs on a cliff face containing dozens of other panels, each depicted on a separate slab of rock; until the relationships among all these panels are worked out, interpretations of any one are premature. I have given relationships which seem to appear, but I feel that I can say nothing about the supernova possibility.

I will now briefly discuss the eight remaining glyphs whose meaning can be approximately though conjecturally resolved under the astronomical hypothesis.

Eight Determinable Examples

Figure 13.3A   Ly-1

The relevant figure consists of a crescent with a cusp occulted by a large circle; it occurs within a panel complex enough to allow us to decide the possible presence of an astronomical meaning and some of what is depicted. Leaving aside the crescent for a moment, other figures on the glyph have a clear positional and figural correspondence to stellar groups (figs. 13.3B and 13.3C). From upper left to lower right on the line drawing these are:

1. The constellation of Lyra with Vega prominently displayed
2. Andromeda forming the body of the Iguana
3. A complex of Draco and Ursa Major, with the line of Ursa Minor leading to Polaris is indicated
4. The constellation of Virgo, with perhaps the star Arcturus (Alpha Bootis) indicated

Since the position of the crescent figure in relation to these other figures is on the ecliptic, it is probably lunar. Furthermore, this position is quite near the Crab Nebula. The circle occulting its cusp could therefore consistently refer to the 1054 supernova.

Since the design is incised on a horizontal boulder, it can be viewed from either direction: (*A*) If the crescent's lower cusp is regarded as occulted, the depiction could consistently refer to the original waning crescent–supernova appulse of 5 July 1054. The crescent figure is depicted as the appulse would have appeared on the eastern horizon; the other figures are depicted as they appear facing north (fig. 13.3B). (This "turning" viewpoint exists on other Great Basin glyphs; examples are in Mayer 1975, fig. 5, and especially in Mayer 1976.) Virgo would have been below the horizon at this time.

13.3. A: *PRA 151k from ARF photo.*
B: *Andromeda region from* Norton's Star Atlas.

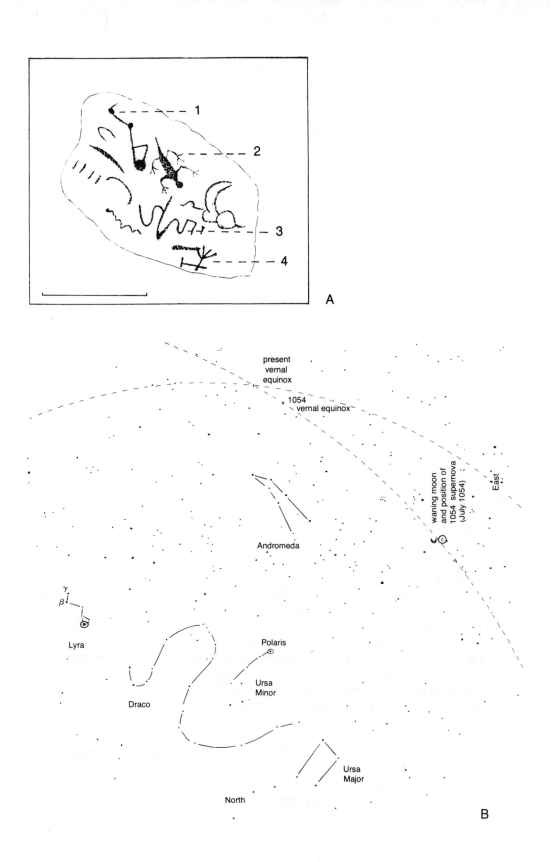

A

present
vernal
equinox

1054
vernal equinox

waning moon
and position of
1054 supernova
(July 1054)

East

Andromeda

γ
β

Lyra

Draco

Polaris

Ursa
Minor

Ursa
Major

North

B

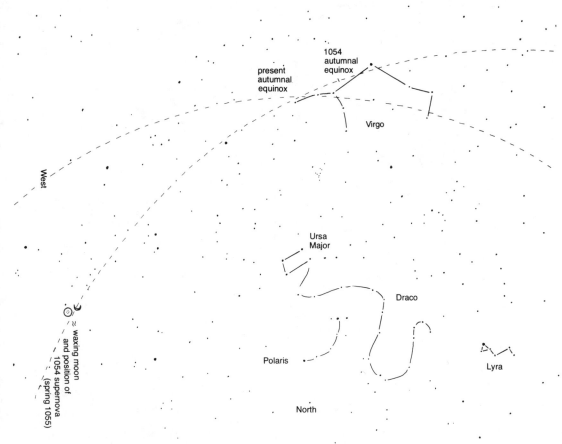

The following labels appear within the figure:

1054 autumnal equinox

present autumnal equinox

Virgo

West

Ursa Major

Draco

Polaris

Lyra

North

waxing moon and position of 1054 supernova (spring 1055)

S & T, 12ʰ

13.3.C: *Virgo region from* Sky and Telescope.

(*B*) Viewing the design from the other direction, the crescent appears in a waxing form (fig. 13.3C). The waxing crescent would have been in appulse with the supernova in the spring of 1055, when the supernova would still have been a bright object. The moon-supernova would be viewed facing the western horizon; the other figures again viewed facing north. Virgo would have appeared near the zenith at this time. From these correspondences it seems possible that this ingenious design was intended to be viewed from either direction.

Further evidence that the petroglyph refers to the 1054 supernova appears in the relatively large size and importance of Lyra in relation to the other stellar groups: in 1054 the solstitial colure would have passed between Gamma and Beta Lyra.

The more geometrically formed lines in the lower left are undetermined at present; they may be a count, perhaps referring to the number of lunations between the initial waning moon–supernova appearance and the waxing moon–supernova appulse the following spring.

Figure 13.4A　　　　　　　　　　　Ly-1

An especially interesting example of a waning crescent whose lower cusp is occulted by a large concentric circle (cf. Miller's White Mesa example) is shown in figure 13.4A. This example occurs by itself on a boulder but in a straight row of three boulders possibly depicting lunar events. While one cannot be absolutely certain that a relationship among these exists, it seems reasonable from their proximity and placement to assume one; the results of an examination of these relationships follow.

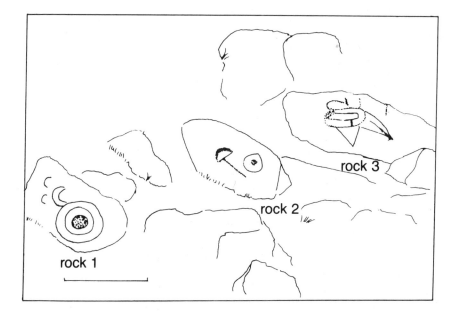

13.4. A: *From ARF photo.*

Rock 1: The concentric circle has been associated with the summer solstice point in other panels (Mayer 1976). If this is its meaning here and if the crescent is lunar, the amplitude of the waning crescent indicates that the sun would have been about 24° to 36° to the east and, therefore, the event would have taken place in mid or late July (Gregorian). (The two faint crescents to the left may be a count of days of crescent visibility remaining.) However, the similarity of this figure to Miller's White Mesa example suggests that the concentric circle could refer to the 1054 supernova. In this case the sun would have been nearer the summer solstice

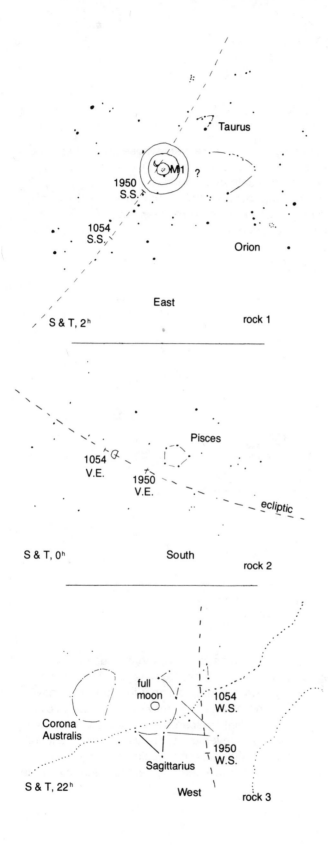

Taurus

M1

1950
S.S.

?

1054
S.S.

Orion

East

S & T, 2ʰ

rock 1

Pisces

1054
V.E.

1950
V.E.

ecliptic

S & T, 0ʰ

South

rock 2

full
moon

1054
W.S.

Corona
Australis

1950
W.S.

Sagittarius

S & T, 22ʰ

West

rock 3

point, which in 1054 was about 12.8° east of its present position, and the event would have taken place in early or mid July. This is consistent with the supernova data.

Rock 2: If the crescent refers to a last-quarter moon, it would occur near the vernal equinox position and about six days earlier than the event depicted on rock 1 (see fig. 13.4B).

Rock 3: Two places on the ecliptic correspond to this figure, the Sagittarius region (winter solstice) and the Orion-Taurus region (summer solstice). From figure 13.4B it can be seen that the fit to the winter solstice region is much better, though the ambiguity may be deliberate. This panel then would depict the position of a full moon about thirteen days earlier than rock 1.

If the moon was viewed in morning twilight in each case, that on rock 3 would appear in the west, on rock 2 on the meridian, and on rock 1 in the east. Lunar phases which set before morning twilight do not appear.

Although tentative, evidence from the relationship among the boulders suggests that the crescent on rock 1 is indeed lunar and that the concentric circle depicts either a summer solstice point or the 1054 supernova.

Figure 13.5   SBr-211

The relevant figure on this petroglyph is a waxing crescent inside a circle, with its lower cusp occulted by a circle. It occurs within a diagonally grouped set of figures, between a thin waxing crescent at the upper right and a thin waning crescent at the lower left; this suggests that a single visible lunar cycle is being depicted. We can extract further information about this cycle from the glyph, which may help us decide whether the occulted crescent is a supernova depiction.

First of all, we have seen from an investigation of other Great Basin petroglyphs that the "two joined circles" often refer to the stars Castor and Pollux of Gemini (Mayer 1976). Furthermore, the vertical form of this figure has consistently referred to the eastern, rising form of Gemini. In this glyph, however, the eastern form of Gemini is found in conjunction with the waxing, western form of the moon at the upper right. This discrepancy can be shown to be probably deliberate: If the moon's position at its first visibility as the thin waxing crescent is just south of the star Pollux (110° on the ecliptic), as indicated on the glyph, then at the end of a

---

13.4.B: Rock 1, *waning crescent viewed at dawn over eastern horizon; around summer solstice point.*
Rock 2, *last quarter crescent viewed at dawn on meridian; around vernal equinox point.*
Rock 3, *full moon viewed at dawn over western horizon; around winter solstice point.*

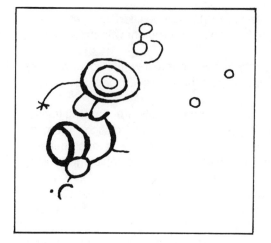

13.5. *CRA 226b, SBr-211.*

single sidereal month (27.3 days) it would arrive back at this point as a thin waning crescent. The sun would have been about 14° west of the 110° point at the beginning of the cycle (i.e., just north of Nu Gem., 6° east of the present summer solstice) and 14° east of this point at the end (i.e., north of Beta Cancer). In other words, at the end of this lunar cycle the depicted configuration of Gemini would be visible in the east before sunrise and would hold a waning crescent at the 110° point. The figure at the upper right would therefore be a composite figure, a kind of visual equation, stating the beginning and the end of the depicted sidereal month.

If the topmost crescent figure refers to the first appearance of the waxing moon near Beta Gemini, two days of crescent invisibility would have occurred near the summer solstice. This then is the first sidereal month following the summer solstice, at a time when the new moon would be near that point. This could not have occurred in 1054, since the waning moon–supernova configuration occurred in early July. In 1055 a new moon occurred near the supernova in June, but the extremely thin waning moon near the supernova at the end of the July sidereal month would probably have been invisible.

Therefore, if this interpretation of the glyph is correct, the occulted crescent inside a circle could not refer to the crescent moon–supernova appulse. It may refer to earthshine on a crescent moon whose lower cusp is near a bright star or planet; it may also refer to the sequence of lunar phases, passing through waxing crescent, full, and waning gibbous forms. Its position between thin waxing and waning crescent figures suggests this possibility, and the joined concentric circle would in this case indicate passage of these phases through solstitial and equinoctial points.

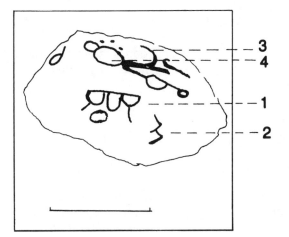

13.6. *PRA 154l, Ly-1.*

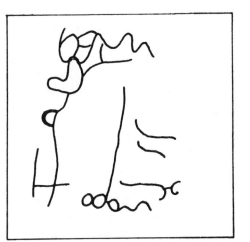

13.7. *CRA 48w, Iny-272.*

Figure 13.6      Ly-1

This petroglyph can be correlated with the Belt of Orion (*1*) and the region around the present summer solstice as it appears in the western sky in March and April. The figure to the right of the Belt corresponds to Cassiopeia but is mirror imaged (*2*).

The prominent crescent figure (*3*) has a waxing form, the lunar form at the western horizon; it could, however, also consistently refer to a curve formed by the stars of Auriga. The large circle at the crescent's base is in the position of the Crab Nebula (*4*). However, this crescent-circle figure could not refer to the initial waning moon–supernova configuration, which appeared in the east. It is interesting though that a waxing moon–supernova appulse occurred in the months of March, April, and May of 1055; this is consistent with the glyph. Two other possible supernova depictions have occurred at this site (figs. 13.3 and 13.4).

Figure 13.7   Iny-272

This glyph shows the same region of sky above the western horizon as figure 13.6 and again shows a waxing crescent in conjunction with a large circle, near the upper cusp in this case. It occurs at a California site and has a very different style from Figure 13.6. The wavy line to the right of the upper crescent has been shown to refer to the Milky Way when in conjunction with a "three joined circles" figure (Mayer 1976) and could also do so here. The lower, sharply etched waning crescent is depicted too close to the waxing crescent to refer to the waning crescent of a few days before and is unexplained at present.

Like Figure 13.6, this mainly western glyph could not depict the initial waning moon–supernova appearance but could consistently depict the waxing moon–supernova appulse the following spring.

Figure 13.8A   ⊕ Ch-71

Since the thin crescent moon is a horizon phenomenon, this petroglyph was probably meant to be viewed from the direction in which it appears in Figure 13.8A. That the crescent figure in fact depicts an eastern waning moon can be seen from the figures above it, which correspond in form and position to the prominent stellar groupings of Cassiopeia and Corona Borealis at 22^h. (The rayed semicircle has been frequently correlated with Corona Borealis [Mayer 1976]). The waning moon would have been very near the present summer solstice, and the sun therefore at least 17° (more likely 29°) to the east. Therefore, unless this is a very old glyph, an early morning sky in July is depicted.

The figure to the right is a quite accurate representation of the Taurus region (fig. 13.8B); the ovals enclose "blank" areas seen only under excellent conditions. The contrived hourglass figure incorporating the Hyades may be an oblique reference to the constellation Hercules marking the winter solstice, as the Hyades mark the summer solstice; such references to the opposite side of the sky have been found in several other Great Basin stellar petroglyphs.

Although the large circle to the right of the crescent is very near the position of the Crab Nebula, it may not depict the initial appearance of the supernova, since the crescent appears rather far to its east; it may instead refer to the following morning, when the moon would have been a thinner crescent 13° to the east of the supernova. Could it be that the careful depictor of this event overslept on the morning of 5 July 1054 (Julian)?

If this is a supernova depiction, the smaller circle would refer to Zeta Taurus. Of course, these circles may simply refer to planets.

13.8. A: *PRA 329b from ARF photo.*
B: *the Taurus region from* Norton's Star Atlas.

A

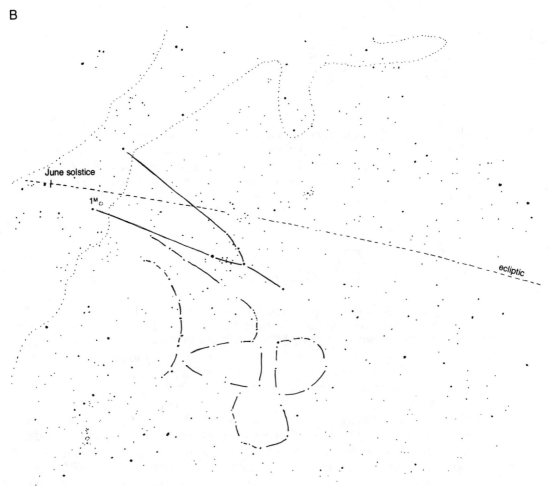

June solstice

1^M

ecliptic

B

Norton's Map 5 [PRA 328d and 329b, ARF photos, Ch-71]

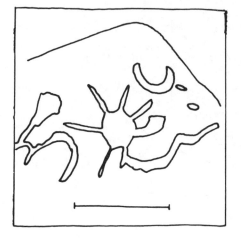

13.9. *PRA 323e from ARF photo.*

Figure 13.9   Ch-71

This petroglyph, occurring at the same site as figure 13.8A, also clearly depicts a waning crescent moon, again with two objects (possibly planets) to its south. It is difficult to estimate the slope of the ecliptic from this view but it seems quite small, which at least rules out a period around the autumnal equinox as subject of the glyph. If this does refer to the same event as figure 13.8, the moon would be depicted a few hours or at most a day earlier.

Figure 13.10A   Tul-176

The relevant figure in this pictograph from a California site is the lower half of a waxing crescent, with a large circle near the cusp. The glyph as a whole probably refers to a two-month sequence of luni-solar events over an area of the ecliptic near the present summer solstice: lunar crescents appear to be used to estimate the sun's position and to time its arrival at the solstice.

The summer solstice area of the ecliptic seems to appear twice: once above the truncated crescent and again at the top of the glyph in the form of three dots. (For a similar treatment of Nu, Mu, and Eta Gemini see fig. 13.6.) In each case a waxing crescent appears just to the west (*right*), implying a sidereal lunar cycle. At the beginning of this first sequence the sun would be at about 33° south of Alpha Aries; at the end at about 60°, south of the Pleiades (fig. 13.10B).

The second sequence evidently refers to a synodical month, from the first

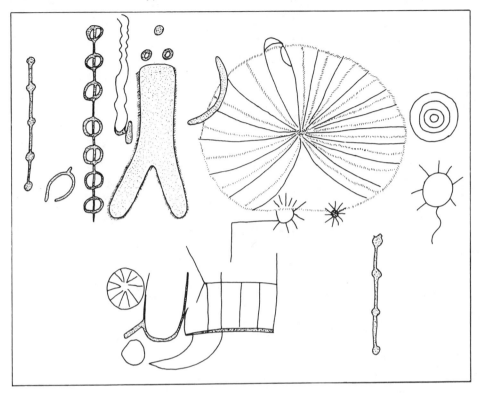

13.10. A: *CRA 369, Tul-176, rock painting in red, white, and black; no color coding appears in CRA.*

appearance of the waxing moon just west of the triangle Nu, Mu, and Eta Gemini (very near the summer solstice) to the first appearance of the waxing moon just west of Delta Cancer. These two first appearances are indicated by a single thin waxing crescent figure, and the ecliptical position of the cycle by the composite

figure ⅄ . The sun at the beginning of this cycle would be at about 60°, and at the end it would be near 90°, the summer solstice. A rectilinear figure extends from the left sun figure, marking this place.

The shell figure has its center at a point corresponding to Polaris, and its lines or spaces counted counterclockwise may indicate days; this is corroborated by the waning crescent figures three "days" before the thin waxing crescent.

Since the truncated lunar crescent seems positioned about 10′ east of the position of the Crab Nebula, the large circle near its lower cusp is probably not the 1054 supernova; it may refer to a planet. The predominately western form also rules out this glyph as a depiction of the initial appearance of the supernova.

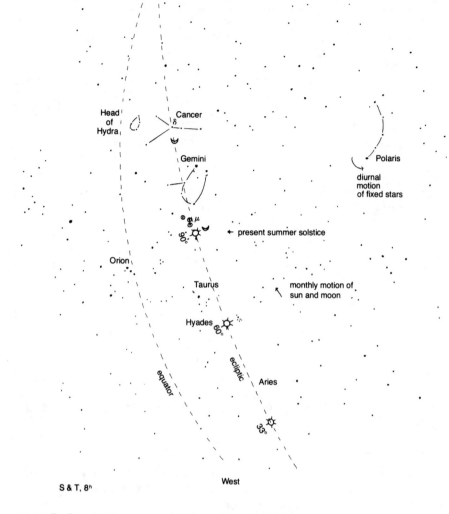

13.10.B: *Gemini Taurus region from* Sky and Telescope.

Conclusions

First, figures 13.5, 13.6, 13.7, and 13.10A do not seem to be depictions of the initial waning moon–supernova configuration. However, figures 13.6 and 13.7 may indicate the waxing moon–supernova configuration of the spring of 1055. (It is interesting that figure 13.6 occurs at site Ly-1 where four other possible supernova depictions also occur.)

Furthermore, figures 13.5 and 13.10A, both occurring at southern California sites, share some unexpected characteristics: both seem to depict sidereal lunar cycles near the summer solstice and both compress a lot of information about the cycle into a single ingenious diagram. These examples could almost be called visual equations. Their crescent-circle figures may be lunar-planetary conjunctions.

Since these doubtful cases contain forms similar to the ones accepted as supernova depictions by Miller, they might have been accepted by him as depictions of the supernova, if the archaeological evidence were consistent. Unfortunately such evidence may not be as significant as hoped in all cases, since, on the one hand, petroglyph sites could have been used intermittently over long periods of time (PRA, p. 234) and, on the other hand, some of them may have been sacred places far removed from living centers.

Second, figures 13.3A, 13.4A, 13.8A, and 13.9 seem to offer positive evidence for Miller's hypothesis. However, figure 13.9 is a marginal case because of the simplicity of the design and is included in the discussion because of interesting similarities with figure 13.8A, which occurs at the same site (Ch-71). Evidence for figure 13.4A is also rather tentative, as explained in the discussion; however, it occurs at the same site (Ly-1) as figure 13.3A, which is perhaps the strongest positive case presented here. Although these examples are consistent with the supernova possibility, all four of them could have other explanations. Most obviously, the relevant large circles could depict planets or (if concentric) solstice points, but it is curious that planets at this position on the ecliptic should be recorded so persistently with the crescent moon.

Concerning the planetary possibility, three of the eight discussed examples carry a small "flange" (single projecting line) on the relevant large circles (figs. 13.3A, 13.5, and 13.7). Such a flanged circle has been shown to have a probable planetary reference on the great panel at Spanish Springs, Nevada (Mayer 1976). Other incidences of flanged circles in all the examples are shown in table 13.1. Since crescents and sun signs are sometimes flanged (e.g., fig. 13.4A, rock 2, and fig. 13.10A), the line may indicate "movement."

Direction of the Cusps

From the eight examples discussed and also from the indefinite examples, it can be seen that the orientation of the crescent is consistent with the horizon form and position of the other astronomical figures in all but two cases, figures 13.3A and 13.5. (These relationships are shown in table 13.1.) Furthermore, there are coherent astronomical reasons for the two apparent exceptions, as the comments on figures 13.3A and 13.5 show. Because of this evidence of deliberate care and precision in recording the direction of the crescent, it seems unnecessarily generous of Miller's hypothesis to accept both forms. I therefore suggest that the following condition be considered as an addition to the hypothesis: that the petroglyph makers did not make mistakes in depicting the direction of the crescent. Although this condition may sometimes lead us astray, it seems we will be less often wrong than if we assume the opposite, in the case of American Indians.

Orientation of the Petroglyph

Miller and most subsequent investigators, in deciding whether a petroglyph is a depiction of the 1054 supernova, have emphasized the visibility of the Crab Nebula from the place of the depiction. This seems to be a rather unnecessary limitation on Miller's hypothesis. After all, we are dealing with the recording of a remembered event; the petroglyph would probably not have been executed in the predawn hours in which the supernova first appeared, because it would have been difficult to see; and if we assume that the petroglyph maker rushed to the nearest slab of rock the next morning to record what he had seen, there is no reason why that slab should have a particular orientation, any more than a slip of note paper should have a particular orientation for us. Again, the petroglyph maker may have waited until he reached a sacred place to record the remarkable event (note in table 13.1 the concentration of possible depictions at site Ly-1), and the sacred spot need not have been oriented to the supernova. Or he may have waited for a particular ceremony to record the occurrence, the place of recording not being exposed to the supernova. Of course it may be the case that the petroglyph makers were quite meticulous about having the heavenly prototype shine directly down upon its chthonic counterpart; but it does not seem necessary to assume this to be true. Indeed, it appears to be something which needs to be shown.

Summary of Evidence

1. A number of crescents appear in southwestern petroglyphs.
2. Crescents closely associated with large circles or pits are not unique. Fifteen previously unnoted examples are given.
3. Orientation of lunar cusps is usually consistent with the horizon forms of associated asterisms depicted on the glyph.
4. Eight possible supernova depictions have been found which have forms similar to Miller's examples and which are determinable under the conditions of the astronomical hypothesis. Of these, four appear to be consistent with the initial waning moon–1054 supernova appulse.

Acknowledgments

I would like to thank the Archaeological Research Facility, University of California, Berkeley, under the direction of Professor R. Heizer, for permission to use photographs from its files. Thanks are also due to Sky Publishing Corporation for permission to use hand copies of star charts from *Sky and Telescope* and *Norton's Star Atlas*; the University of California Press for permission to reproduce line drawings from R. Heizer and M. Baumhoff, *Prehistoric Rock Art of Nevada and Eastern California* (copyright © 1962 by the Regents of the University of California; reprinted by permission of the University of California Press); and Ballena Press, P.O. Box 711, Ramona, California 92065, for permission to reproduce line drawings from R. Heizer and C. Clewlows, Jr., *Prehistoric Rock Art of California* (1973).

14

Anasazi Solar Observatories

Ray A. Williamson
Howard J. Fisher
Donnel O'Flynn

Introduction

Solar observing for the purpose of establishing a yearly calendar or marking religious ceremonies has been a strong part of historic Pueblo Indian practice. In her thorough review of nineteenth- and twentieth-century sun-watching practices of the Pueblo Indians, F. H. Ellis (1975) raises the question of the existence of prehistoric sun-watching stations or observing sites. Our discoveries in Chaco Canyon (Williamson et al. 1975) support and extend her assertion that the ancestors of historic Pueblo Indians had similar sun-watching practices and even suggest that the Anasazi who inhabited Chaco Canyon until about A.D. 1250 carried their observations to a more sophisticated level than is true of their descendants. Our more recent observations and transit measurements confirm this finding and demonstrate the existence of a variety of possible solar observatories in the canyon. In this paper we will discuss the range of possible forms of Anasazi solar observatories and relate them to our studies in Mesa Verde National Park and Hovenweep and Chaco Canyon National Monuments.

We use the general term "solar observatory" even though we are well aware that in many respects it may be a misleading designation. In the modern understanding of the word an observatory is simply a building which is specially constructed as a repository for observing instruments. For our present purposes, we intend it to refer to a building or a site which has a demonstrable alignment to one or another significant solar direction, *whether or not it could actually be used to observe the sun*.

What might a prehistoric Pueblo observatory look like? Differentiating with respect to their possible use, we can postulate four types. Actual sites, of course, may incorporate features of one or more of these types. We propose the following sequence of prototypes which form a natural progression, from structures suitable for the simple measurement of celestial phenomena to those which are strictly geometrical in their final manifestation. As we will show, our measurements of ancient buildings confirm the suitability of this sequence.

We identify as type 1 an observatory which is used solely for gaining information, that is, the building or observing station is used as or with an instrument. Its function is to allow observers to watch the sun in order to extend their understanding of the motion of the sun or to determine a calendar. A historic example is the horizon calendar reported by Stephen (1936, p. 29) to be in use by the Hopi. Important ceremonial dates are determined by referring to the horizon positions of the sun as seen from known geographical locations.

A type 2 observatory is a structure which is built directly from observations of the sun such that the phenomena which guided its construction are manifestly observable in the completed building. It is not meant to extend knowledge but may be used to establish certain specified dates or to allow the observation to be part of a ceremony or observance. A type 2 structure will contain a feature which is distinguished by the fact that it lends additional drama or clarity to the phenomenon in question. For example, while at Zuni, at the winter solstice, Cushing (1941, p. 129) noted that "many are the houses in Zuni with scores on their walls or ancient plates embedded therein, while opposite, a convenient window or small porthole lets in the light of the rising sun, which shines but two mornings in the three hundred and sixty-five on the same place."

A type 3 observatory is built directly from observations of the sun but the phenomena which guided its construction are not directly observable. The directions are incorporated into the structure but not necessarily observationally manifest in the completed building. Those historic pueblos which are oriented to the cardinal points are an example here (Stubbs 1950). For instance, an east-west sight line which was determined by observing the sunrise or sunset at an equinox in the early phases of construction may be intentionally obscured by a wall or intervening building built at a later date.

A type 4 building incorporates an astronomically significant direction but one which, because of local horizon features, could not have been determined at the actual building site. Instead, the building alignments would have been determined at a location at which direct observations could be made and would then be translated to the desired site geometrically by means of some sort of instrument. The obvious grid pattern of the historic pueblos might be an example of this type of building; for here only *one* of the parallel lines is directly established from the sun, the others determined geometrically from it.

Horizon Observing Stations

In October and December of 1974, Donnel O'Flynn conducted an extensive search of the Chaco Canyon terrain to determine whether there were any likely horizon observing stations in the canyon or on its rim. Using the National Park Service archaeological survey, the Chaco Center's roadway survey, and C. Cochran's rock art survey of the canyon, he searched for natural or artificial features in the vicinity of Pueblo buildings, stairways, sun glyphs, or road intersections which could be used as horizon markers. He located only two possible solstice markers and one possible equinoctial marker. We expected a small number of possibilities because, except for the canyon walls, Chaco Canyon has very few sharply deline-ated natural features, such as rock chimneys or buttes. The surrounding terrain viewed from the rim is largely featureless.

The two supposed solstice observing sites are at opposite ends of the canyon, one east of Wijiji and the other near Penasco Blanco. Both are exactly suited to observing the winter solstice sunrise and share the attributes of being near a painted sun symbol and an ancient roadway. The equinoctial site is connected with Casa Rinconada and will be discussed in the section devoted to that kiva.

Wijiji Site

This possible ancient solstice observation post is located about 1 km east of Wijiji on a shelf on the wall of a rincon (site no. SJ 931). At the head of a set of stairs leading up out of the rincon is a white painted sun or morning-star glyph. About 500 meters across the rincon to the east of the glyph is a natural rock chimney which when viewed from the glyph site has an apparent diameter of about 25' arc. To an observer placed in front of the sun glyph (fig. 14.1), the rock chimney is located at an azimuth of 118°45' and altitude of 0°52'. The chimney could thus have been used as a foresight for a winter solstice sunrise observation. Because the chimney is just a few minutes of arc narrower than the apparent diameter of the sun, it makes an excellent and very accurate device for determining the exact date of the winter solstice.

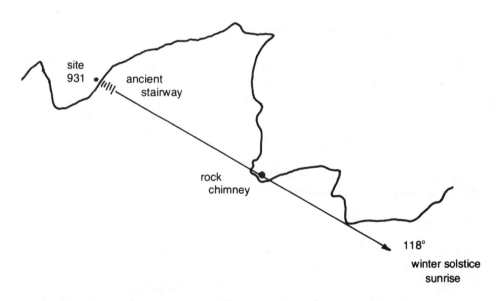

14.1. *Sun glyph marking a sun-watching station east of Wijiji on the north wall of Chaco Canyon (contour at 6,500 ft.).*

The sun glyph is definitely considered to be Anasazi (Cochran 1973 and Hayes 1974, private communications), although there are several Navaho as well as Anasazi glyphs nearby. There is no indication of just where an Anasazi observer might have placed himself for the sunrise observation. To see the sun rise directly behind the foresight today, an observer has to stand on the ledge some 14 meters to the north of the sun glyph. Because of the slight difference in the sun's obliquity in A.D. 1100, one would have to stand 2 meters farther north to witness the same appearance.

Lending credence to the use of this site as an observing post is the fact that the terrace or ledge is well sheltered from the weather and was significantly warmer than the plain below when confirmatory observations were made on 19–21 December 1974. It was also possible to use a collaborator stationed above the ledge to warn the solstice observer when to expect the first gleam of the sun.

If our supposition about the use of this location is correct, why was the sun symbol not drawn at the local winter solstice sunrise azimuth (A = 119°11') from the foresight? Two obvious possibilities occur. It may have been placed next to the road to mark the ledge as a sacred place from which solstice observations were to be made. Second, it may have been placed there to indicate the proper place from which to observe the sun prior to the winter solstice. Such observations would serve as a warning that the solstice would occur soon. Looking toward the foresight from the sun glyph, one sees the sun rising just behind the foresight sixteen days before the winter solstice, perhaps signaling the beginning of solstice observances or preparation rituals.

Penasco Blanco Site

The Chaco Canyon pictograph which has been suggested as a possible record of the A.D. 1054 supernova is located 650 meters east of Penasco Blanco (Brandt et al. 1975). Because of the sun symbol associated with the suspected supernova representation, the relatively clear view of the eastern horizon above from the pictograph site, and its close proximity to a major ancient roadway, this seemed to be a horizon observing station. We were not disappointed in our expectation. Whereas below the pictograph site itself the horizon is only indifferently visible, an easy walk along the ancient roadway from Penasco Blanco brings one to a shallow depression in the cliff face just above the pictograph. From this location the edge of a cliff face located at an azimuth of 120° could have been used as an aid for marking the winter solstice sunrise beyond.

Fajada Butte

One surprise in our survey was that we found no evidence of Fajada Butte being used as an observing post. To a modern astronomer this natural feature, which stands by itself in the canyon, seems an obvious site for a solar observatory. There is evidence of habitation of the butte, but in our inspections on two separate occasions, we did not find any obvious solstice markers on the horizon as seen from the top of Fajada Butte. Nor did we observe any evidence of man-made solstice markers, such as those we had previously found near Casa Rinconada and Pueblo Bonito (Williamson et al. 1975).

We consider both the Wijiji and the Penasco Blanco winter solstice sites to be examples of a type 1 observatory. If they were indeed used to observe the sun, they were probably used primarily for setting the date of the winter solstice ceremony. That they are marked by clear sun symbols and are near an ancient roadway may indicate the spots as places to mark the observance as well as to set a date. An example of this sort is reported at Zuni (Cushing 1941, p. 128; Stevenson 1904, p. 149). Cushing reports:

> Each morning, too, just at dawn, the Sun Priest, followed by the Master Priest of the Bow, went along the eastern trail to the ruined city of Ma-Tsa-Ki, by the riverside, where, awaited at a distance by his companion, he slowly approached a square open tower and seated himself just inside upon a rude, ancient stone chair, and before a pillar sculptured with the face of the sun, the sacred hand, the morning star, and the new moon. There he awaited with prayer and sacred song the rising of the sun. Not many such pilgrimages are made ere the "Suns look at each other," and the shadows of the solar monolith, the monument of Thunder Mountain, and the pillar of the great gardens of Zuni, "lie along the same trail." Then the priest blesses, thanks, and exhorts his father, while the warrior guardian responds as he cuts the last notch in his pine-wood calendar, and both hasten back to call from the house-tops the glad tidings of the return of spring.

If the Chaco Canyon observing sites were used in a manner similar to Zuni practice at Matsaki, they properly belong to type 2 as well.

Man-Made Structures

We have previously found that the axes of symmetry of the Great Kivas Casa Rinconada and Pueblo Bonito A are aligned north-south (Williamson et al. 1975). Other astronomical alignments are evident in Casa Rinconada and in Pueblo Bonito.

Casa Rinconada

One of six known Great Kivas in Chaco Canyon, Casa Rinconada is located on the south side of the canyon across from Pueblo Bonito and Chetro Ketl. It is typical of other Great Kivas in having wall niches, floor vaults, a built-in stairway, and a fire box. It is atypical, however, in being located on top of a low hill set apart from any major dwellings and in having a wall which extends above ground. Wild claims for Casa Rinconada as a solar and lunar observatory have appeared in the popular literature (Kaplan 1974). We find that most of these claims lack adequate supporting evidence, but the kiva does have solstice and equinox alignments related to the wall niches which may have been intentional on the part of the builders.

Casa Rinconada has two sets of wall niches. One set is composed of twenty-eight niches approximately evenly spaced around the kiva about 75 cm above the primary bench (fig. 14.2). These niches are of uniform construction, about 30 cm on a side. The remaining set of six niches is placed about 30 cm lower and the niches are on the average 4–6 cm larger than those in the first set. There are two of these on the east wall of the kiva and four on the west wall (fig. 14.3). In addition to the wall niches, there is a window in the northeast wall above niche A and a niche in the southeast wall above and to the north of niche 20.

Following a suggestion by C. Cochran, we have determined that sunlight

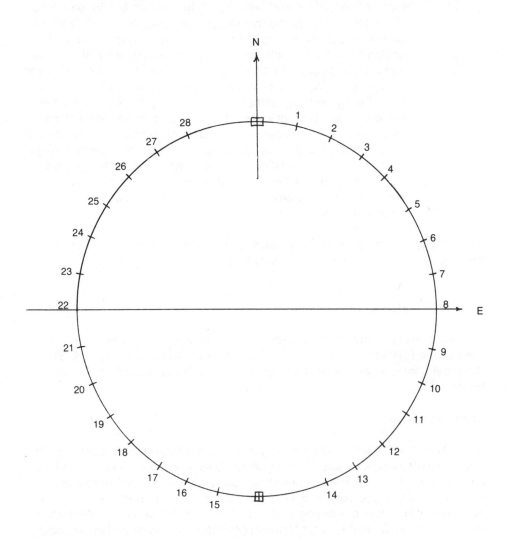

14.2. *Casa Rinconada: the twenty-eight regular niches.*

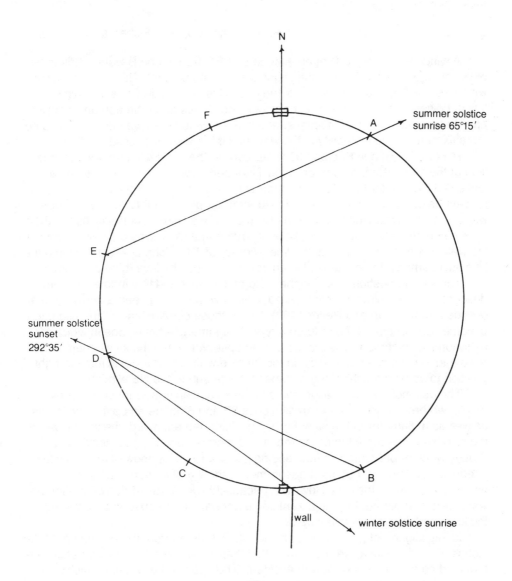

N

F

summer solstice
sunrise 65°15'

A

E

summer solstice
sunset
292°35'

D

C

B

wall

winter solstice sunrise

14.3. *Casa Rinconada: the six irregular niches.*

passing through the northeast window will illuminate niche E for four or five days
at the summer solstice. The window defines an artificial horizon. The line between
niche E and the northeast window lies at an azimuth of 65°15' and an altitude of
6°. The apparent horizon of the canyon walls is only 3°. Thus, the sun will appear
on the distant horizon some fifteen minutes before it illuminates the niche.

We can only speculate about a summer solstice sunset line in the kiva, but
if the relationship between niche E and the northeast window is indicative of other
possible solstice alignments, it seems plausible to postulate that there was a window above niche D similar to that above niche A. The azimuth of the niche B–niche
D line is 292°35'.

A window over niche D at an altitude of 9°04' from niche B would satisfy the physical requirements for admitting light to illuminate niche B. This would place the window some 30cm below the rim of the kiva. This supposition must remain speculation, however, since the wall just above niche D was found broken down (Vivian and Reiter 1960). We can at least suggest that a window above niche D would be more likely to cause instability in the wall than if the wall were solid.

Morgan (quoted in Kaplan 1974) discovered that, at the winter solstice, the light of the sun enters the corner of the T-shaped south doorway and illuminates niche D. It seems that this finding depends largely on the accidental nature of the present height of the wall which is constructed perpendicular to the south doorway (fig. 14.3). When the kiva was in use, the wall was almost certainly higher than in its reconstructed form. It is possible of course that there was a small window in the wall. It is also possible that the line—corner of T to niche D—was built into the kiva but not meant to be manifest to an observer within the kiva (type 3 alignment).

The same question arises in the case of the niche E–NE window alignment described above. What we have called a window may have been a doorway to an outside room (Vivian and Reiter 1960). Under these circumstances, the alignment becomes one of type 3. For it to be a type 2 alignment—that is, one in which the astronomical alignment was manifest to an observer within the kiva—there would have had to have been a window in the outside wall of that room in just the right position to admit the light of the summer solstice sun to the NE window.

The question of type 3 alignments in the kiva is an important one. For example, we have found that the small niches 22 and 8 define an east-west line as as well as a diameter of the kiva (fig. 14.2). Extended eastward, the line between the niches grazes the edge of the mesa 400 meters east of Casa Rinconada. Cloudy weather prevented us from seeing just where the shadow of the mesa falls at equinoctial sunrise, but our measurements show that it should fall directly across the center of the kiva. However, because the kiva was roofed over after the walls were completed, this alignment could not have been observed from within the kiva; and thus it falls into type 3.

Is this alignment purposeful or accidental? Judging from the placement of the niches around the kiva, we are certain that their positioning follows a carefully determined pattern inconsistent with accident. The spacing between the niches is uniform. For example, niches 1–14 and 15–27 are spaced an average 11°8' ± 23' apart. Except for niche 28, they are also placed quite symmetrically about the north-south line (fig. 14.2). Furthermore, taken in pairs, niches 1–13 and 15–27 define diameters of the kiva. Each of these diameters intersects the other diameters within 15 cm of the geometrical center of the kiva.

We feel that reconstruction causes little error in our results for Casa Rinconada. The angular measurements of the niches, in particular, are very little affected, because, as the photographs taken after excavation and before reconstruction make clear, none of the set of twenty-eight niches was significantly changed by reconstruction. The original interior heights of the second set of six larger niches are generally unknown, but that information would not materially affect our findings. The interior vertical faces of this set of niches were also little changed by reconstructions; therefore, our angular measurements probably accurately reflect the original values (Vivian and Reiter 1960).

Pueblo Bonito

Pueblo Bonito (fig. 14.4) exhibits several cardinal alignments and at least two solstice alignments. As mentioned earlier, the axis of symmetry of Great Kiva A is a north-south line. In addition, the wall to the west of the kiva which divides the pueblo roughly in half is aligned nearly north-south (A = 0°45' ±10'). Furthermore, the western side of the straight south wall is oriented east-west (A = 90°08' ±7'). According to Judd (1964, fig. 5), both these walls and the kiva were built at nearly the same time. The masonry style is characteristic of the so-called Late Bonitian, type 3 masonry (A.D. 1000–1100) which was used at about the same time that Casa Rinconada was constructed.

　　Cardinal alignments *are* of solar significance: a north-south wall casts no shadow at midday, and an east-west wall coincides, on the day of equinox, with the directions of sunrise and sunset, *assuming a plane horizon*. If these phenomena were readily visible at Pueblo Bonito it would be an example of type 2 alignment. But, in fact, the high mesa walls of the canyon make a view of true sunrise and sunset impossible, and so an east-west line at this location corresponds with no *manifest* solar phenomena whatever: a case of type 4 alignment (if the east-

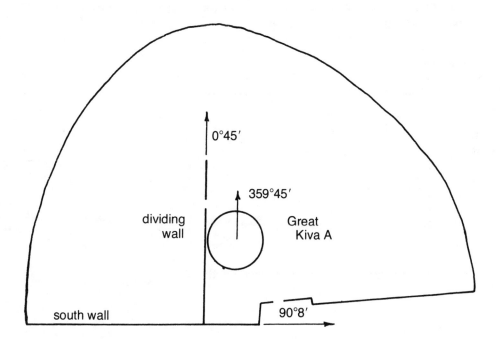

14.4. *Pueblo Bonito.*

west direction was transferred geometrically from some other location) or at least of type 3 (if the east-west direction was determined locally by some indirect means, such as the path of the shadow of a vertical gnomon).

There are several corner doorways in Pueblo Bonito whose orientation may be purposely astronomical. These corner doorways are rare in the architecture of the Anasazi, and Pueblo Bonito contains more than half of the known examples (Judd 1964, p. 28). Judd considers them to be Late Bonitian additions of type 4 masonry. We were unable to measure the azimuths of all six corner doorways (two open to the NE, one to the NW, and three to the SE), but the two we did measure, in rooms 228 and 225B, afford an execellent view of the winter solstice sunrise. As the sun rises, it symmetrically illuminates the opposite corner (fig. 14.5) for a few minutes before the corner passes into shadow. The problem with these doorways used as windows is that they seem to be entrances to inside rooms. The corner doorways are examples of a type 3 observatory, for it seems certain that in the completed pueblo an exterior wall would have interfered with the passage of sunlight into the rooms. While we may postulate the existence of an exterior port, or window, as at Zuni (Cushing 1941, p. 129), in which case the alignment becomes one of type 2, such a postulate is in no way necessary to the claim that this orientation is deliberate. As we have emphasized before, a direction can be astronomically significant even though the structure which embodies it may present no visible phenomena when in the completed state. A type 3 or 4 alignment suggests that a ceremonial or other architectural importance marked it. These alignments are therefore among the most interesting; they might be said to present a case of geometry emerging out of astronomy.

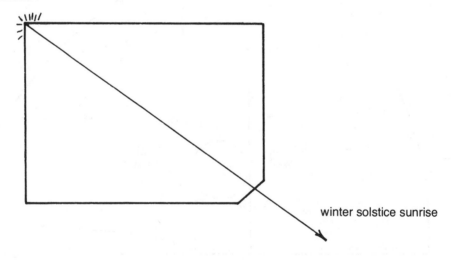

14.5. *Corner doorway and illuminated opposite corner, Pueblo Bonito, room 228.*

Hovenweep

As early as 1919, Fewkes (p. 42) entertained the possibility that the towers of Hovenweep National Monument and those located elsewhere in the nearby Southwest may have been used as astronomical observatories. He rejected this explanation of their use because of the location of some of them. The towers of Hovenweep are commonly constructed in groups with several on the rim of a narrow box canyon and one down in the canyon, such as occurs in the towers at the head of Ruin Canyon. At this site, for example, one cannot even see down the canyon from Square Tower (Fewkes 1919, fig. 6), let alone in any other direction except vertically. Other possible uses of these towers, such as defense (Schulman 1950) or the storage of grain or signaling, have been suggested, but none of these possibilities seems to completely fit their location and structural features. Unfortunately, the resolution of the puzzle of these towers is not aided by the few cultural remains which are found in the ruins. They are helpful in estimating the habitation dates of the towers but are little help in determining their function (Schulman 1950).

The suggestion of their possible use as astronomical observatories has persisted in the literature (Ellis 1975, p. 86) and in the private opinion of some southwestern archaeologists (Hayes, 1973, private communication). This opinion is still seriously considered because their towerlike shape strongly suggests such use and because most of the towers have several small openings, or ports, which could have been used to make astronomical observations.

Spurred by the hope of resolving the question, we have made a preliminary survey of the towers at Hovenweep. Our results show clearly that some of the towers are suitable for making astronomical observations of the sun and stars.

Because we were engaged in a preliminary survey and our time was very limited, we used a transit to determine the average magnetic declination for the area. We then used a Weems and Plath compass to measure the orientation of most of the ports. The ports of Oval Tower and Rimrock House, however, were measured with a transit (table 14.1). Because the acceptance angle of the ports can vary between 1° and 10° depending on where the observer stands, the ½° accuracy of the compass is quite acceptable. It was possible to use an average magnetic declination for the region because, unlike the case in Mexico (Aveni 1973, private communication), the magnetic declination varies relatively little from place to place in small regions of this part of the Southwest. For example, in Chaco Canyon, we found an r.m.s. deviation of less than 1° in magnetic declination from Penasco Blanco to Wijiji. The only problem we did encounter at Hovenweep was that in one or two of the towers steel reinforcing rods were used to stabilize the structures. These we could not measure reliably with a compass, and so they do not appear in table 14.1.

The angles of table 14.1 represent the azimuths of the ports which could have possibly been used to see the horizon. It is important to note here that many of the ports were constructed at an angle other than perpendicular to the walls, implying that the orientation of the port was of some importance to the person who built it. As the data show, orientations to bright stars as well as to the sun are evident.

Table 14.1.
Summary of Hovenweep Measurements

Tower	Azimuth orientation of port	Rise/set of nearest celestial object brighter than magnitude 2.0 (ca. A.D. 1200)†
Rimrock House*	171°52′	None
	242°09′	Beta Canis Major (Mirzam)
Oval Tower*	113°11′	Alpha Canis Major (Sirius)
	151°29′	Gamma Vela
	190°43′	None
	231°29′	Epsilon Canis Major
Horseshoe Tower	23° (no view of horizon)	None
	319°	Alpha Lyra (Vega)
	301°	Sun, summer solstice; Alpha Bootes (Arcturus)
	291°	Moon at maximum southerly inclination to ecliptic on summer solstice
	193°	None
	295°	Beta Gemini (Pollux)
Hovenweep Castle	239°	Sun, winter solstice; Alpha Scorpio (Antares)
	299°	Sun, summer solstice; Alpha Bootes (Arcturus)

*Transit measurements.

†Rise/set azimuth of object was within 2° of port azimuth. Azimuths are measured from the north toward the east along the horizon. Altitude of local horizon has been taken into account.

Although these data show that it was *possible* to use the towers as astronomical observatories, we have not yet determined whether that was their *probable* use. Much more evidence will be needed to establish a convincing case for this hypothesis. If it does prove to be a plausible hypothesis, the towers will represent a form of observatory quite different from those we have reported on above. The orientations of the ports place the towers in the type 2 category, but they would be the first clear examples we know of in the Southwest which could be considered stellar as well as solar observatories.

Sun Temple, Mesa Verde

Although we will report on Sun Temple elsewhere (Williamson and Fisher, in preparation), it is important to include a brief commentary on it here. Sun Temple derives its name from the fact that there is a peculiarly shaped rock attached to the western wall of the structure. Fewkes (1916, p. 21) thought it might be representative of the sun and pointed out that while sitting on the rock with one's back to the wall one clearly could see the setting sun directly in front. In other words, the observer faces west. He called this rock, and the seatlike construction surrounding it, a sun shrine. Fewkes further asserted that the straight south wall (fig. 7) is oriented to the summer solstice sunrise and/or the winter solstice sunset. We have determined that this is not the case, a finding that is supported by Reyman (1975).

In a confusing passage (p. 469) Fewkes seems to assert that the south wall if extended eastward would intersect the horizon 20° north of the east-west line. Our measurements show, quite to the contrary, that the extended south wall would intersect the horizon about 20° *south* of the summer solstice sunrise. The orientation of the south wall is 79°21' ±8' in the eastern direction or 259°21' ±8' in the western direction.

Thus the relation of Sun Temple to the sun seems to be a tenuous one at best. As we will report more fully elsewhere (Williamson and Fisher, in preparation), we set out to discover if the orientation of the wall had another astronomical significance. We found that in A.D. 1200 three bright stars, Procyon, Altair, and Betelgeuse, rose within 1°5 of the easterly azimuth of the south wall and one bright star, Rigel, set within 1°25 of the westerly azimuth of the south wall. In the absence of other confirmatory evidence, we regard this alignment as an inviting possibility which deserves more study. In any event, it is clear that no sure case has yet been made for associating "Sun Temple" with the sun.

Conclusions

It is now clear that there is a variety of solar and possible stellar observatories among the structures left behind by the Anasazi. What we and others have found so far indicates that the Anasazi had a considerable range of sophisticated astronomical knowledge and practice. We must now begin to integrate our data with other information which has already been gathered (Reyman 1971) and to consider what meaning these solar observatories might have had for the lives of their builders. A thorough examination of this question is not possible here, but we can make some tentative suggestions.

We know from historic Pueblo practice that the exact determination of the winter solstice and often of the summer solstice is crucial to the ceremonial and agricultural interests of Pueblo society (Ellis 1975; Parsons 1939a). We believe we have clear evidence that the Anasazi also watched the sun to establish these dates.

Not only did they observe the sun to establish a calendar, but at least some segment of the Anasazi population also incorporated their knowledge of the yearly cycle of the sun into their dwellings and ceremonial structures. In some cases, such as Pueblo Bonito, this may have been done in order to time rituals, but in others, such as Casa Rinconada, there seems to have been a conscious attempt to reflect the crucial celestial phenomena in earthly structures.

Casa Rinconada seems to be a special place, set apart from the major pueblos yet centrally located in the grid pattern of the ancient roads (Ebert and Hitchcock 1973). It represents in graphic symbolic form the essential features of the Pueblo cosmic view.

The cardinal directions are clearly indicated by its geographical placement and orientation and by the symmetrical arrangement of the floor features and wall niches. The time of the summer solstice and possibly the winter solstice can be established from within the kiva. The sipapu, a structural feature representing the place of emergence from the underworld, is elaborately constructed. Other kiva features whose functions are not yet clearly understood may add to this picture. In the future it will be important to understand whether Casa Rinconada is the result of isolated thought patterns or the culmination of years of more mundane astronomical practice among the Anasazi. Reyman (1971, p. 307), who suggests that Casa Rinconada and other great kivas are examples of Mexican influence in the Southwest, seems to favor the former possibility. We prefer the latter, if only because the practice of observing the sun seems to be widespread in Pueblo culture and is an obvious necessity for an agricultural society. A particular difficulty in answering this question at this time is the fact that we do not know the ages of some of the sites, and so we do not yet know whether there is an age sequence of solar observatory types.

The results of the Chaco road survey should also be taken into account in understanding the role that astronomy may have played in the life of the Anasazi. For example, some of the roads may very well be astronomically aligned. But even if the roads and the study of solar motions were completely separated in the mind of the Anasazi, they both, along with the architecture of the pueblos, are manifestations of a high level of intellectual achievement in Pueblo life in Chaco Canyon.

We are necessarily cautious about the possible role of astronomy at Mesa Verde and at Hovenweep. Reyman's work at Mesa Verde (1971, pp. 188–227) is far from complete and in some instances it is of questionable accuracy (Reyman 1975). Whether there are solar observing sites in Mesa Verde remains to be seen. Certainly, if our initial results at Hovenweep are confirmed in the future work we plan there, it promises to be a rich repository of astronomical alignments. In any event, it is certainly the case that there still remains much to be done in the Southwest in order to fully comprehend the astronomical practice of the Anasazi.

Acknowledgments

We wish to express our thanks to Walter Harrison, superintendent of Chaco Canyon National Monument, and to Ronald Switzer, superintendent of Mesa Verde National Park, for their wonderful hospitality while we were making these measurements. Special thanks are due National Park Rangers Jim Court and Clarion Cochran for their aid and guidance. Tom Lyons was helpful in providing useful aerial photographs of Chaco Canyon. We appreciate Al Hayes's persistent skepticism which helped us to avoid flights of fancy. Donnel O'Flynn is grateful to the Watson Foundation for the generous support which made his part of this research possible.

15

The Inca Calendar

R. T. Zuidema

Introduction

Most Spanish chroniclers in the sixteenth and seventeenth centuries report that the calendar of the Incas consisted of twelve months and was, in their own words, very similar to ours. Some authors in the nineteenth and early twentieth centuries indulged in highly fantastic and unfounded calendric schemes that were reputed to be Incaic, but these consisted more of the dross of simplistic Western ideas about primitive and archaic calendars.

Some students made a serious attempt; Nordenskiold (1925), for example, analyzed the "quipus" (knotted strings) and their calendrical content. In a sense even this was all guesswork as he had no ethnohistorical data to support his conclusions. Most students from the seventeenth century on stuck to the twelve month names and left it at that. Some modern students (e.g., Muller 1929, 1972) have tried to check out the Inca data on solar risings and settings, but as they did not know the place from where these were observed and as they hypothesized the wrong center of observation, they could not arrive at reliable reconstructions of the observational system.

Notwithstanding the apparent simplistic calendrical system of the Incas, there are many loose data, inconsistencies, and contradictions that do not fit into it. The well-informed indigenous chronicler Felipe Guaman Poma de Ayala (1936, ff. 893, 894 [pp. 883, 884]) is adamant about the fact that the Incas had an elaborate and precise calendar; he even gives us the picture, along with the name and address, of a calendar specialist—Juan Yumpa, from Uchucmarca in the province of Lucanas, whom he calls an "astrologuer-poet, who knows the round of the Sun and the Moon, eclipse and of stars and comets, hour, sunday, and month and year and of the four winds of the world for sowing the food since of old." Jose de Acosta (1954) in his famous chronicle, "Natural and moral history of the Indies," compares the Peruvian calendar favorably to the Mexican one (book 6, chap. 3). The work of recent scholars on the modern Andean agricultural and ceremonial calendar (Brownrigg 1973; Escobar et al. 1967) also demonstrates a high complexity, even if it has to be computed now by way of the Christian calendar.

Acosta had a direct knowledge of the complexity of the Inca calendar, as he refers (book 6, chap. 19) to the *ceque* system of Cuzco. This consisted of 328 *huacas* ('sacred shrines') in and around Cuzco which, in groups of an average of eight *huacas*, were aligned into forty-one directions (the *ceques*, or lines) toward the horizon. The *ceque* system was used for different social and ritual purposes. An explicitly expressed purpose (according to the priest Cristobal de Molina and the lawyer Juan Polo de Ondegardo, who did a painstaking research of recording it in the decade of 1560–1570 [Lohman Villena 1967]) was, however, also as a counting device for the calendar, each *huaca* standing for one day in the year, and as a system of sight lines for observing astronomical events on the horizon. The *ceque* system as a calendar was also mentioned by other students who knew about it—like Juan de Matienzo, the son-in-law of Polo de Ondegardo. At the moment we do not need to analyze why these students, or why the Jesuit Bernabe Cobo who preserved it in his chronicle, did not further analyze the *ceque* system as a calendar, as was done in the case of the Mexican and Maya calendars. One reason may be that in the Inca case the calendar was recorded on quipus in terms of an abstract theory of political organization, which has to be analyzed first, and not in terms of an elaborate system of gods, animals, and color directions, as it was preserved in Mexican pre- and postconquest codices. If we want to study the pre-Spanish Andean calendar, we will have to make the jump into insecurity through a study of the Inca theory of political organization and of an abstract *ceque* system.

In my rereading of the Spanish chroniclers for a study of Inca symbolism in religion and rituals and for a study of the iconography of pre-Spanish art, I also concentrated my attention on an analysis of the calendrical aspects. However, I want to treat most of these data as consequences of the calendar, to be explained by it, and not as information for its reconstruction. In the case of the preconquest data, I am aware so far of only two textiles that represent intricate calendrical accounts of all the days in a full solar year. I will analyze these first, as they set the stage for the kind of numerical computations that we also find in the *ceque* system as an Inca calendar. Here I have concentrated on three aspects that are perhaps necessary in any calendar as a description of astronomical events.

The first aspect involves the existence of schematic time units as defined by Neugebauer (1942) in the case of the Egyptian calendar. A schematic time unit is any fixed amount of days that repeats itself through time *independently* and that can be used to describe and measure astronomical time units. Such schematic time units are, of course, of importance to the administration of a centralized political organization. I will suggest that a first application of the *ceque* system was concerned with the recording of these schematic time units.

The second aspect involves the measurement of astronomical time units. In this case, the *ceque* system was used differently as a quipu for recording the measured astronomical time units.

The third aspect involves the use of the *ceque* system for observing astronomical events in terms of risings and settings of the sun, the stars, and possibly the moon. This, then, was still another use of the *ceque* system, independent from the two others.

Earlier fieldwork done in 1953 together with Dr. Manuel Chavez Ballon (see Zuidema 1964), as well as ongoing fieldwork started in the summers of 1973 and 1975, was primarily concentrated on exactly locating as many *huacas* as possible, especially those that were used as markers (*sucanca*) for astronomical observations. This work has advanced considerably and much use has been made of modern toponyms, data on old and new maps, data from chronicles and documents in general pertaining to the Cuzco area, and mythological and ritual data on Inca culture in general. Certain results of this work, for example, pertaining to the directional sequence of the *ceques*, will be used in the present paper. Nonetheless, much work still has to be done and a full discussion pertaining to the location of the *huacas* with their religious, ritual, and mythological significance must await another occasion. For a more elaborate discussion of the *ceques* and *huacas* used for the observation of sunrise and sunset during the solstices, see Zuidema (1976). Additional reasons for concentrating in this paper on numerical values in the *ceque* system are that this analysis can be done mostly independently from the location of the *huacas* and that arguments developed here may be helpful in locating the *huacas*. The discussion of Inca month names and their monthly rituals will also be kept to a formal statement of the problem as, again, a fuller understanding is dependent on an analysis of the numerical problems involved in the *ceque* system.

The most important reason, however, for choosing this approach in opening a discussion of Andean calendrical and astronomical problems lies in the nature of the *ceque* system itself. Knowing its functions as a day-to-day account of the whole year and as a system of astronomical observation, we would expect to have 365 or 366 *huacas* and 36 *ceques*, not 328 *huacas* and 41 *ceques*. These and other numbers are squarely based on sidereal lunar computations and not on solar ones, whereas "solar" numbers are only secondarily embedded into this lunar system. The problem of lunar astronomical observations is far more complex than solar because of the more erratic movements of the moon. A precise location of the *huacas* and an understanding of the Inca techniques of astronomical observation are therefore also dependent on a better understanding of the Inca "theory of the moon" and this is what this paper will mostly deal with.

Preconquest Calendars

The Calendar in the Huari Textile (Museum of Anthropology, Munich)

The textile (fig. 15.1) consists of two parts, sewn together, that are identical except for the mirror symmetry in the human figures. Figure 15.2 delineates the color scheme. Each part has 10 rows of 36 circles. Three vertical columns of 10 circles each correspond to one human figure. The 12 figures could represent months of 30 days in a year of 360 days (Catalog Mexico-Peru 1968, no. 630, fig. 91).

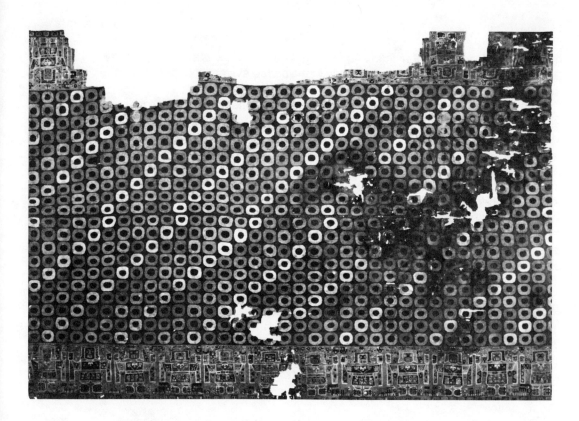

15.1. *The Huari textile.*

Moreover, the circles are organized on diagonals by way of the 5 colors: white (W), red (R), brown (Br), yellow (Y), and blue (Bl). Counting from the upper left corner to the lower right corner, there are 45 diagonals: first 9 partial ones, then 27 whole ones of 10 circles each, and then 9 partial ones. The following diagram represents the color scheme, each letter standing for one diagonal.

W	R	Br	Y	Br
W	R	Bl	Y	Br
W	R	Br	Y	Bl
W	R	Br	Y	Br
W	R	Br	Y	Bl
W	R	Br	Y	Br
W	R	Bl	Y	Br
R	W	Br	Y	Br
R	W	Bl	Y	Br

57W	59R	51Br	72Y	52Br	Totals of circles
15R	13W	21Bl		20Bl	

72	72	72	72	72

W	R	Br	Y	Br	W	R	Bl	Y	Br	W	R	Br	Y	Bl	W	R	Br
R	Br	Y	Br	W	R	Bl	Y	Br	W	R	Br	Y	Bl	W	R	Br	Y
Br	Y	Br	W	R	Bl	Y	Br	W	R	Br	Y	Bl	W	R	Br	Y	Br
Y	Br	W	R	Bl	Y	Br	W	R	Br	Y	Bl	W	R	Br	Y	Br	W
Br	W	R	Bl	Y	Br	W	R	Br	Y	Bl	W	R	Br	Y	Br	W	R
W	R	Bl	Y	Br	W	R	Br	Y	Bl	W	R	Br	Y	Br	W	R	Br
R	Bl	Y	Br	W	R	Br	Y	Bl	W	R	Br	Y	Br	W	R	Br	Y
Bl	Y	Br	W	R	Br	Y	Bl	W	R	Br	Y	Br	W	R	Br	Y	Bl
Y	Br	W	R	Br	Y	Bl	W	R	Br	Y	Br	W	R	Br	Y	Bl	W
Br	W	R	Br	Y	Bl	W	R	Br	Y	Br	W	R	Br	Y	Bl	W	R

| I | II | III | IV | V | VI |

| ababa | cbcbc | efefef | cdcdc | babab | dcdcd |

Y	Br	W	R	Br	Y	Bl	W	R	Br	Y	Br	W	R	Bl	Y	Br	R
Br	W	R	Br	Y	Bl	W	R	Br	Y	Br	W	R	Bl	Y	Br	R	W
W	R	Br	Y	Bl	W	R	Br	Y	Br	W	R	Bl	Y	Br	R	W	Br
R	Br	Y	Bl	W	R	Br	Y	Br	W	R	Bl	Y	Br	R	W	Br	Y
Br	Y	Bl	W	R	Br	Y	Br	W	R	Bl	Y	Br	R	W	Br	Y	Br
Y	Bl	W	R	Br	Y	Br	W	R	Bl	Y	Br	R	W	Br	Y	Br	R
Bl	W	R	Br	Y	Br	W	R	Bl	Y	Br	R	W	Br	Y	Br	R	W
W	R	Br	Y	Br	W	R	Bl	Y	Br	R	W	Br	Y	Br	R	W	Bl
R	Br	Y	Br	W	R	Bl	Y	Br	R	W	Br	Y	Br	R	W	Bl	Y
Br	Y	Br	W	R	Bl	Y	Br	R	W	Br	Y	Br	R	W	Bl	Y	Br

| VII | VIII | IX | X | XI | XII |

| efefe | dcdcd | e'f'e'f'e' | dcdcd | b'a'b'a'b' | dcdcd |

15.2. *Color scheme and arrangement of the Huari textile.*

Each row represents a group of 5 diagonals; in each column there are 9 diagonals representing 72 circles. The last two rows invert the order of the white and red circles. Brown and blue alternate in the third and fifth columns. Blue occurs in 5 rows, alternating with brown; therefore, blue never occurs twice in a row, but brown does occur twice in 4 rows (1, 4, 6, 8). Because of these inversions and alternations we can take the first two columns as a group ($2 \times 72 = 144$ circles) and the last three columns as a group ($3 \times 72 = 216$ circles). The diagonals and their colors seem to express a double system based on a division of $5 \times 9 = 45$ diagonals and a division of $5 \times 72 = 360$ circles in terms of their colors.

The system of the 12 standing figures does not exactly duplicate that of the circles. Each figure has a different scheme of combining colors in the face, headdress, shirt, staff, feet, and so on. A regular sequence of 3 groups of 4 figures can be found in the color of the face, the feathers of the crown, and the feet of each single figure. The groups could represent seasons of 4 months each. Under each figure, with one exception, is a row of 5 similar but much smaller faces; under the third figure are 6 faces.

The colors of the smaller faces under each figure do not correspond to the latter. Under each of the three sequences of 4 figures we detect, however, the following pattern in the color scheme of the smaller faces that, when certain variations are taken into account, could be called a recurring pattern (e′, f′, a′, and b′ show a slight difference in the color scheme from e, f, a, and b):

I	II	III	IV
a b a b a/	c b c b c /	e f e f e f/	c d c d c
V	VI	VII	VIII
b a b a b/	d c d c d /	e f e f e /	d c d c d
IX	X	XI	XII
e′f′e′f′e′/	d c d c d /	b′a′b′a′b′/	d c d c d

(As this color scheme was, however, studied from a color slide, which on this point was not completely clear, it should be checked against the original.)

In conclusion, we have 12 big faces, 61 small ones, and a total of 73. Counting each face for 5 days (as in 11 cases one big face and 5 smaller ones would correspond to 30 circles), this means the 73 faces represent a year of 365 days ($5 \times 73 = 365$). Because of the irregularity mentioned we conclude that the textile refers to two different concepts of a year: one of 360 days, with "schematic" (Neugebauer 1942) months of 30 days, and one of 365 days. The second number could be interpreted in two different ways. Either it may have indicated the real number of days in the solar year (but then an extra day would have had to be added, not accounted for in the textile, in every leap year) or the numbers 5 and 73 could have been used in a schematic way together with 72 ($= 8 \times 9$). Later we will observe that the Incas probably recognized:

$5 \times 73 = 365$ days as the solar year
$8 \times 73 = 584$ days as the Venus year
$9 \times 73 = 657$ days as a double sidereal lunar year ($328 + 329$)

So far we have described one half of the textile. The other half is identical in terms of the circles. The twelve figures, however, show a reversed order because of a mirror symmetry of the two halves. The whole textile, then, represents a double solar year with a reversed hierarchy in the second year of the circles as "governed" by the 12 figures.

15.3. *The Inca textile.*

The Calendar in the Inca-Period Textile (Kosok 1965, fig. 34)

In this textile (fig. 15.3) the days are represented by rectangles, each within a rectangular frame. Pairs of dark-colored frames alternate in each row and each column with pairs of light-colored frames. So there are groups of 4 frames. The alternation is irregular in one section of two rows, but this fact may be due partially to (modern?) repair of the textile. Each frame consists of an upper and lower part of different colors; the frames in one pair alternate the positions of the colors. The rectangles have a choice of 5 different designs, but so far I have not been able to discover any regularity in this pattern.

The nature of the repairs in the textile does not invalidate the existence of the following numbers of rectangles: Three rows are separated from the rest of the textile both by double lines and by an irregular number of rectangles. The upper row has 32 rectangles, a row near the center has 37, and the lower row has 30 rectangles. Seven regular rows are in the upper part and four in the lower, each consisting of $7 \times 4 = 28$ rectangles. These 11 rows clearly refer to sidereal lunar months of 27⅓ days rounded off to 28 days. The 13 months of 28 days form a year of 364 days, which is 1½ days short of a solar year. In this case the upper and lower irregular rows may have served to add up for this deficiency, although the number of rectangles seems too high for that purpose. Kosok suggested that the middle row of 37 rectangles could refer to a period of 3 solar years and 27 synodical months. If his idea were correct, we could as well suggest that the two rows of 30 and 31 rectangles referred to the two possible lengths of each of the 12 solar months in a solar year of 365 days. At the moment these suggestions will not help us further. However, it is clear from the textile that in pre-Spanish Peru a sidereal lunar calendar existed which utilized months of 27⅓ or 28 days ordered by groups of 4 days. We will find this conclusion corroborated by the data on the Inca calendar in the Spanish chronicles.

The Months in the Incaic Solar Year

The Number of Months and Their Names

While all the chronicles agree that the Incas had 12 months, contradictory data give us a notion that the system was more complex than most chroniclers want us to believe.

The four most important Inca ceremonies (called Raymi) were those following the two solstices and the two equinoxes, the celebration of which started at the first new moon. The months (called Quilla, or -quix 'moon') were synodical; we would expect, therefore, that the year of 12 synodical months (354 days) would fall behind with the solar year (365 days). However, we read nothing of the intercalation of an extra month every three years.

The concordance with the Christian month names also is confused. An Incaic month may be equated to different Christian months; whereas one chronicler may give two different names to a single month, another one may use them for two months. These discrepancies occur mostly in the period from March to July. Comparing the different sources we come to the reconstruction of the set of 14 names in table 15.1. Most chroniclers give the names in pairs and will combine, at one place or another in the calendar, two names in one month or else they will suppress a name. However, there are hardly any discrepancies concerning the general order of the names.

Some chroniclers (Guaman Poma, f. 260; Polo 1916, chap. 7) mention that the Incas added one or two days to certain synodical months in order to catch up with the solar year. However, they do not explain how such an intercalation, which thereby creates a system of solar months, can be accomplished. The beginnings

Table 15.1.
The Inca Months

Raymi	Quilla	
Capac Inti raymi *(solstice, December)*	. . . .	
Capac raymi	Camay quilla Hatun Pucuy quilla Pacha Pucuy quilla	
(equinox, March) Inca raymi		Ayriguay
	Hatun Cuzqui	Aymoray
Inti raymi	Aucay Cuzqui	Cauay
(solstice, June)		
		Chahuahuay
	Anta Cituay	Tarpuy quilla
Coya rami		
	Cituay	
(equinox, September)		
Uma raymi	Puchayqui	
Ayarmaca raymi	Catarayquis	

of these solar months were determined by way of a set of pillars on the horizon observed from Cuzco. All these data support our later conclusion that the Incas had a complicated system of simultaneously using four different types of months:
1. Synodical months of 29 or 30 days
2. Solar months of 30 days or longer
3. Sidereal months of 27⅓ days
4. Months of 23, 24, or 26 days
(Although Bertonio, in his Aymara dictionary, [1912], does not give a full list of Aymara month names, the following data are useful for comparative purposes:

Autipacha	time of hunger
Auti	month of August, or close, when it does not rain
Haccha auti	from Corpus Christi till two months later
Hiska auti	from September till the third when it is not so dry
Hiska	(1) urine of women and of all female animals or (2) small

Bertonio, then, mentions two 2-month periods in the dry season from June till September, all with names derived from the word *auti* 'hunger'. Perhaps the word *Anta*, used by Gonzalez Holguin [1952] in the month name of Anta Cituay, is a bastard form of the same word *auti*.)

The Beginning Dates of the Solar Year

The solstices and equinoxes were the rest points in the year, and either point or
set of points could be used for beginning the year. Other nonsolstitial or nonequi-
noctial beginnings are also mentioned. Various chroniclers say, for instance, that
originally the year began in January but that one king changed it to December.
Part of this problem can be solved by observing that the two solstice feasts were
celebrated in the months before these events, so that one could take either the
beginning or the end of this feast as New Year. The reappearance of the Pleiades
in May was also an important event for announcing the June solstice.

We may question, however, if the shift from January to December really did
refer only to this type of problem. Many chroniclers mention the coexistence of an
earlier agricultural and sidereal calendar as used by the lower classes and a later
political and solar calendar as used by the Incas in the administration of their
empire. The two beginning dates of the agricultural year were in February and
August, when, according to Guaman Poma and modern indigenous ideas, the
"Earth opens"—a belief related to the fact that at those times plowing was done
(Guaman Poma, ff. 894, 1124). Again to modern (J. Earls, personal communication) and old belief (Guaman Poma, f. 894 [p. 884]): the sun does not move from its
solstitial points on the horizon to dates respectively in February and in August.
Guaman Poma fixed the two days of June and August (in terms of the Christian
calendar) on San Juan (June 24) and on Santiago (July 25). The latter day is
understandable, as the Peruvians soon after the conquest replaced their old Thunder and Lightning god, also equated with Venus, with Santiago (Saint James) as
their god of war and agriculture. The Inca month of August must also have been
dedicated to the Thunder god because, when the Inca king initiated the new agricultural year at that time, he did this in a dress symbolizing this god (Guaman
Poma, f. 250; Zuidema MS). Today the period of San Juan to Santiago is still
used as a calendric unit in southern Peru (Brownrigg 1973). Contrary to all astronomical evidence, Guaman Poma (ff. 894, 895 [pp. 884, 885]) mentions that the
days are longer than the nights from the December solstice to August while the
nights are longer from August to December. His conclusion, however, that therefore the moon "governs" the latter period refers to a better observable astronomical fact recorded in the Inca calendar. We will observe later how a solar calendar
may have been more important during the dry season (related to the northern
upper Hanan moiety of Cuzco) and a synodic lunar calendar more important during the wet season (related to the southern lower Hurin moiety).

The problem discussed here also involves shifts of either rituals (Guaman
Poma, ff. 257, 239) or month names ("Discurso" in Maurtua, p. 156; Duviols, p. 25)
to an earlier date in terms of the Christian calendar. These shifts, when corrected,
point to a beginning date of the year somewhere in February. We will discuss later
a possible way in which the periods of the December solstice to February and from
the June solstice to August were defined in the pre-Spanish calendar.

Schematic Periods of 8, 10, 15, and 30 Days

Such trustworthy sources as Betanzos (chap. 18), Avila (chap. 18), and Guaman Poma (ff. 235, 260) make us aware of a schematic month with the fixed number of 30 days which the Incas divided both into two half months of 15 days and into 3 periods of 10 days. I have the feeling that they used these weeklike periods mostly as a calculating device for describing astronomical periods of a solar calendar; however, no other chroniclers mention these periods.

The week of 8 days is described from Ecuador (Ortegon, in Oberem, p. 235) to Bolivia (Matienzo, p. 53), in early sources which refer to local customs. The Incas used this week especially in relation to the custom of the king changing wives every 8 days; the rotating wives served him with their whole retinue, which was brought to Cuzco from their place of origin (Pedro Pizarro, pp. 49, 63; Cobo, book 12, chap. 37). After a year (but, as we will see, this was not a solar year) the Inca would return to the first wife. This week of 8 days was also used in market cycles (Garcilaso, book 6, chap. 35) and in the cyclical service of priests in the Temple of the Sun in Cuzco. Probably under the influence of the European calendar, Garcilaso added a holiday to each week and therefore speaks of 9-day weeks as the rotation period of priests of the sun in Coricancha (Temple of the Sun) (Garcilaso, book 3, chap. 22). Finally, weeks of 8 days were important probably in terms of ritual "months" of 24 days for the celebration of the most important Inca feasts, especially the Capac Inti raymi, the December solstice feast (Garcilaso, book 6, chap. 23; Molina, pp. 49–58).

Today, the cyclical and weekly type of service used by women on haciendas around Ayacucho is called *suyu*; a word used in the same way by Gonzalez Holguin in 1608 for groups of people in general. The week of 8 days is also still important in modern agricultural activities (Brownrigg 1973; Mrs. Rosa Gamarra-Thompson, personal communication).

Seasons of 3 and 4 Months

In an earlier analysis of the Inca calendar, principally based on data from Guaman Poma, I described an internal order of the 12 months consisting of a descending hierarchy in the seasons January–March and April–June, when the sun moves on the horizon from south to north, and an ascending hierarchy in the seasons July–September and October–December, when the sun moves from north to south. Although this description is still accurate for one use of the calendar, the problems of the whole system are far more complicated. The following analysis will again be based principally on Guaman Poma's (ff. 235–260 [pp. 894, 895, 1130–1167]) and Molina's descriptions of monthly rituals and agricultural activities.

First, there were the two half years from solstice to solstice with the solstitial feast in the month preceding this solar event. There were also two half years crosscutting the first ones from equinox to equinox. October–March was the wet half year and April–September was the dry one. The feast of the king and that of the queen were celebrated, respectively, just after the March equinox and just before the September equinox. The ritual activities in these four seasons also refer to another hierarchical relationship. The four months around the two solstices (December–January, June–July) were dedicated to the cult of the sun. The four months around the two equinoxes (September–October, March–April) show a relationship to the cult of water, that is, to the creator god, Viracocha, and to the moon-goddess. The four inbetween months were dedicated to agriculture, to death, to the Thunder god as the god of war and of all atmospheric events, and to Venus. In May the Inca would finish the agricultural year by ritually harvesting (that is "killing") a special field in Cuzco; in August he would ritually plow the same field ("conquering, killing" the earth) both acts being accompanied by victory songs ("Discurso" in Maurtua, p. 177). November was dedicated to the cult of the dead (when the seeds were in the ground) and February was the month when most illnesses would occur and when new virgin ground would be plowed.

Besides the four seasons of three months each, Guaman Poma also mentions three seasons of four months each. August–November was dedicated to sowing and this period was counted in terms of synodic months. The Inca opened the period by ritual plowing, and in the last month watches were installed to guard against the theft of irrigation water. During December–March (the time of heavy rains) plants had to grow and ripen. In the first month was the great feast of the sun and the rites of initiation and in the last month watches in the field guarded against theft. The months of April–July were used for harvest and were dedicated to the sun. In the last month, land was redistributed for the next agricultural year. Matienzo (p. 55) mentions the four-month period also in Inca administration and Guaman Poma (ff. 265, 288) and Sarmiento (chap. 31, 47) mention it for the crowning of a new king.

Periods of 2, 3, 4, 5, 8, 10, and 16 Years

Periods of more than one year may have had astronomical significance. Two and eight years are mentioned in relation to bridge building (Thompson and Murra 1966), three or six years for the renewal of *acllas* (virgins of the Sun) in their *acllahuasi* (house of *acllas*) (Las Casas, chap. 140; Murua II, chaps. 10, 19), and five years for the age classes; four-year periods are mentioned for communal hunts or *chaco* (Murua). Periods like these are still agriculturally important for the following period of land.

Finally, Sarmiento reports (chap. 31) how the king Pachacuti Inca (who himself worshipped the god of Thunder and of Venus as his personal god) kept the crown prince for 16 years in the Temple of the Sun till his initiation. For this event he invented a new solar ritual establishing four temples of the sun outside Cuzco. These temples probably indicated the directions of observation for sunrise and sunset during the solstices. The 16 years of preparation for the rising sun may have been based on the equation of 16 solar years to 10 Venus years ($16 \times 365 = 10 \times 584$).

The Ceque System

Introduction

The *ceque* system has been compared to a giant quipu, laid out over the Cuzco valley and the surrounding hills that served in the local representation of the Inca cosmological system, in its spatial, hierarchical, and temporal aspects. The *ceque* system was used at different times of the year for different purposes and by different classes of people for recording superimposed cycles of ritual events. To understand the different calendrical cycles that were represented and integrated into one system, it will be necessary to distinguish and separate the layers of meaning attached to each event and its cycle. Not only can the *ceque* system be metaphorically compared to a quipu but every local group did in fact record its *ceque* system, that is, its political, religious, and calendrical organization on a quipu (Matienzo, p. 119), and the local keepers of these records, the *huacaca-mayoc* or *villcacamayoc* (specialists of the *huacas* and *villcas*, i.e., of the sacred shrines and objects) (Cook, book 13, chap. 22; Molina 1943, pp. 69–77), had to give account of them to the national administration.

The meaning of the *ceque* system can be explained best by way of the feast of the Capac hucha, when children were sacrificed (Molina, pp. 69–77) in Cuzco during the two solstitial feasts (Guaman Poma, ff. 247, 259, 262, 263). At that time, the ritual and calendrical (Matienzo, p. 120) value and rank of all the *huacas* in the empire, of every village, town, province, were reassessed. The representatives of these sent presents and children to the Inca in Cuzco. Some were sacrificed there while others were sent back and sacrificed at home. These *capac hucha* (also called *cachahui* or *cachahuaco*, from *cacha*, 'messenger') followed a straight line (*ceque*) on their way home and did not go by way of the roads (Duviols 1967, pp. 26, 27, 38; Molina 1943; Rostworowski 1970, pp. 23–24).

The *huacas* of the *ceque* system in Cuzco were also recorded on a quipu. On the basis of this information, Molina wrote "Relacion de las huacas" (an account of the *huacas*) of Cuzco for the bishop of Cuzco. Polo de Ondegardo gave a similar account, from a quipu (Matienzo, pp. 119, 120), to the viceroy. Both accounts are from around 1570 and it is probable that their information, as preserved in the chronicle of Cobo, derived from the same quipu. Many of the place names and *huacas* mentioned by Molina in his description of the calendrical feasts of Cuzco coincide with those of the *ceque* system.

Guaman Poma mentions as a name for secretaries *quilla uata quipoc* (f. 359) "the quipu specialist for months and years" and as a name for accountants and treasurers *hucha quipoc* (f. 351), using the same word, *hucha*, as that for the human sacrifices. Gonzalez Holguin also has a similar name, *hucha yachak*, for secretary. For us, the most important fact is the calendrical reference in the names given by Guaman Poma. In a drawing of the *hucha quipoc* (f. 360) he shows a man with a quipu and a tablet of 20 squares with black and white points in each of the squares (fig. 15.4). The tablet was used for counting numbers and for "setting down feasts and sundays and months and years." We will argue later that the tablet may have had a calendrical function.

15.4. *The quipu specialist for the months and years. (From Guaman Poma, f. 360.)*

The reason why the *capac hucha* walked in a straight direction was probably because they had to follow a specific *ceque*. Since the *ceques* were considered to go out from the Temple of the Sun and since specific *huacas* also had a function in terms of astronomical observation, we may assume that the *ceques* were used as sight lines for the observation of solar, lunar, and stellar risings and settings. For the purpose of this paper it is of great importance that the *ceques* going straight N, W, and E could still be determined, because the *huacas* on these *ceques* are still precisely known.

The Order of the Ceques

The *ceque* system consisted of 41 *ceques* (lines) radiating from the Temple of the Sun in Cuzco and organizing 328 *huacas* in and around the city. Both numbers are of calendrical importance as $8 \times 41 = 12 \times 27\frac{1}{3} = 328$, 8 being the number of days in the Andean week, 12 the number of solar months in the year, and $27\frac{1}{3}$ the number of days in the sidereal lunar month. One *ceque* consisted of two lines running parallel to each other and not, as Cobo claims, one being the continuation of the other. However, for different calendrical reasons they were counted either as one or two. Finally, in his conclusion, Cobo does not say that there were 41 or 42 *ceques*, but 40.

The number 40 was important in the Inca theory of political organization. Local groups were matched, in an ascending order of size, to a hierarchical order of 100, 500, 1,000, 5,000, 10,000 and 40,000 (not 50,000!) families. The province of Cuzco, compared to a unit of 40,000, consisted of the city of Cuzco, the valley of Cuzco, and an outer zone of (probably 40) different non-Inca kingdoms that had received the honorary rank of Incas-by-privilege. In a special rite during the equinoctial feast of Cituay in September, 400 warriors had to "drive out the illnesses from Cuzco," each group of 10 following one *ceque* (Cobo, book 13, chap. 29). In this context we may understand why Polo de Ondegardo once mentions "more than 400 huacas" (p. 55) and at another place (p. 43) specifies the number as 340: 12 *sucancas* (observation posts on the horizon) and 328 *huacas*. Therefore, our first conclusion is that to the 40 or 41 *ceques* could be attached the schematic number values of either 8 ($8 \times 41 = 328$) or 10 ($10 \times 40 = 400$).

The distribution of the 40 (41, 42) *ceques* was not regular in the case of one of the four divisions of Cuzco. We will follow step by step how the Incas arrived at the actual distribution of the *ceques* since it is important for an understanding of the calendar.

The area surrounding Cuzco was first divided into a northern upper moiety called Hanan-Cuzco, and a southern lower moiety, Hurin-Cuzco. These moieties were themselves halved to produce four parts, *suyu*. A straight W-E line was formed by the first *ceque* of Chinchaysuyu (NW) and the last *ceque* of Antisuyu (NE). The last *ceque* of Chinchaysuyu went straight north, separating this quarter from Antisuyu. The last *ceque* of Collasuyu, going 37° E of S, divided Hurin into two unequal parts: a small Collasuyu section (SE) and a large Cuntisuyu section (SW). Each *suyu* had groups of 3 *ceques* with the individual called either:

Collana, a, 'principal, first'
Payan, b, 'second, middle'
Cayao, c, from *calla* 'origin'
A similar hierarchical order was applied to the groups of *ceques* (1, 2, 3) and to the
suyus I, II, and III. In the latter context of primarily local and not hierarchical organ-
ization, Cuntisuyu (IV) represented an extra group in opposition to the first three.
Cuntisuyu reversed the internal hierarchical order of the other *suyus*. The scheme
is delineated in fig. 15.5.

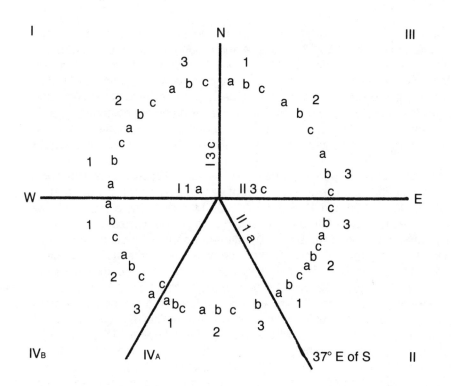

15.5. *Scheme of the* ceque *system.*

The *huacas* and their *ceques* are enumerated in Cobo's "Relacion de los
ceques" in the following order:
    I 3 c b a, 2 c b a, 1 c b a
    III 1 a b c, 2 a b c, 3 a b c
    II 3 c b a, 2 c b a, 1 c b a
IV_B 3 b, 2 c b a, 1 c b a, IV_A 3 c-a, 2 c b a, 1 c b a
In four cases, the generic name of the *ceque* was replaced by the name of the
group associated with it (see IV g, V a). The fourth *ceque* of Cinchaysuyu (I 2 c)
was called Payao and the fifth one (I 2 b) Cayao. Probably Cobo here made an

error, the fourth *ceque* being Cayao and the fifth Payan. I corrected this error.

If we accept that Cobo's order of enumeration is based on Inca information, then we might conclude that the *huacas* and *ceques* of I and II are enumerated in ascending order. In IV the order may have been descending because of a reversed hierarchical value of the terms Collana, Payan, and Cayao (see V b). The Incas arrived at the number of 14 or 15 *ceques* in Cuntisuyu by first dividing this *suyu* into two parts, A and B. A comparison to the political organization of nearby San Jeronimo clearly demonstrates this intention (Zuidema 1964, pp. 222–223, 241–242). The Incaic organization there was ranked as one of 500 families. The 5 *pachacas* (*pachaca* = a group of a hundred) of San Jeronimo corresponded to the 4 *suyus* of Cuzco with Cuntisuyu, IV, matching the two last *pachacas*. From this comparison we might expect that the two halves of Cuntisuyu would also contain 9 *ceques* each, making a total for Cuzco of 5 × 9 = 45 *ceques*. A first reduction to 42 was obtained by *not* redoubling *ceques* 3 a b c. The final reduction to 41 resulted from joining *ceque* b to part B of IV and *ceques* c and a, taken as one, to part A. The suggested reduplication and reduction enable us to reconstruct the original situation:

Original situation   *Final situation*

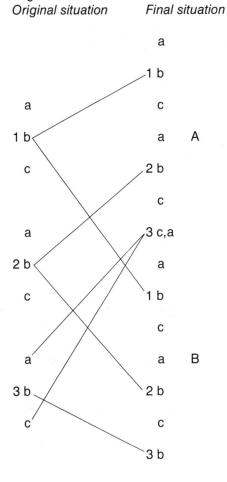

Later when I use the subscripts A and B (e.g., IV$_A$ 1 b) I will be referring to the final situation unless specific reference to the original situation is made.

The number 42 (or 41 or 40) was mentioned elsewhere in Peru in similar contexts. In two cases we can also study a similar reduction from 45.

Copacabana

The Incaic Temple of the Sun in Copacabana, on Lake Titicaca, was served by 42 "nations" from all over the empire (Ramos Gavilan 1621). The list consisted of:
1. One descent group of the Inca high nobility, called Sucsupanaca, to which always belonged the High Priest of the Sun
2. The two groups of Hanan- and Hurin-Cuzco
3. The four groups of Inca-by-privilege, Huaro, Quihuar, Papre, and Chilque
4. Thirty-eight other nations
Altogether, there were 45 groups although Gavilan specifically mentions the number 42. One reduction he applied was by joining Huaro and Quihuar and also Papre and Chilque. A similar reduction was used in similar contexts and on the same groups by Guaman Poma (ff. 84, 85, 750, 740) and in certain colonial documents. A further reduction could be achieved by taking Sucsupanaca as one group and Hanan- and Hurin-Cuzco as another. The total then would be one group of Inca high nobility, one group of Inca low nobility, and 40 other non-Inca groups. Of these 42 groups, 41 served the *panaca* (sisterhood or the grouping or household of the sisters and female cousins of a certain man) to which the High Priest of the Sun belonged, probably in calendrical ritual. Cobo may have referred to a similar situation in a village near Lake Titicaca when he says (book 14, chap. 17): "Once when I was present at the procession of Corpus Christi [i.e., the Catholic feast that replaced the old June solstitial celebration] in a village of Collao, I counted 40 dances, each different from the other, in which they imitated by way of their dress, their singing, and their dancing the different nations to which they belonged."

The Ritual of First Plowing in Hurin-Haucaypata

There were two "plazas of the Sun" in Cuzco: one of Hanan-Cuzco, Hanan-Haucaypata ("the plaza of rejoicing of Hanan"), in the center of town, and one of Hurin-Cuzco, Hurin-Haucaypata. The latter was close to the Temple of the Sun but outside the ceremonial part of the town within the confluence of two rivers. Calendrical festivities, with the Inca present, were carried out in both plazas. The second one was close to the field where the rituals of first harvesting, in May, and of first plowing, in August, were carried out. We will describe the latter feast (Rostworowski 1970b, pp. 165–166).

The Inca sat on his throne of gold (a pyramid) with his 4 councilors as chiefs of the 4 *suyus* of the empire behind him. They were described as chiefs of 100,000 families. Behind the 4 councilors were seated the chiefs of 10,000 families; there were 10 of these in each *suyu*. In the last position were seated the ambassadors of the provinces, who were apparently also divided into 40 groups. First, the Inca plowed a certain distance alone; next the 4 councilors plowed twice that distance; finally, the 40 chiefs with the rest of the people plowed till the end of the morning. In the afternoon, the 45 dignitaries (Inca, 4 councilors, 40 chiefs) who each had a golden digging stick played games while the other people continued plowing. The hierarchy involved was the same as in Copacabana and a similar type of reduction of the number of dignitaries was probably applied, the 4 councilors counting as one.

The Organization of Priests in Allauca

In an article on the ancestral organization of the village of Allauca (Zuidema 1973, from Hernandez Principe 1622) in the department of Ancash, central Peru, I analyzed the following organization of male and female priests distributed over its 4 *ayllus* (a vague or extended family by common agreement):

	First *ayllu*	Second *ayllu*	Third *ayllu*	Fourth *ayllu*
Male priests	8	8	4	4
Female priests	12	16	6	8

The numbers in the third and fourth *ayllus* are, for both men and women, half of those in the first and second *ayllus*, respectively. The first and third *ayllus* together and the second and fourth *ayllus* together each have 12 male priests. In a similar example from Cuzco, the Inca had 12 councilors: 4 from I, 2 from III, 4 from II, and 2 from IV (Guaman Poma, ff. 183, 365; Santacruz Pachacuti, p. 256). In the case of female priests of Allauca, the first and second *ayllus* together have 28 (28 is the number of days in a sidereal month). Together with the number of priests in the third and fourth *ayllus*, there are 42 female priests, as many as the number of *ceques* in Cuzco. The description of Allauca is all the more important for our purposes as it is given in the context of human sacrifices (*capac hucha, cachahui, ceque*). We can conclude, therefore, that we are dealing here with the only specific description of a *ceque* system in Peru with a calendrical reference (numbers 12, 28, 42) similar to the *ceque* system of Cuzco.

The Kingdom of Nampallec in Lambayeque

The last example is from the pre-Inca and pre-Chimu kingdom of Nampallec (Cabello Valboa, book 3, chap. 17) in the north coast valley of Lambayeque. This organization consisted of 12 towns, including the capital, which were originally governed by the 12 sons of the second king in a legendary dynasty of 12 kings. These kings were served by 40 court officials who were each sent as a specialist by a different village.

The Possible Schematic Calendrical Number Values Implied in the Ceque System as Compared to Those of the Textile

Giving the *ceques* a number value of either 8 or 10, we could hypothesize about the *ceque* system as a schematic calendrical system in three different ways.
1. Accepting an original situation in Cuntisuyu of 9 *ceques* and a number value of

10 for each *ceque*, we could arrive at the number 12 × 3 × 10 = 360. Betanzos
mentions a schematic year of 360 days plus 5 extra days, and schematic months
of 30 days divided into half months of 15 days.
2. Reduplicating the number of *ceques* in Cuntisuyu, we first arrive at an amount
of 45 *ceques*. Giving these a value of 8, we would arrive at a year of 360 days divided into 45 weeks of 8 days (45 × 8 = 360). In the Huari textile there were 12
figures, 36 columns of 10 circles each, and 45 diagonals dividing the same number
of circles in 5 color groups of 72 circles each (5 × 72 = 45 × 8).
3. By way of reducing the number of *ceques* in Cuntisuyu, we arrive at a total of 41
ceques which correspond to an actual number of 328 (8 × 41) *huacas*. We will
observe later that not only was the number of *ceques* in Cuntisuyu reduced from
18 (2 × 9) to 14, but also the number of *huacas* on each *ceque* was reduced as
compared with those of the *ceques* in the other *suyus*. The Huari textile also contained 3 × 9 diagonals, each with a full number of 10 circles and 2 × 9 diagonals
with reduced numbers. The other Inca-period textile showed us the importance of
the numbers 4 and 28 (an approximation of 27⅓).

Earlier I mentioned that according to Pedro Pizarro the Inca was served every
8 days by another wife and that after a year he would come back to the first wife.
The description of a feast in Quito in 1639 (Pablo Herrera, p. 88) mentions that a
man of Inca nobility represented the Inca king and that he was accompanied by 40
wives. This suggests that the original Inca king had one principal wife and 40 secondary ones, who served him in the 41 weeks of a calendrical year of 328 days.
Because, in the *ceque* system, the first *ceque* of Chinchaysuyu was not called
Collana but Capac ('royal'), we may assume that the principal wife, who as queen
was her husband's full sister, was represented by this *ceque*.

Herrera (1916, chap. 13) describes how, once after a war, the Inca king "established as law that there could not enter into Cuzco more than one thousand Collas at a time and that before this number left there could not enter others." Accepting that the province of the Collas was given the rank of having 40,000 families, we
can conclude that the Inca week of 8 days, the market cycle, the priest cycle, the
king having 40 secondary wives, and the regulation of the Colla contingent in Cuzco (which example probably was given as a specific case of a more general rule)
all took part in a general system of taking turns (*mitta*), integrating the social, economic, ritual, and calendrical spheres, for which the *ceque* system with its 41
ceques and 328 *huacas* was the technical instrument.

The Political Subdivisions of Cuzco, the Groups of Ceques, *and the*
Measuring of Astronomical Time Units by Way of Ceques *and* Huacas

The Political Subdivisions of Cuzco

So far we have discussed the formal organization of the *ceque* system and we
have suggested certain correlations between this formal system and another one
consisting of schematic years, months, and weeks. Only after establishing such a
formal and schematic system can one describe the astronomical time units which

were measured by it. This fact is just as true for the modern student who wants to reconstruct the Andean calendar as it was for the Inca administration who wanted to use the same calendar in their whole empire. A mythical explanation says that it was for this reason that one Inca king divided the year into 12 months, because "in this way the generally accepted order would be such, from Quito to Chile, that they never would lose track of time" ("Discurso" in Maurtua, p. 150).

Astronomical values like the half-year periods between when the sun is in perihelion and aphelion, synodical months, solar months, sidereal lunar months, and possibly the Venus cycle were expressed by way of the numbers of *huacas* in the groups of *ceques* and combinations thereof. These combinations were explained in terms of the political and religious organization of Cuzco. Certain facets of this organization will have to be discussed before we can tackle the astronomical problem.

The anonymous chronicler best introduces the organizational problem when he mentions how one king "divided the population of Cuzco into 12 parts and ordered that each part would take up the names of its month and of the occupation carried out then, and that at the beginning of its month the group would come out on the central plaza, announcing its month and playing trumpets in order that everybody would know" ("Discurso" in Maurtua, p. 150).

Cobo also refers to this fact. On the one hand, he mentions the names of these 12 groups, each being associated with a certain group of 3 *ceques* of which it took care; on the other hand, he associates each group of 3 *ceques* with a specific *sucanca* on the horizon of Cuzco which indicated sunrise or sunset at the beginning of a specific month. Nonetheless, it is difficult to match the *ceque* system to these statements of Cobo, as the latter refer to a solar calendar and the totals of *ceques* and *huacas* fit only into a lunar calendar. So far, we can accept that certain associations were made between political groups and groups of *ceques* and months; however, they were *not* one-to-one associations. We become aware of this problem when discussing the association of the two non-Inca towns in the valley of Cuzco with the *ceques* and months.

Besides the Inca city of Cuzco at the west end of the valley, the town of Sanu (today San Sebastian), situated in the center of the Cuzco valley, represented the pre-Inca kingdom of the Ayarmaca, which was north of Cuzco. The town of Oma (today San Jeronimo), at the east end, represented in the valley an original kingdom of which the towns of Urcos and Huaro (some 40 km SE of Cuzco) formed the center. People from these towns had the special occupation, carried out outside of Cuzco, of being priests and confessors to the Inca high nobility. Sanu and Oma are not mentioned on any *ceque*, but they are situated between III 3 c and II 3 c. The Ayarmaca of Sanu gave their name to *ceque* III 3 b which was close to the town, and, since the people of Oma worshipped as their ancestress a Mama Anahuarque (Rostworowski 1962, p. 137), we may assume that they took care of *ceque* IV$_B$ 3 b which was also called Anahuarque. This *ceque*, however, was not in the direction of the town of Oma. Whereas the high nobility of Cuzco celebrated its initiation feasts in December (Capac Inti raymi), the Ayarmaca did so in November (Ayarmaca raymi), and the people from Urcos (including those from Oma) had their initiation feast in October (Oma raymi) (C. Molina 1943, pp. 46–48).

These data, although helpful, still leave us completely confused about the association of political divisions with groups of *ceques* and months. The high nobility of Cuzco, who belonged to Capac ayllu ('the royal descent group') and who celebrated Capac Inti raymi, took care of the group of *ceques* I 1. We can relate Ayarmaca to III 3 and Oma to IV 3. But only the name Anahuarque suggests the association of the month Oma raymi, called after the town of Oma, to IV 3. In the two other cases we will have to suggest later, on astronomical grounds, that the month Ayarmaca was related to IV 2 and the month Capac Inti raymi to IV 1. Drawing a positive conclusion from a negative result, we must reaffirm that there was not a one-to-one relation of a political division with a group of *ceques* and with a specific month.

The problem of the association of the other 10 political divisions with groups of *ceques* is extremely complex and we will mention here only the results of our research.

The rank and function of each of these divisions were indicated in three different ways:

1. By the rank of its *suyu* and its group of *ceques*
2. By the mythical association to one of the former Inca kings
3. By the specific religious cult related to each group and its ancestor

The situation in Hanan-Cuzco was as follows:

I 1 (Collana)	<u>10</u>	<u>8</u>	(Collana) III 1
	Sun	Viracocha	

I 2 (Payan)	<u>9</u>	<u>7</u>	(Payan) III 2
	Thunder		

I 3 (Cayao)	<u>6</u>	Ayarmaca	(Cayao) III 3

The descending hierarchy was from I 1 to III 3 and is shown in correlation with the numbers of the last (10) to the first (6) king of Hanan-Cuzco. We must consider this distribution as regular in comparison to other similar examples. The first three groups were related respectively to the cult of the three major gods of the Inca pantheon. The cult of the visible Sun was of primary concern to Inca government. Thunder and Venus, considered as sons of Sun, were worshipped as gods of war and agriculture. Viracocha, the creator god, as the real, invisible sun, was considered ancestor to the priestly hierarchy. The three gods, then, were part of a solar cult within a solar calendar.

The following two political divisions of lesser importance had chthonic associations. The last group was non-Incaic. Because of the numbers of *huacas* involved, I will henceforth call I 1, I 2, and III 1 the major groups of *ceques* and III 2, I 3, and III 3 the minor ones.

The association in Hurin-Cuzco of groups of *ceques* with political divisions was not regular, although the latter derived their origin from a dynasty of five kings with a similar internal structure as those of Hanan-Cuzco. Some of the changes were due to the reduplication and reduction of *ceques* in IV and their reversed hierarchy. Of the major groups of *ceques*:

II 2 now belonged to the descendents of the fifth king, corresponding to the tenth king (I 1) in Hanan-Cuzco.

II 1 now belonged to the descendents of the fourth king, corresponding to the ninth (I 2) in Hanan-Cuzco.

IV 3, containing *ceque* Anahuarque (IV$_B$ 3 b), did not belong to an Inca group, but probably to the town of Oma.

Of the minor groups of *ceques*:

II 3 belonged to the descendents of the third king, corresponding to the eighth in Hanan-Cuzco.

In Cuntisuyu we only know that IV$_B$ 1 belonged to the descendents of the first king. We have no data on the second king; therefore, we cannot draw any conclusions about the original situation in IV, except for the fact that these two other political divisions belonged to minor groups of *ceques* (IV 2 and IV 1).

We already mentioned the council of 12 nobles to the Inca king. Comparing the situation in Cuzco to that of Allauca, it seems most reasonable to suggest that only the 6 major groups of *ceques* were related to these councilors. That is:

4 from I 1 and I 2
2 from III 1
4 from II 2 and II 1
2 from IV 3

We will discover later that it was this group of *ceques* that defined the solar year by their number.

The Numbering of Huacas *in the* Ceque *System*

Cobo and Polo de Ondegardo mention explicitly 328 *huacas* of the *ceque* system. There were, however, some extra *huacas*. Here I will discuss to what extent the extra *huacas* might have affected the total number of *huacas* for the calculation of astronomically important numbers.

First, there were the 12 *sucanca* (Herrera, book 4, chap. 5; Polo), or 14 (Cobo), pillars used for astronomical observation. Both chroniclers mention these in addition to the total of *huacas*, although they do not give their names and locations in a special list. Of some *sucanca* we know, however, that they also functioned as regular *huacas* in the list of 328. Molina (pp. 26, 27) mentions two other *sucanca*, but these are located beyond the *ceque* system. Therefore, there is no reason to suppose that the *sucanca* were also used for counting extra days.

Second, the Temple of the Sun itself was counted as an extra *huaca*, although it was "not placed in the *ceque* system" (Cobo, p. 186). I want to propose that the temple could be counted, when necessary, as an extra *huaca* of IV$_B$. Different data support this suggestion. Santillan (p. 47) includes the whole of Cuzco, as the center of Inca political organization, in Cuntisuyu. Guaman Poma (f. 183) relates the high priest of Cuzco, serving in the Temple of the Sun, to Cuntisuyu. Of its two subdivisions, IVₐ (37 *huacas*) and IVв (43 *huacas*), the latter one has more *huacas*, indicating its relatively higher importance. Whereas in the other three *suyus* some *ceques* started at the foot of the Temple of the Sun and others were farther removed from it, it was only in IVв that three *ceques* (1 a, 1 b, and 3 b) started from *huacas* within the Temple of the Sun. In IVₐ all *ceques* started on the edge of Cuzco. Finally, *ceque* IVв 3 b, called Anahuarque, is the longest single *ceque* of the whole system. For this reason I propose, too, that the descending hierarchy of the *ceques* and groups of *ceques* in IV, or at least in IVв, was inverted in opposition to their order in the other *suyus*.

Third, at the end of the description of the *ceques*, Cobo mentions 4 extra *huacas* that belonged to "different *ceques* that were not placed in the same order as the others when the investigation was made." Apparently (Cobo, book 13, chap. 28; Molina, pp. 64, 65), these *huacas* had a special function in relation to the beginning and the end of the irrigation system. One *huaca*, Tocoripuquio, should be found on *ceque* I 2 a but was forgotten: Cobo says that *ceque* I 2 a has 11 *huacas* although he mentions only 10. The name of another "extra" *huaca*, Quiquijana, was in fact also mentioned on *ceque* II 2 a.

I propose, therefore, that the last two extra *huacas*, not mentioned here, also corresponded to 2 of the 328 *huacas* and that we can take this number as having been intended by the informants in their description of the *ceque* system to Polo de Ondegardo. In the next paragraph I will show that there is also an internal consistency of the total of 328 *huacas* by way of the distribution of the numbers of *huacas* belonging to each group of three *ceques*.

The last problem we have to deal with here is the distribution of the *huacas* in Cuntisuyu. Although the number of *ceques* was augmented here, as was the space given to this *suyu*, the number of *huacas* was not. The different order of the *ceques* did, however, redistribute the *huacas* into other groups of other numbers. In the following diagram of the number of *huacas* in the *ceque* system, I will include for Cuntisuyu:

1. The original number of *huacas* in a situation of 3 × 3 ceques
2. The number of *huacas* in the later situation

The number of *huacas* in the original situation conforms completely to the pattern in the other *suyus* and I will analyze this distribution in the next paragraph. In the later situation the *huacas* are redistributed into the two major groups, IVв and IVₐ, with the number of *huacas* 43 and 37 respectively. Here I want to interpret the possible calendrical meaning of this secondary redistribution.

We noticed before that Cuntisuyu played a double role within the organization of 4 *suyus*. First, it is a *suyu* like the 3 others with a distribution of 3 × 3 = 9 *ceques* and with number values for the *huacas* of the 3 groups of *ceques* similar to those of the other *suyus*. Second, comparing the organization of 4 *suyus* in Cuzco to that of the 5 *pachacas* in San Jeronimo, we discovered that Cuntisuyu alone corresponded to the fourth and fifth *pachacas* of this non-Inca town, worshipping as their ancestress Mama Anahuarque. Similar 5-fold models were integrated in Cuzco into the 6-fold divisions of the *ceque* system in, respectively, Hanan-Cuzco and Hurin-Cuzco. The *panacas* of the 5 kings in each moiety were related to the first 5 groups of *ceques* and the non- and pre-Inca population to the sixth group. Apparently, a similar 6-fold geographic division of the whole Cuzco area was also known. Around Cuzco, 4 other temples of the sun were recognized, corresponding to the 4 *suyus*; but there were 6 sacred mountains: one in each of the 4 suyus, a fifth in Antisuyu, and a sixth in Cuntisuyu. The last two were close to the E-W line dividing Hanan- and Hurin-Cuzco (Sarmiento, chap. 31). The two southern mountains, Huanacauri in Collasuyu and Anahuarque in Cuntisuyu, were related to the pre-Inca population of Cuzco and to their Inca conquest. Elsewhere I have argued that the 6-fold division of Hanan-Cuzco can be interpreted as the imposition of one 4-fold division upon another in the following way:

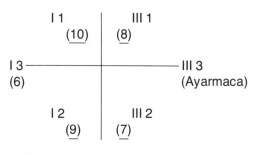

and

```
I 1, I 2  |  III 1, III 2
──────────┼──────────────
   I 3    |     III 3
```

My argument is now that the data on Cuntisuyu also reveal a superimposition of one 4-fold model upon another one and that describing them within a 6-fold model the situation is this:

```
  I    |   II
───────┼────────
 III   |   IV
───────┼────────
 IVₐ   |   IV_B
```

According to this model we can consider the following totals of *huacas* in the *ceque* system:
1. I + II + III represent a unit similar to that of the three major groups of *ceques* in the organization of Hanan-Cuzco (see also next section). The total of the *huacas* is 85 + 85 + 78 = 248. This number was used in Babylonian astronomy, and in other

systems derived from it, as a close approximation of the period of 9 anomalistic months (9 × 27.55 = 247.95), useful for the prediction of lunar eclipses (van der Waerden 1974, pp. 244, 245).

2. I + II + III + IV represent a system of 12 sidereal months (328 = 12 × 27⅓) corresponding to another system of 12 solar months (see following sections).

3. I + II + III + IV + IVₐ, counting the *huacas* of IVₐ a second time, backward, gives a total of 328 + 37 = 365, the number of days in the solar year. Perhaps a division of this total into 248 (I + II + III) and 117 (IV + IVₐ) may help us to understand the division of the year into 3 seasons of 4 months each as given by Guaman Poma. He claims that the 4-month season of August to November is governed by the moon and that then the nights are longer than the days. One conclusion of the analysis in the next section will be that the Incas had 4 months of 29 days and 8 months with a medium length of 31 days. The division mentioned here could have been another useful way to relate IV with its 117 *huacas* (IV + IVₐ) to 4 synodical months and I + II + III to the 8 solar months (8 × 31), being equal to 9 anomalistic months.

4. I + II + III + IVₐ + IVв, containing 365 + 43 = 408 *huacas*, is close to that counted on the second textile of the Inca period: 407 squares (32 + [7 × 28] + 37 + [4 × 28] + 30). The squares in the corners of the textile are, however, difficult to count and the total may therefore be either 406 or 408. This total may explain why Polo de Ondegardo and Acosta mention 328 as well as "more than 400" *huacas* for the *ceque* system. We remember, moreover, that in the Situay raymi (September equinox) 400 warriors would follow the 40 or 41 *ceques* (10 warriors for each *ceque*). Four hundred eight days is close to the period of 15 nodical months (15 × 27.2 = 408).

The Astronomical Significance of the Number of Huacas

Introduction. Professor T. Barthel, of Tubingen, suggested to me (personal communication) that in different cases the sum of a group of *ceques* with a high number of *huacas* (a major group) and a group with a low number (a minor one) indicates the value of a double sidereal lunar month. This suggestion led me to the discovery of an overall system involving sums of *huacas* of two or more groups of *ceques*.

The more important *suyus* (I and II) each have 2 major groups of *ceques* with values of 29 or more *huacas*. III and IV each have only one major group. In I, II, and III, these are higher-ranked groups. In IV, group 3 has the highest number. The numbers are those of a synodical month (29 or 30) or some days more (31 or 33), as suggested by Guaman Poma (f. 260) for adapting a synodical month to a calendrical one. The numbers of the minor groups of *ceques* are significantly lower but also show a regular pattern: III 2 and IV 2 each have 24 *huacas*, I 3 and III 3 of Hanan-Cuzco have 23 *huacas*, and II 3 and IV 3 of Hurin-Cuzco have 26 *huacas* (table 15.2).

The perihelion and aphelion. The total of the higher numbers in Hanan-Cuzco (33 + 29 + 31) is 93; that in Hurin-Cuzco (30 + 29 + 30) is 89. These numbers could be used for calculating the half year from March equinox over June solstice

Table 15.2
Arrangement of Huacas *in the* Ceque *System*

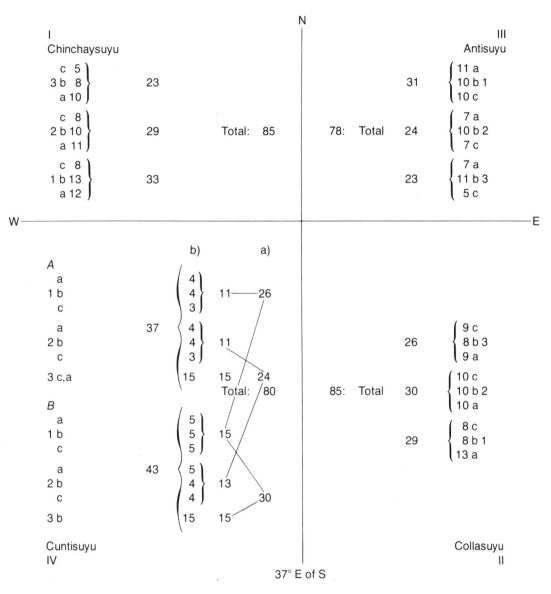

N

I
Chinchaysuyu

c 5
3 b 8 } 23
a 10

c 8
2 b 10 } 29   Total: 85
a 11

c 8
1 b 13 } 33
a 12

III
Antisuyu

31   ⎰ 11 a
     ⎱ 10 b 1
       10 c

78: Total 24   ⎰ 7 a
                 ⎱ 10 b 2
                   7 c

23   ⎰ 7 a
     ⎱ 11 b 3
       5 c

W ——————————————————————————————— E

b)   a)

A
  a   ⎰ 4 ⎱
1 b   ⎰ 4 ⎱ 11 —— 26
  c   3

  a   37 ⎰ 4 ⎱
2 b   ⎰ 4 ⎱ 11   26   ⎰ 9 c
  c   3   ⎱ 8 b 3
                                               9 a
3 c,a   15   15   24
            Total: 80   85: Total 30   ⎰ 10 c
B   ⎱ 10 b 2
  a   ⎰ 5 ⎱   10 a
1 b   ⎰ 5 ⎱ 15
  c   5   29   ⎰ 8 c
                                             ⎱ 8 b 1
  a   43 ⎰ 5 ⎱   13 a
2 b   ⎰ 4 ⎱ 13
  c   4   30
3 b   15   15

Cuntisuyu   Collasuyu
IV   II

37° E of S

to September equinox when the sun is in aphelion (186 days) and the other half year when the sun is in perihelion (179 days). If we accept that the solstices fall halfway between the equinoxes (the solstices are difficult to fix on a specific day since the sun rises and sets at the same place on the horizon during different days, whereas during the equinoxes it moves fastest from one day to another), then we could say that the numbers 93 and 89 were used for calculating from equinox to solstice and from solstice to equinox back again. This would give us the values of: $(2 \times 93 = 186) + (2 \times 89 = 178) = 364$.

In this case, the Temple of the Sun could have been added as an extra *huaca* to make a full solar year ($364 + 1 = 365$). The number 186 belonged to Hanan (I and II), the northern moiety of Cuzco. During that time of the year the sun also rises and sets north of the E-W line. The number 179 was in the same way related to Hurin (II and IV) and the south. We remember that it was probably also the 6 major groups of *ceques* that gave to the Inca his council of 12 persons. (Each representing one solar month?) From these data we conclude that each of the 6 major groups of *ceques* may have served 2 months in the calendar of 12 solar months. Analyzing first the case of Hanan-Cuzco I suggest that:

1. I 1 (33 *huacas*) indicated the two longest months around the June solstice (June 21), that is (in terms of the Christian calendar), from May 20 to July 24. These months were dedicated to the state cult of the Sun.

2. I 2 (29 *huacas*) indicated the months from April 21 to May 19 and from July 25 to August 22 and was dedicated to the cult of the Thunder and ritually to the first harvesting and first plowing, respectively.

3. III 1 (31 *huacas*) indicated the months from March 21 (equinox) to April 20 and from August 23 to September 22 (equinox), dedicated to the cult of Viracocha and ritually to water and irrigation.

We remember that according to Molina the year started "around the middle of May" and according to Guaman Poma the sun "sat still" in his solstitial seat till Santiago (July 25), which date he took as the first one of the month of August. The two days in May and July are close approximations in defining the period of the two solstitial months dedicated to the cult of the Sun. Apparently, Molina took the first day for starting his description of the ritual and solar year while Guaman Poma took the last day for describing the agricultural cycle in the year.

The perihelion and the synodic months. In Hurin-Cuzco we found as a value for the 6 solar months the number 178. That is, one day longer than 6 synodic months ($6 \times 29.5 = 177$) and one day short of the half year when the sun is in perihelion. The values of the *huacas* in the major groups of *ceques* of Hurin-Cuzco (30, 29, 30) could be used to describe the solar months in terms of synodic months. Because of the irregularities mentioned in Hurin-Cuzco, it is more difficult to decide upon the exact relationship of each group of *ceques* to two months. I would suggest the following relationships:

1. II 2 (30 *huacas*) indicated the two months around the December solstice from November 21 to January 20. The name of the fifth king, whose descendents took care of the *ceques* in II 2, was Capac Yupanqui, a synonym of Tupac Yupanqui (tenth king) and a name employing Capac ('royal') as do the two solstitial months of December (Capac Inti raymi and Capac raymi Camay quilla). Capac Yupanqui also had a specific relationship to the cult of the Sun (Guaman Poma, ff. 100, 101; Murua, book 1, chap. 11).

2. II 1 (29 *huacas*) indicated the two months from January 21 to February 18 and from October 23 to November 21. The *ceques* here were taken care of by the descendents of the fourth king who occupied in Hurin-Cuzco the same position as those of the ninth king in Hanan-Cuzco. The number of *huacas* in both cases was also the same.

3. IV 3 (30 *huacas* and 31 *huacas*) indicated the two months from February 19 to March 20 and from September 23 to October 23.

In conclusion, we might say that the particular phase of the moon that governed the September equinox in a specific year would recur also in the next December solstice and the next March equinox. After that day, this relationship of phase of the moon to solar month would change rapidly and so, after the following solstitial month of July, it would be very different. This fact might explain why we do find more month names during this season of 4 solar months (April to July) than there are months, since this would be the time for making necessary adjustments. We remember also the statement of the anonymous chronicler that each of the 12 political divisions in Cuzco had its name in common with a month. We found possible evidence for that statement only in one case: that of the town of Oma with the month Oma raymi and of the group of *ceques* to which *ceque* Anahuarque (IV 3) belonged. Our present explanation of the relationship between solar months and synodic months supports that statement.

The sidereal period of 73 nights (?). Having discovered the regularity and significance of the number of *huacas* in the major groups of *ceques*, we might ask if a case could be made for any regularity in the numbers constituting the minor groups.

In IV and I together and in III and II together there are, in each case, 73 (26 + 24 + 23) *huacas* belonging to the minor groups of *ceques*. In this case the axis of division is not the W-E line but a N-S line (5 × 73 = 365). The period of 73 days could have been used to correlate the solar year with the sidereal lunar year (a double sidereal lunar year, including the Temple of the Sun once: 328 + 329 = 657 = 9 × 73) and the Venus cycle (8 × 73 = 584). Rauh has made a case for the Incaic use of a 73-day period, observing that Inca wooden bridges were rebuilt every 8 years, making the 8-year period a significant interval (Rauh, quotes in Thompson and Murra 1966). In section III c, I mentioned the possible importance of the period of 16 years for integrating solar and Venus rituals into one system.

I want to suggest in the next section that a 73-night period (possibly divided into periods of 36 and 37 nights) was used in sidereal time reckoning, especially in relation to the sidereal lunar calendar. In opposition to the major groups of *ceques* with solar relationships, the minor groups had chthonic relationships, that is, to the heaven at night.

The sidereal lunar months and their possible relationship to the solar year. In the data from the *ceque* system (8 × 41 = 12 × 27⅓ = 328 *huacas*), the sacerdotal organization of Allauca (28 + 14 = 42 female priests), the Inca period textile, and other pre-Spanish examples in Peruvian art and architecture, we find convincing evidence that the sidereal lunar month was important in preconquest Andean culture. But we do not have any ethnohistorical or modern anthropological information on how such a calendar might have been used. One reason is that probably it was an exclusively female calendar. The following hypothetical suggestions are therefore based only on the significance of the numbers in the *ceque* system with the hope that this line of reasoning might be conducive to the discovery of new data confirming or rejecting it.

   After 27⅓ days the moon will take the same position against the stars as before. The time at night, however, will be different. An 82-day period (3 × 27½ = 82) would have been convenient to see the moon at the same time of night against the same stars. The number of *huacas* in the four *suyus* are, however, only rough approximations:

   I: 85 *huacas*
   II: 85 *huacas*
   III: 78 *huacas*
   IV: 80 (or 81) *huacas*

Following the suggestion of Dr. Barthel, each major group of *ceques* can be combined with a minor one and will give a very close approximation of 2 sidereal months in their combined number of *huacas*. The most elegant combinations are:

$$\left.\begin{array}{l} 31 + 23 = 54 \\ 33 + 23 = 56 \end{array}\right\} \quad 110$$

$$\left.\begin{array}{l} 30 + 24 = 54 \\ 29 + 26 = 55 \end{array}\right\} \quad 109 \qquad \text{Total: 328}$$

$$\left.\begin{array}{l} 30 + 24 = 54 \\ 29 + 26 = 55 \end{array}\right\} \quad 109$$

   These periods describe the sidereal lunar year as a completely independent cycle in terms of double sidereal lunar months (fig. 15.6).

   The numbers of these double months are built up from one solar month unit and another unit considerably lower. It is therefore reasonable to suppose that the sidereal lunar calendar was also integrated into the solar year. Taking into account
(*1*) the double use of each of the 6 high numbers 33, 31, 30, 30, 29, 29 around a W-E axis and
(2) a similar double use of the 6 low numbers 26, 24, 23, 26, 24, 23, but around a N-S axis,
we develop the model in fig. 15.6. In each of the following periods the moon would be in the same sidereal position at the beginning and at the end (the dash indicating that three letters under it represent one calendrical position):

QPpab: 30 + 24 =   54
RQPpabc: 29 +   54 + 26 = 109
SRQPpabcd: 30 + 109 + 23 = 162
qpPAB: 24 + 31 =   55
rqpPABC: 26 +   55 + 29 = 110
srqpPABCD: 23 + 110 + 33 = 166

These periods are calculated for the half year from the December to the June solstice. The same numbers would account for the half year from the June to the December solstice. Using the double sidereal lunar months in this way, within the

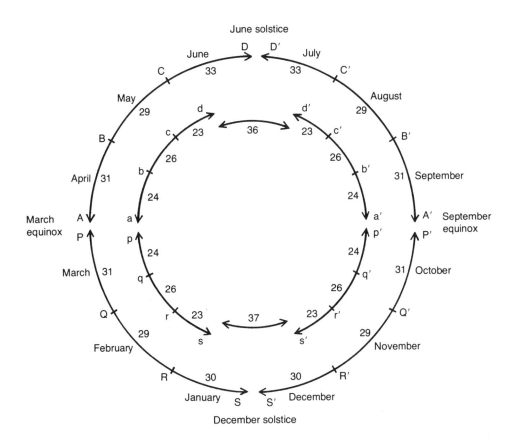

15.6. *Hypothetical yearly cycle showing lunar months integrated into solar year.*

context of the solar year and its solar months, would leave a gap in the sidereal time reckoning of 36 days around the June solstice and 37 days around the December solstice. Together, they are equal to any of the other four periods (73 days) of the sidereal year. A double lunar cycle, based on 328 + 329 = 9 × 73 nights, could therefore be left intact and would also be combined with a solar year in a cycle of 12 solar months.

We remember how a Venus cycle of 10 Venus years can be described in terms of 16 solar years. Similarly, 10 double lunar cycles of 657 (328 + 329) days equal 18 solar years. The periods of 3 years (Las Casas 1958, chap 140; Murua 1968, book 2, chap. 18) are mentioned for the renewal of the *acllas* (the virgins of the Sun) in their *acllahuasi* (house of the *acllas*); it may be that these years were calculated on the basis of lunar cycles. Six lunar cycles are equal to 5 solar years, the normal period used in the Inca age-class system.

Representation of a double sidereal month in Guaman Poma and in the Huari textile. In the introduction to the *ceque* system, I mentioned that Guaman Poma (f. 361) discusses a *quipucamayoc* ('quipu specialist') who was concerned with the assessment of local *ceque* systems (as indicated by his name *hucha quipoc*) and who was called (f. 359) a *quilla uata quipoc*, the quipu specialist for months and years. He was responsible for counting numbers "for setting down feasts and sundays and months and years." This man is shown in a drawing (f. 360) with a quipu and a kind of abacus (fig. 15.4). Wassen (1940) has made a strong case saying that only the abacus was used for calculations like adding and subtracting and that the quipu served for recording the final numbers arrived at. However, since it is explicitly said that this man was concerned with the calendar, I want to suggest here another possible use of the abacus.

In a total of 20 squares, that is, 4 columns and 5 rows, there are 5 × (5 + 3 + 2 + 1) = 55 circles: 32 of these are white and 23 are black. The numbers are of the same magnitude as those found in the *ceque* system for respectively:

1. A double sidereal month
2. The number of *huacas* in a major group of *ceques* representing a solar month (of 30 days) to which, in the words of Guaman Poma (f. 260), could be added one or two days according to the moon
3. A minor group of *ceques*, having chthonic associations

As the number 55 is the best whole number approximation to a double sidereal lunar cycle (2 × 27⅓ = 54⅔), we could imagine that white and black pebbles or kernels of corn were used for making the adjustments that Guaman Poma mentions in the correlation of a solar month to a sidereal cycle by changing the ratio of the two types of pebbles. A suggestion for such possible adjustments was made in the preceding section.

Earlier I indicated the importance of the period of 73 days, with its subdivisions of 26, 24, and 23 days, for relating a calendar consisting of solar months to one of sidereal lunar months. A similar relationship may be detected also in the Huari textile. On the basis of the organization of the circles in groups of 5 diagonals each, we discovered the importance of the number 72 (being the total of circles in all the first diagonals of each group of 5, of all the second diagonals, etc.). Because of certain irregularities in the color scheme of the diagonals, the total of 72 in four of the five cases was divided into two groups of 57 + 15, 59 + 13, 51 + 21, ar.d 52 + 20 circles respectively; that is, the average division was of 54¾ and 17¼ circles, the first value being a very close approximation to the number of nights in 2 sidereal lunar months.

It is premature to guess how in the case of the textile the numbers 54¾, 72, and 73 (the total of the frontal figures and faces) exactly were used. The important thing is that these totals were represented in a calendar that otherwise stresses the existence of a year of 12 months of 30 (3 × 10) days and that a similar use of those numbers could have been made as in the *ceque* system.

The Ceque *System and Astronomical Observation:*
A Preliminary Discussion

Introduction

Cobo and Polo mention that each group of 3 *ceques* was related to a *sucanca*, a pillar on the horizon as observed from Cuzco, which indicated the beginning of a month by the rising or setting of the sun at that place. In the case of three *huacas* Cobo also specifies their calendrical function as a *sucanca*. Our primary concern in the field work carried out during the summer of 1975 was to find these *huacas* and the *ceques* on which they were located. For different reasons, however, we were obliged to try to locate *all* the *ceques*. The map of the *ceque* system (fig. 15.7) is a first draft. For a general idea, I am confident that it is correct. I could locate *huacas* as place names from almost all the *ceques* with the help of old and modern maps, with data from other chroniclers, and by going into the field and questioning modern inhabitants.

Tentatively, I have drawn all the *ceques* as straight lines from the Temple of the Sun for the following reasons:

1. Except for *huacas* in or very near Cuzco, most of the *huacas* found could be considered as lying on straight lines.

2. Many of the place names referred to a general area (hacienda, mountain, etc.) and not to a specific rock or other exactly definable place. One of the exceptions was the next-to-the-last *huaca* of *ceque* II 1 a, called Guarmichaca. (This was the ninth *ceque* of Collasuyu in the sequence of *ceques* as used by Cobo. I will indicate this sequence also when referring to specific *huacas*.) There are, at this place, ruins of a small Inca site, still known under that name, from which one can see Cuzco. The Temple of the Sun (now the church of Santo Domingo) was 37° E of magnetic north and its observation enabled me to define the first *ceque* of Collasuyu and its direction.

3. In the section dealing with the *capac hucha*, we observed that a child, sent home to be sacrificed, followed a *ceque* as a straight line. In modern indigenous agricultural practices this concept of *ceque* is still used to indicate the area from one line to the next. In some cases, when a *huaca* did not lie on its *ceque* in the *ceque* system, Cobo says so. While keeping the concept of *ceque* as a straight line, *huacas* of one *ceque* could be found to the right or left with some margin of freedom.

4. For the purpose of this research I was more interested in the *huacas* near the horizon (as seen from Cuzco) than in the nearby *huacas*. Therefore, the first ones have influenced my choice in the direction of a *ceque* as a straight line. In future research I hope to refine the whole map of the *ceque* system and give more exact locations of *huacas*.

In the following sections I will discuss the general data on Inca observatories and then the problem of location in Cuzco. In our fieldwork so far we were more successful in locating the *ceques* on which the solstitial *sucancas* were located than in locating the observation post(s). The latter cannot be identified with the Temple of the Sun as the center of the *ceque* system.

It will be understood from the data in this section that the *ceque* system was used in Inca astronomy quite independently from its use as a quipu in calendrical computations.

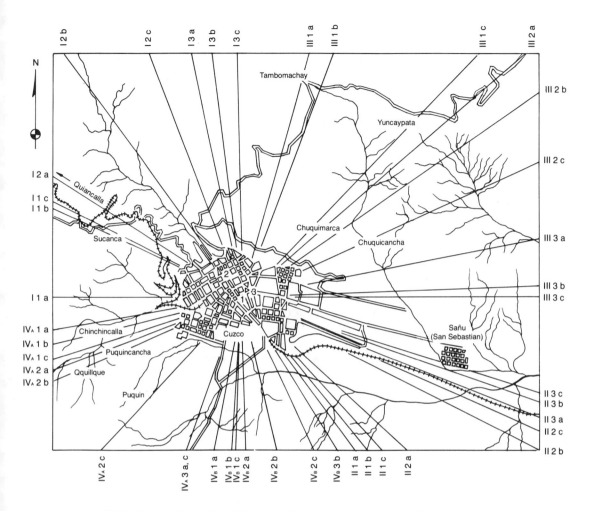

15.7. *Map of the city of Cuzco with* ceques *superposed.*
(1) Coricancha (Temple of the Sun);
(2) Hanan-Haucaypata;
(3) Hurin-Haucaypata (Limapampa).

The Observatories

There are two traditions about the observatories in Cuzco: the first is that of Polo and Cobo and to this tradition we have already alluded. The other tradition is that of Betanzos (chap. 15) and Sarmiento (chap. 30), who both have very similar data, and of the anonymous chronicler ("Discurso" in Maurtua, p. 151) and Garcilaso (book 2, chap. 22). I will first analyze the second tradition.

All four chroniclers mention a group of four pillars for making one observation of a specific solar rising or setting. They all give some measures, in *pie*, *paso*, *vera*, *estado*, or *legua*, which I will convert into meters. The central pillars were smaller and were used for an exact observation; the outer pillars were bigger and helped to predict the approaching event.

According to Sarmiento (1947), the inner pillars were 16.72 meters apart and the outer ones 50.16 meters ($3 \times 16.72 = 50.16$) from each other. Betanzos gives the measurements as 8.36 meters for the inner ones and 41.80 meters for the outer ones. They do not give the distance from the center of observation to the posts; but, perhaps, this can be estimated. The height of the outer pillars was 4 meters.

According to the anonymous chronicler, the inner pillars were 69.65 meters apart, the outer ones 278.6 meters, and the distance of the center of observation 11,144 or 16,716 meters, that is, either 40×278.6 or 60×278.6. The angle of view of the outer posts would be about 1°. These distances between the pillars are satisfactory for good observations of one solar rising or setting. But the anonymous chronicler claims that when the sun arrived at one of the outer pillars (and he mentions these *sucanca* in relation to sowing in August), at that time the people living higher in the mountains would start sowing, whereas the people down in the valley started their sowing when the sun moved between the inner pillars.

Finally, Garcilaso mentions that the inner pillars were 50 meters apart and the outer pillars 150 meters. The pillars were observed on the skyline, but he does not know from where they were observed; he suspects the Temple of the Sun. His measurements seem to be of the same magnitude as those of the anonymous chronicler; both mention much higher values than do Betanzos and Sarmiento.

In fact, the latter authors seem to be describing a different system. Observations were not from Cuzco to the horizon, but from a flat place outside the city and higher up in the mountains where the Incas could set up a system of poles and observe them from a nearby place (perhaps from some 2,000 m, comparing their measurements to those of the anonymous chronicler). The wooden poles were used for actual observations. On the basis of these observations, a more elaborate and durable system with towers of stone was set up.

The chroniclers also do not agree on the day in the year for which the pillars were set up. The anonymous chronicler mentions only one set of pillars in the west for observing the opening of the agricultural year in August. Sarmiento says that the beginning of sowing was observed with pillars in the west and the beginning of harvest with pillars in the east. The dates would be around May and August. Probably the two sets of pillars could be used in relation to both events. Such a hypothesis could mean that both sets were used for one and the same event in May and in August, that is, for two days equally distant from the June solstice; or the data could mean that one set was used for indicating the beginning of May (April 21) and the end of August (August 23), while the other set was used for the end of May (May 20) and the beginning of August (July 25). In the case of the latter hypothesis, I am using the *ceque* system as a quipu, counting days by *huacas*. (See previous section.)

Garcilaso mentions four sets of four pillars for observing the rising and setting of the sun at the time of the two solstices.

None of the chroniclers mention *sucanca* for observing the equinoxes, but Garcilaso refers to a system of two gnomons for this purpose. In this case, the shadow of the gnomon itself was observed, so there was no need of any kind of horizon observation.

Despite the difficulties and insecurities of interpretation, I think that these four sources give us a better interpretation of the system of observation used by the Incas than do Polo and Cobo. Polo indirectly mentions ("Errores," p. 43) that there were 12 *sucanca* (i.e., the total of *huacas* which he mentions, 340, minus the total mentioned by Cobo, 328, equals the 12 *sucanca*). Since he claims (p. 16) that there was one pillar for each month and that the one for the beginning of "winter," the December solstice, was called Puncuy (= Puccuy) *sucanca* and the one for the beginning of "summer" Chirao *sucanca*, I concluded that there were 12. Cobo, probably basing his statement on the data of Polo (or Molina?) mentions 14 *sucanca*. To arrive at this number, he may have argued in three different ways:

1. With the expansion of groups of *ceques* in Cuntisuyu, he took 14 groups as corresponding to 14 *sucancas* and 14 months.

2. He excluded Puccuy *sucanca* and Chirao *sucanca* (mentioned also by him) from the 12 indicating the beginnings of the months.

3. Using a system of pillars as mentioned by Polo and Cobo, and observing both sunrise and sunset, one needs a system of 14 and *not* 12 pillars.

June solstice

Chirao	Chirao
July	June
August	May
September	April
equinox	equinox
October	March
November	February
December	January

December solstice

Puccuy	Puccuy

(In my earlier paper on the calendar, I used the 12 pillars as mentioned by Polo, in a similar diagram. Professor F. Lounsbury suggested to me that in fact I would need the 14 pillars.)

However, at the moment I have little confidence that these data or interpretations of Polo and Cobo are correct. My doubts are based on the facts that:

1. Both authors mention only one pillar for one month, although we know that for each observation 4, or at least 2, pillars are needed.

2. Cobo mentions in the *ceque* system only three *huacas* that served as *sucanca* and in each case these consist of 2 pillars.

3. These three *sucanca* are all located on the western horizon; his data agree here with those of the anonymous chronicler and Cieza (*Cronica*, chap. 92), who mentions that only in the west were artificial pillars as *sucanca* set up.

We conclude, therefore, that the informants of Polo (and, indirectly, of Cobo) may have thought of a system of 12 (3 × 4) pillars on the western horizon, consisting of three *sucanca*, each of two smaller pillars, to which were added in each case a higher northern and southern pillar. These higher pillars were probably situated on the two *ceques* next to the one of the *sucanca* and for this reason we may not have detected them yet. Furthermore, it is logical to suppose that *sucancas* only were set up on the western horizon. Only here, as the anonymous chronicler observes, were the mountains and the horizon near to Cuzco. We will notice from the data in the *ceque* system that the observation points in the east, beyond the valley, consisted of prominent natural features of the mountains.

The Sucancas *and Other* Huacas *of Astronomical Significance as Mentioned in the* Ceque *System*

Garcilaso remembers how he had seen the *sucancas* in his youth but that later they were destroyed by the Spaniards. He did not know from which point in Cuzco they were observed; but he said that once the *sucanca* are located it is easy to reconstruct the center of observation. For us, it was easier to locate the *ceques* on which the *sucanca* were situated than the center of observation. Therefore, I will discuss first the *sucanca* on the western horizon and then the other *huacas* of astronomical significance.

Cobo calls only one of the three *huacas* that served as *sucanca* by this name; but he says of this and two other *huacas* on the western horizon that they consisted of two artificial pillars and he indicates their calendrical function. We could not exactly locate the *huacas* themselves, as they were destroyed by the Spaniards, but, especially in the first two cases, we were quite successful in locating all the other *huacas* of their *ceques*. Therefore, on the basis of a description of the *sucanca*, of the direction of its *ceque* and of the adjacent *ceques*, and of the fact that, seen from Cuzco, it had to be on the horizon, we could indicate the area where each *sucanca* had to be located (fig. 15.7).

1. Quiancalla (I 2 b, sixth *ceque*, ninth *huaca*), which means "from where one sees (*callan*) dawn (*quia*) or sunrise," indicated the June solstice ("the beginning of the summer" in the words of Cobo).

2. Sucanca (I 1 b, eighth *ceque*, seventh *huaca*) indicated that "then the people had to start sowing maize."

3. Chinchincalla (IVʙ 1 b, thirteenth *ceque*, third *huaca*) "was a big mountain with two pillars; when the Sun arrived, it was time to sow."

In the case of the latter two *sucancas*, we do not know if they indicated the beginning of a month or any other specific day within the agricultural cycle. Perhaps the name *chinchi* can help us. Gonzalez Holguin (1952) and Lira (1944) refer to a shrub, Chinchircuma, as "a yellow flower that is like feathers," and Lira also refers to a fruit of a thorny shrub, *Chinchi chinchi*, which was used against fevers. We know that the Incas started sowing when, in August, "a thorny plant was in bloom with yellow flowers" ("Discurso" in Maurtua, p. 149). Therefore, we might bring the *huaca* Chinchincalla in relation to this "thorny plant with yellow flowers," and the possibility exists that this *sucanca* indicated the beginning of the month of August (although such an interpretation would bring us additional difficulties).

Another *ceque* that we can consider in relation to the three discussed is the first *ceque* of Chinchaysuyu (I 1 a). All its *huacas* outside Cuzco are near the W-E line, as are the *huacas* of the last *ceque* of Antisuyu (III 3 c).

If Quiancalla served for observing the June solstice, we should expect the *huaca* used for observing the December solstice to be in the opposite direction. In fact, we do find mentioned in Collasuyu a *huaca* (II 2 a, fourth *ceque*, eighth *huaca*), Guancarcaya ("from where one observes the drum"?), "which is a canyon like a gate . . . It was dedicated to the Sun and they offered him children in certain feasts that they had there." Because of its closeness to other huacas like Intipampa (II 2 b, fifth *ceque*, eighth *huaca*), "the plaza of the Sun," and Omotourco (II 2 b, fifth *ceque*, tenth *huaca*), which is also mentioned by Molina (p. 26) in relation to a *sucanca* and a solstitial ceremony (pp. 26, 48), we may conclude that Guancarcaya itself serves as a *sucanca* for observing sunrise during the December solstice.

Both solstitial *huacas*, Quiancalla and Guancarcaya, are situated, in their respective *suyu*, on the fourth *ceque* from the W-E line. This coincidence seems to be intended. Therefore, we may pay more attention to the fact that in Antisuyu a *huaca* was mentioned on the sixth *ceque* (i.e., on the fourth *ceque* north of the W-E line) Chuquicancha (III 2 c, sixth *ceque*, third *huaca*), as "a temple of the Sun." Nearby were two places, Susurpuquio (Molina, p. 20; or Susumarca, III 2 b, fifth *ceque*, eighth *huaca*) and Callachaca (Santacruz Pachacuti, pp. 237, 247; III 2 a, fourth *ceque*, third *huaca*; III 2 b, fifth *ceque*, eighth *huaca*; III 2 c, sixth *ceque*, second *huaca*), both mentioned in relation to the most explicit Inca myth of the appearance of the sun as a god. Not far from Chuquicancha was another Temple of the Sun bearing a similar name, Chuquimarca (III 1 c, third *ceque*, fourth *huaca*), where the Inca went during the June solstice. I conclude, therefore, that Chuquicancha had a function in relation to sunrise during the same solstitial feast in June. Moreover, I would propose that this temple had a role during the December solstice.

In the case of Quiancalla and Guancarcaya, I suspect that they were used not only for observing, respectively, the sunset in June and the sunrise in December from a central point in Cuzco but also for observing these events from each other as centers of observation toward the other *huaca* as *sucanca*. We may suspect a similar role for Chuquicancha in relation to another *huaca*, Puquincancha (IVa 2 b, tenth *ceque*, second *huaca*), as Temple of the Sun with a special function during the December solstice (Molina, pp. 60, 67). Using Puquincancha for observing a sunrise behind Chuquicancha during the June solstice and Chuquicancha for observing sunset behind Puquincancha during the December solstice might also explain another mythical reference to Chuquicancha in Callachaca. Once, during a severe drought (a reference to the dry season in June), rains (a reference to the wet season in December) only fell over Callachaca and only there produced a good crop (Santacruz Pachacuti, p. 247). (For a more detailed discussion of the *huacas* mentioned in this paragraph, see Zuidema 1976.)

The Center(s) of Astronomical Observation

The anonymous chronicler says explicitly that the *sucanca* were observed from the middle of the plaza in Cuzco where a stone pillar was erected on top of an elevation, called Osno (= Ushnu). It is clear, then, that the center of astronomical observation was not in the Temple of the Sun as the center of the *ceque* system. However, after having located the *huacas* of *ceque* I 2 c to which the *huaca* Quiancalla belonged as the *sucanca* of sunset during the June solstice, we realized that, while some suburbs of Cuzco can be seen from there, the Incaic part of the city cannot be seen. On the other hand, there is an open view in the solstitial direction toward the Inca fortress of Sacsahuaman, which is situated in a plain to the northeast above Cuzco. Checking this information out, we observed sunset during the June solstice from Sacsahuaman, that is, from a round Inca structure there called Muyucmarca ('the round building') which was a Temple of the Sun. The point observed was within the area as described for the *huaca* and *sucanca* Quiancalla.

During our field work, we made astronomical observations to various points on the horizon from the Temple of the Sun in Cuzco (Coricancha), from different points on the plaza, from atop the cathedral, and from Muyucmarca on Sacsahuaman. We worked under the assumption that all three could have been used by the Incas for astronomical observation. Only later did I realize that neither Coricancha nor the plaza near the cathedral was intended by the anonymous chronicler to be taken as the center of observations.

Cuzco had two plazas called Haucaypata ('Plaza of rejoicing'); both had an Ushnu and both were used for state rituals. Hanan-Haucaypata was in the upper half of Cuzco where the plaza of the king was also situated. Hurin-Haucaypata, belonging to the lower half (Hurin), was not far from Coricancha but was outside the ceremonial part of Cuzco. Today, as in colonial times, this plaza (or part of it) is known as Limapampa. Nearby were the sacred fields where the king did his ritual first plowing and first harvesting. The field was called Sausero (II 3 b, second *ceque*, third *huaca*); Limapampa was the first *huaca* of this *ceque* (II 3 b, second *ceque*, first *huaca*). Another field nearby, Guanaypata (III 3 a, third *ceque*, fourth *huaca*)—where according to the Inca origin myth a golden bar had sunk into the ground indicating that the city should be built there (Sarmiento, chap. 13)—had a "wall that had been built there by the Sun." Probably this wall, but certainly the Ushnu on Hurin-Haucaypata, was used for astronomical observations (III 2 b, fifth *ceque*, first *huaca*) (Cobo, book 13, chap. 32; Molina, pp. 29, 30, 36).

The conclusion reached here can be checked out in future fieldwork in two ways:
1. The position of Hurin-Haucaypata can be observed in relation to the crossing of the solstitial lines from Quiancalla to Guancarcaya and from Chuquicancha to Puquincancha.
2. Sarmiento and Betanzos mention two other observatories in flat areas above

and outside Cuzco. Possibly, Chuquicancha and Muyucmarca on Sacsahuaman, which were both temples of the sun, served this function. The position of Hurin-Haucaypata in relation to both these places can also be studied. Guaman Poma (ff. 261, 262, 263, 894) mentioned that solar observations were made from temples of the sun with windows. His description would probably fit structures like Muyucmarca.

Once the astronomical value of the places mentioned here is well assessed, we will then be able to study the calendrical importance of Sucanca (I 1 b) and Chinchincalla (IVв 1 b) and probably of many other *huacas* on the horizon as observed from Hurin-Haucaypata.

General Conclusions

A general problem of ethnohistorical studies on the Incas is that most Spanish chronicles were written forty years or more after the conquest. They reflect less what the Spaniards really saw of an empire in its full glory than what they interpreted from the elaborate and idealized memories of their older Inca informants who lived in a colonial society.

The *ceque* system, because of its intricate and systematic character, could be proven to be the most important exception to this general situation. Comparing it to the two pre-Spanish textiles, we find the same numbers discussed: 8; 27 or 28; 54, 55, or 56; 40, 41, or 42; 72 or 73. The Huari textile gives greater stress to the solar calendar with lunar numbers embedded into it; the Inca textile and the *ceque* system stress a sidereal lunar system containing solar and synodical lunar numbers. On the basis of a common astronomical theory, there seems to be a rather undogmatic concern, comparing the three calendars, in translating the astronomical data into a regular calendar. For instance, both the Huari textile and the *ceque* system started from a base of 45 diagonals, or *ceques*. In the first case 27 diagonals keep their full numbers of circles and 18 (2 × 9) diagonals have their numbers reduced, making 8 the average total of circles on a diagonal and 360 the general total of circles in the textile. In the case of the *ceque* system, 27 *ceques* also keep their original significance. But now, first, the number of the 18 other *ceques* themselves is reduced to 15 or 14 and, second, the number of *huacas* on each of these *ceques* is reduced, bringing down the total from a hypothetical 360 (45 × 8) to 328 (41 × 8). Concluding the comparison: the Huari textile starts from a situation of 45 × 8, reducing it to 41 × 8.

Ethnohistorical data have been supportive for the assumption of an 8-day week and a possible 10-day week also for the significance of a schematic month of 30 days, a synodic month of 29 or 30 days, and a solar month of 30 to 32 days. There is, however, no written evidence of the use of a sidereal month. The analysis of this paper may help to discover how Andean peoples actually observed this event. Here the data analyzed in another paper (Zuidema 1976) might be worth considering. The *ceque* indicating the setting of the sun during the June solstice contained also a *huaca* (Capipa[c]cha "the waterfall in the river Capi"; i.e., the "root" [capi] of Cuzco) where the Inca would bathe at new moon before June solstice and where another ritual dedicated to the moon was carried out at full moon after the December solstice. This and other *ceques* may have been used, then, in a special way to measure the movement of the moon along the horizon. Another possibility is that the Incas had knowledge of some form of a zodiac with "lunar mansions." Modern data on indigenous constellations collected recently by Urton (to be published) bring more order to the data on Inca constellations.

In this paper it has been my intention to establish a basis for the numerical analysis of the textiles and the *ceque* system. Later it may also be possible to interpret the number of *huacas* belonging to the individual *ceques*. Besides locating the *huacas* more precisely in the field, further research should also analyze the exact association of *panacas* (the "royal *ayllus*") with groups of *ceques* or to individual *ceques*, the similar association of the nonroyal *ayllus* in the organization of Cuzco, and the relationship of both kinds of groups to the Inca month. Then a better understanding of various mythological and ritual data can also be reached and their importance to the calendar better understood.

Acknowledgments

Support for this study, which is gratefully acknowledged here, was received from the National Science Foundation during the summer of 1973, when I carried out fieldwork in Cuzco, and during my year of sabbatical leave of 1973–74. During the summer of 1975, I received further support for carrying out fieldwork in Cuzco from the American Philosophical Society.

Notes on the Contributors

Anthony F. Aveni, awarded a Ph.D. in astronomy from the University of Arizona, is professor of astronomy at Colgate University, where he has taught since 1963. His involvement in pre-Hispanic studies developed out of his interest in the history of astronomy. With the support of the National Science Foundation, in 1970 he began a series of research field trips to Mexico, Guatemala, Honduras, and Peru in order to study the astronomical orientation of pyramids and temples. He has since published several articles on native American astronomy and has edited *Archaeoastronomy in Pre-Columbian America* (Austin: University of Texas Press, 1975), which resulted from the first meeting of archaeoastronomers at Mexico City in 1973.

John C. Brandt (B.A. in mathematics, Washington University, and Ph.D in astronomy and astrophysics, University of Chicago) has taught at the University of California, Berkeley, and is now chief of the Laboratory for Solar Physics and Astrophysics of the NASA-Goddard Space Flight Center, Greenbelt, Maryland. His papers span the subjects of solar wind, comets, and galaxies. His interest in rock art, originally a hobby, has begun to develop into a serious research interest.

John B. Carlson, an astronomer, received his Ph.D. in radio astronomy from the University of Maryland in 1977, but his early interest in archaeoastronomy has already resulted in a wide range of publications. His areas of research include the Olmec compass, geomancy, and astronomical methods of the ancient Mesoamericans.

Michael P. Closs is a professor in the Department of Mathematics at the University of Ottawa. His interest in the Maya world has developed quite recently, but he has already begun to produce important publications on the Maya Venus calendar and the problem of correlating Maya and Christian dates.

John A. Eddy is a research associate at the High Altitude Observatory of the National Center for Atmospheric Research, Boulder, Colorado. As a solar physicist, he has research interests in solar-terrestrial relationships and the sunspot cycle about which he has produced several important works. His first archaeoastronomical study, published in *Science Magazine* in 1975, involved an investigation of the Big Horn Medicine Wheel in Wyoming, a topic upon which he elaborates in his contribution to the present text. The National Geographic Society has supported some of his research.

Howard J. Fisher has been tutor in physics at St. John's College since 1965, when he received his A.B. from the University of Rochester.

Sharon L. Gibbs received her undergraduate education at Colorado State University and a Ph.D. in the history of science from Yale University. She was research associate in the history of astronomy at Colgate University and is presently with the U.S. National Archives in Washington, D.C. Trained in the history of western science, she has produced a book, *Greek and Roman Sundials* (New Haven: Yale University Press, 1976). Her work in the present volume represents her first look at native American science.

Horst Hartung, an architect, has been since 1951 professor of pre-Columbian architecture at the University of Guadalajara. His research in pre-Columbian studies has produced numerous papers dating back to 1955. His text *Die Zeremonialzentren der Maya* (Graz: Akad. Druck-u. Verlag., 1971) is a basic work on Maya city planning.

David H. Kelley, a Harvard Ph.D. in archaeology, is well known in the community of Maya scholars for his many basic contributions to the understanding of early writing systems. His most recent book is *Deciphering the Maya Script* (Austin: University of Texas Press, 1976). Kelley is professor of archaeology at the University of Calgary.

Dorothy Mayer, a former graduate student in philosophy at the University of California, Berkeley, has been interested in petroglyphs since 1972. Her studies originated in a basic background in the philosophy and history of science and mathematics. She has since published several articles on their interpretation.

Donnel O'Flynn, after earning a liberal arts degree from St. John's College in 1972, won a Watson Foundation fellowship to study archaeoastronomy.

Judith Remington received her master's degree in anthropology from the University of the Americas, where she did extensive field work among the Maya-speaking natives of Guatemala. She is currently a Ph.D. candidate in anthropology at Northwestern University. Her contribution to this book is the first publication of material contained in her thesis.

Linda Schele, an artist and art historian, is research associate at the Dumbarton Oaks Center for Pre-Columbian Studies in Washington, D.C., as well as professor of art history at the University of South Alabama. In the past three years she has produced landmark papers on the decipherment of hieroglyphic inscriptions at the Maya city of Palenque.

Waldo Wedel, recently retired as senior archaeologist at the Smithsonian Institution, has had a long and impressive career as a North American archaeologist since receiving his Ph.D. in 1936. Two of his best known books are

Prehistoric Man on the Great Plains (Norman: University of Oklahoma Press, 1961) and *An Introduction to Kansas Archaeology* (Washington, D.C.: Smithsonian Institution, 1959).

Ray A. Williamson earned his B.A. in physics from Johns Hopkins University and his Ph.D. in astronomy from the University of Maryland. He was associated with the University of Hawaii before becoming assistant professor of astronomy at St. Johns College, where he is also assistant dean of faculty. In addition to his astronomical interests in interstellar matter and galactic nebulae, his most recent archaeoastronomical interests include Pueblo astronomy. He is currently being funded by the National Geographic Society to study ancient astronomical systems at Chaco Canyon, New Mexico.

R. Thomas Zuidema received a Ph.D. in anthropology from Leiden University in the Netherlands. He is well known to all students interested in the Inca civilization, having published over fifty articles on Inca political and social organization, both present and past, while working in Peru for twenty-five years. Zuidema is currently professor of anthropology at the University of Illinois, Champaign-Urbana.

References

Acosta, J. de. 1954. *Historia natural y moral de las Indias* (1590). *B.A.E.*, vol. 73. Madrid.

Allis, S. 1918. Letters from Samuel Allis, May 3, 1834, to January 16, 1849, pp. 690–741 in Letters concerning the Presbyterian mission in the Pawnee country, near Bellvue, Nebraska, 1831–1849. *Kansas Historical Collections* 14:1915–1918.

Arriaga, P. J. 1920. *La extirpacion de la idolatria en el Peru* (1621). Lima.

Aveni, A. F. 1972. Astronomical tables intended for use in astroarchaeological studies. *American Antiquity* 37:531–540.

———. 1975. Possible astronomical orientations in ancient Mesoamerica. In *Archaeoastronomy in pre-Columbian America*, edited by A. F. Aveni, pp. 163–190. Austin: University of Texas Press.

———, ed. 1975. *Archaeoastronomy in pre-Columbian America*. Austin: University of Texas Press.

———, and S. L. Gibbs. 1976. On the orientation of ceremonial centers in central Mexico. *American Antiquity* 41:510–517.

———; S. L. Gibbs; and H. Hartung. 1975. The Caracol tower of Chichen Itza—an ancient astronomical observatory? *Science* 188:977–985.

———, and R. M. Linsley. 1972. Mound J, Monte Alban: Possible astronomical orientation. *American Antiquity* 37:528–531.

Avila, F. de. *See* Trimborn, H., and A. Kelm.

Bardawil, L. W. 1976. The principal bird deity in Maya art—an iconographic study of form and meaning. In *Segunda Mesa Redonda de Palenque*, edited by M. G. Robertson, pp. 195–210. Pebble Beach: Robert Louis Stevenson School.

Bernal, I. 1962. *Bibliografia de arqueologia y etnografia: Mesoamerica y norte de Mexico: 1514–1960*. Mexico City: INAH.

Bertonio, L. 1612. *Vocabulario de la lengua Aymara*. Juli, Peru.

Betanzos, J. de. 1880. *Suma y narracion de los Incas . . .* (1551). Madrid.

Blom, F. 1924. Report on the preliminary work at Uaxactun. *Carnegie Institution of Washington Yearbook* 23:217–219. Washington, D.C.

Boller, H. A. 1868. *Among the Indians eight years in the far west: 1858–1866*. Philadelphia.

Bowditch, C. P. 1910. *The numeration, calendar systems and astronomical knowledge of the Mayas*. Cambridge, Mass.: Harvard University Press.

Brandt, J. C.; S. P. Maran; R. A. Williamson; R. S. Harrington; C. Cochran; M. Kennedy; W. J. Kennedy; and V. D. Chamberlain. 1975. Possible rock art records of the Crab Nebula supernova in the western United

States. In *Archaeoastronomy in pre-Columbian America*, edited by A. F. Aveni, pp. 45–58. Austin: University of Texas Press.

Bronowski, J. 1973. *The ascent of man*. New York: BBC/Little Brown and Co.

Brown, L. A. 1963. The Fort Smith Medicine Wheel, Montana. *Plains Anthropologist* 8:225–230.

Brownrigg, L. A. 1973. A model of the Andean system of time dispersed and congregated ritual calendars. Symposium 607, Andean time: Ritual calendars and agricultural cycles. Paper presented at the 72nd meeting of the American Anthropological Association, New Orleans.

Buckstaff, R. N. 1927. Stars and constellations of a Pawnee sky map. *American Anthropologist*, n.s. 29:279–285.

Burkitt, R. 1930–31. The calendar of Soloma and other Indian towns. *Man* 30(80); 31(160).

Cabello Valboa, M. 1951. *Miscelania Antartica* (1586). Lima.

Carlson, J. B. 1975. Did the Olmec possess a magnetic lodestone compass? *Science* 189:753–760.

Carr, R. F., and J. E. Hazard. 1961. Map of the ruins of Tikal, El Peten, Guatemala. *Tikal Reports*, no. 11. Philadelphia: University of Pennsylvania Press.

Caso, A. 1960. *Interpretacion del Codice Bodley 2858*. Mexico City: Soc. Mex. Antr.

———. 1964. *Interpretacion del Codice Selden 3135 (A. 2)*. Mexico City: Soc. Mex. Antr.

———. 1967. *Los calendarios prehispanicos*. Instituto de Investigaciones Historicas. Mexico City: Universidad Nacional Autonoma de Mexico.

Cieza de Leon, P. 1945. *La cronica del Peru* (1551). Buenos Aires: Coll. Austral.

———. 1967. *El senorio de los Incas*. Lima: Inst. Estud. Peruanos.

Closs, M. P. 1976. New information on the European discovery of Yucatan and the correlation of the Maya and Christian calendars. *American Antiquity* 41:192–195.

Cobo, B. 1956. *Historia del Nuevo Mundo* (1633). *B.A.E.*, vols. 91–92. Madrid.

Codex Chimalpopoca. 1945. *See* Velasquez, P.

Codex Telleriano-Remensis. 1830. *See* Kingsborough, E. K.

Coe, M. D. 1973. *The Maya scribe and his world*. New York: Grolier Club.

———. 1975a. Death and the ancient Maya. In *Death and the afterlife in pre-Columbian America*, edited by E. P. Benson. Washington, D.C.: Dumbarton Oaks.

———. 1975b. Native astronomy in Mesoamerica. In *Archaeoastronomy in pre-Columbian America*, edited by A. F. Aveni, pp. 3–31. Austin: University of Texas Press.

Coe, W. R. 1967. *Tikal: A handbook of the ancient Maya ruins*. Philadelphia: University of Pennsylvania Press.

Crosby, H. 1975. *The cave paintings of Baja California*. La Jolla: Copley Books.

Cushing, F. H. 1941. *My adventures in Zuni*. Santa Fe: Peripatetic Press.

Dempsey, H. H. 1956. Stone "medicine wheels"—memorials to Blackfoot war chiefs. *Journal of Washington Academy of Sciences* 46:177–182.

Dibble, C. E., and A. J. O. Anderson. 1950–59. *Sahagun's general history of the things of New Spain: A translation*. Santa Fe: School of American Research.

Digby, A. 1974. Crossed trapezes: A pre-Columbian astronomical instrument. In *Mesoamerican archaeology: New approaches*, edited by N. Hammond, pp. 271–283. Austin: University of Texas Press.

Discurso de la sucesion y gobierno de los Yngas. In Maurtua, *Juicio de limites entre el Peru y Bolivia*, vol. 8. Lima: Chunchos.

Dittrich, A. 1936. Die Korrelation der Maya-chronologie. Reprinted from *Abhandlungen der Preussischen Akademie der Wissenschaften*. Berlin.

Dorsey, G. A. 1904*a*. Traditions of the Skidi Pawnee. *Memoirs, American Folk Lore Society*, no. 18.

———. 1904*b*. Mythology of the Wichita. *Carnegie Institution of Washington*, pub. 21. Washington, D.C.

———. 1906. The Pawnee: Mythology. *Carnegie Institution of Washington*. Washington, D.C.

———. 1907*a*. The Skidi rite of human sacrifice. In *15th session of the International Congress of Americanists* 2:65–70. Quebec.

———. 1907*b*. Social organization of the Skidi Pawnee. In *15th session of the International Congress of Americanists* 2:71–77. Quebec.

Dow, J. 1967. Astronomical orientations at Teotihuacan: A case study in astro-archaeology. *American Antiquity* 32:326–334.

Duffield, L. F. 1965. The Taovayas village of 1759: In Texas or Oklahoma? *Great Plains Journal* 4(2):39–48.

Dunbar, J. 1882. The Pawnee Indians: Their habits and customs. *Magazine of American History* 8:734–756.

———. 1918. Letters from Rev. John Dunbar, September 6, 1831, to May 7, 1849, pp. 570–689 in Letters concerning the Presbyterian mission in the Pawnee country, near Bellvue, Nebraska, 1831–1849. *Kansas Historical Collections* 14:1915–1918.

Dunlevy, M. L. 1936. A comparison of the cultural manifestations of the Burkett (Nance County) and the Gray-Wolfe (Colfax County) sites. *Chapters in Nebraska Archeology*, no. 2, pp. 147–247.

Duran, D. 1971. *Book of the gods and rites and the ancient calendar*. Translated and edited by F. Horcasitas and D. Heyden. Norman: University of Oklahoma Press.

Duviols, P. 1967. Un inedit de Cristobal de Albornoz: La instruccion para descubrir todas las guacas del Peru y sus camayos y haziendas (1582). *Journal de la Societe des Americanistes* 56(1):7–40.

Ebert, J. I., and R. K. Hitchcock. 1973. Spatial inference and the archaeology of complex societies. Paper presented at Mathematics in Social Sciences Board Conference, Santa Fe.

Eddy, J. A. 1974. Astronomical alignment of the Big Horn Medicine Wheel. *Science* 184:1035–1043.

———. N.d. Archaeo-astronomy of North America: Cliffs, mounds, and medicine wheels. To appear in *In search of ancient astronomies*, edited by

E. C. Krupp. New York: Doubleday.

————, and R. G. Forbis. 1975. An examination of medicine wheels in Alberta and the U.S. for possible astronomical use. Paper presented at the 1975 Plains Conference, Lincoln.

Ellis, F. H. 1975. A thousand years of the Pueblo sun-moon-star calendar. In *Archaeoastronomy in pre-Columbian America*, edited by A. F. Aveni, pp. 59–87. Austin: University of Texas Press.

Escobar, G.; R. P. Schaedel; and O. Nunez del Prado. 1967. *Organizacion social y cultural del sur del Peru*. Mexico City: Inst. Indigenista Interamericano.

Espinoza Soriano, W. 1974. El habitat de la etnia Pinagua: Siglos XV y XVI. *Revista de Museo Nacional*, vol. 40. Lima.

Fernandez, O. 1964. *Cronicas del Peru*, vol. 2. Madrid: Atlas.

Fewkes, J. W. 1897. Tusayan Katcinas. *Bureau of American Ethnology Annual Report* 15:267–312. Washington, D.C.

————. 1898. The winter solstice ceremony at Walpi. *American Anthropologist* 11:65–87, 101–115.

————. 1900. Hopi Katcinas. *Bureau of American Ethnology Annual Report*, no. 21. Washington, D.C.

————. 1916. *Excavation and repair of Sun Temple, Mesa Verde National Park*. Washington, D.C.: Office of the Secretary, Department of the Interior.

————. 1917. A prehistoric Mesa Verde pueblo and its people. *Smithsonian Institution Annual Report 1916*, pp. 461–468. Washington, D.C.

————. 1919. Prehistoric villages, castles, and towers of southwestern Colorado. *Bureau of American Ethnology Bulletin*, no. 70. Washington, D.C.

Flannery, K. 1972. The cultural evolution of civilizations. *Annual Review of Ecological Systems* 3:399.

Fletcher, A. C. 1902. Star cult among the Pawnee—a preliminary report. *American Anthropologist*, n.s. 4:730–736.

————. 1903. Pawnee star lore. *Journal of American Folk Lore* 16:10–15.

————. 1904. The Hako: A Pawnee ceremony. *Bureau of American Ethnology Annual Report*, no. 22, part 2, pp. 5–368. Washington, D.C.

————. N.d. Field notes on the Pawnees (MS 4558 [93 & 95]). National Anthropological Archives, Smithsonian Institution, Washington, D.C.

Flores, E., and L. Delaye. 1974. Trazos astronomicos y geometricos en el Caracol de Chichen Itza: Analisis por computadora. Paper presented at 41st International Congress of Americanists, Mexico City.

Forbis, R. G. 1970. A review of Alberta archaeology to 1974. *National Museum of Canada, Publications in Archaeology*, no. 1, pp. 1–49.

————, and J. M. Calder. 1971. Archaeological investigations of the Majorville Cairn, Alberta. Department of Archaeology, University of Calgary.

————, and H. M. Wormington. 1965. An introduction to the archaeology of Alberta, Canada. *Denver Museum of Natural History Proceedings*, no. 11, pp. 1–248. Denver.

Forstemann, E. W. 1906. Commentary on the Maya manuscript in the Royal Public

Library of Dresden. *Papers of the Peabody Museum, Harvard University* 4(2). Cambridge, Mass.

Fuson, R. H. 1969. The orientation of Mayan ceremonial centers. *Annals of the Association of American Geographers* 59:494–511.

Gaitan, M.; A. Morales; H. Harleston; and G. Baker. 1974. La triple cruz astronomica de Teotihuacan. Paper presented at the 41st International Congress of Americanists, Mexico City.

Garcilaso de la Vega (El Inca). 1945. *Comentarios reales* (1609). Edited by A. Rosenblatt. Buenos Aires.

———. 1965. *Royal Commentaries of the Incas and General History of Peru*. Translated by H. V. Livermore. Austin: University of Texas Press.

Gates, W. 1931. A Lanquin Kekchi calendar. *Maya Society Quarterly* 1:29–32.

———. 1932. Pikonchi calendar. *Maya Society Quarterly* 1:78–92.

Gendrop, P. 1974. *A guide to architecture in ancient Mexico*. Mexico City: Minutiae Mexicana.

Gonzalez Holguin, D. 1952. *Vocabulario de la lengua . . . Qquichua* (1608). Lima.

Graham, J. A. 1972. The hieroglyphic inscriptions and monumental art of *altar de sacrificios*. *Papers of the Peabody Museum, Harvard University* 64(2). Cambridge, Mass.

Grange, R. T., Jr. 1968. Pawnee and Lower Loup pottery. *Publications in Anthropology*, no. 3. Lincoln: Nebraska State Historical Society.

Grey, D. 1963. Big Horn Medicine Wheel site, 48BH302. *Plains Anthropologist* 8:27–40.

Grinnell, G. B. 1894. Pawnee star myth. *Journal of American Folk Lore* 7:197–200.

Guaman Poma de Ayala, F. 1936. *El primer nueva cronica y buen gobierno* (between 1584 and 1614). Paris.

Guillemin, G. F. 1968. Tikal: Development and function of the Tikal ceremonial center. *Ethnos* 33:1–35.

Gutierrez de Santa Clara, P. 1964. *Cronicas del Peru*, vol. 3. Madrid: Atlas.

Hartung, H. 1968. Consideraciones urbanisticas sobre los trazos de los centros ceremoniales de Tikal, Copan, Uxmal, y Chichen Itza. In *Acts of 37th International Congress of Americanists* 1:121–125. Buenos Aires.

———. 1971. *Die Zeremonialzentren der Maya*. Graz: Akademische Druck-u. Verlagsanstalt.

———. 1972. Consideraciones sobre los trazos de centros ceremoniales Maya: Influencia de los conocimientos astronomicos en el acomodo de las construcciones. In *Acts of 38th International Congress of Americanists* 4:17–26.

———. 1975. A scheme of probable astronomical projections in Mesoamerican architecture. In *Archaeoastronomy in pre-Columbian America*, edited by A. F. Aveni, pp. 191–204. Austin: University of Texas Press.

———. 1976. El espacio exterior en el centro ceremonial de Palenque. In *Segunda Mesa Redonda de Palenque*, edited by M. G. Robertson, pp. 123–135. Pebble Beach: Robert Louis Stevenson School.

Haviland, W. A. 1968. Ancient lowland Maya social organization. *Middle American*

Research Institution, Tulane University 26:93–117. New Orleans.

Hawkins, G. S. 1968. Astro-archaeology. In *Vistas in Astronomy*, vol. 10, edited by A. Beer, pp. 45–88. New York: Pergamon Press.

Heizer, R. F., and M. A. Baumhoff. 1962. *Prehistoric rock art of Nevada and eastern California.* Berkeley: University of California Press.

———, and C. W. Clewlow, Jr. 1973. *Prehistoric rock art of California.* Ramona: Ballena Press.

Hernandez Principe, R. 1923. *Mitologia andina* (1622). *Revista Inca*, no. 1. Lima.

Herrera, P. 1916. *A punte cronologico de las abroas y trabajos del cabildo a municipalidad de Quito desde 1534 hasta 1714 (primera epoca)*, vol. 1. Quito.

Herrera y Tordesillas, A. de. 1944–47. *Historia general de los Lechos de los Castellanos en las islas i tierra firme del mar oceano* (1601–15). Reproduction of edition of 1726–27. Asuncion, Paraguay.

Heyden, D. 1975. An interpretation of the cave underneath the pyramid of the sun at Teotihuacan, Mexico. *American Antiquity* 40:131–147.

Holguin. *See* Gonzalez Holguin, D.

Husted, W. M. 1963. A rock alignment in the Colorado front range. *Plains Anthropologist* 8:221–224.

Isbell, B. R. 1973. Andean structures and activities: Towards a study of transformations of traditional concepts in a central highland peasant community. Ph.D. Dissertation, University of Illinois.

Jones, H. 1928. Quivira–Rice County, Kansas. *Collections, Kansas State Historical Society 1926–28* 17:535–546.

Joralemon, D. 1974. Ritual blood-sacrifice among the ancient Maya: Part II. Paper presented at the Segunda Mesa Redonda de Palenque, December.

Judd, N. M. 1964. The architecture of Pueblo Bonito. *Smithsonian Miscellaneous Collections* 147(1). Washington, D.C.

Kaplan, H. M. 1974. The mysterious computers of Chaco Canyon. *Empire Magazine, Denver Post*, March 24.

Kehoe, T. F. 1954. Stone "medicine wheels" in southern Alberta and the adjacent portion of Montana. *Journal of Washington Academy of Sciences* 44:133–137.

———. 1974. Stone "medicine wheel" monuments in the northern plains of North America. In *Atti del XL Congresso Internazionale degli Americanisti*, pp. 183–189. Rome.

———, and A. B. Kehoe. 1959. Boulder effigy monuments in the northern plains. *Journal of American Folklore* 72:115–127.

———; A. B. Kehoe; and J. A. Eddy. 1975. Saskatchewan's stone medicine wheels on solstice, 1975. Paper presented at the 1975 Plains Conference, Lincoln.

Kelley, D. H. 1962. Glyphic evidence for a dynastic sequence at Quirigua, Guatemala. *American Antiquity* 27(3):323–335.

———. 1972. The nine lords of the night. *Contributions of the University of California Archaeological Research Facility* 5(16): 53–68. Berkeley: University of California Press.

————. 1976. *Deciphering the Maya Script*. Austin: University of Texas Press.

————, and K. A. Kerr. 1974. Mayan astronomy and astronomical glyphs. In *Meso-american writing systems*, edited by E. P. Benson, pp. 179–215. Washington, D.C.: Dumbarton Oaks.

Kingsborough, E. K. 1830. *Codex Telleriano-Remensis*. Antiquities of Mexico, vol. 2, part 1, pp. 1–149. Mexico City.

Kirkland, F., and W. W. Newcomb. 1967. *The rock art of Texas Indians*. Austin: University of Texas Press.

Koenig, S. 1975. Paper presented at 1975 Conference on Native American Astronomy, Colgate University.

Kosok, P. 1965. *Life, land and water in ancient Peru*. New York: Long Island University Press.

Kubler, G. 1958. The design of space in Maya architecture. In *Miscellanea Paul Rivet*, pp. 515–531. Mexico City.

LaFarge, O., and D. Byers. 1931. The year bearer's people. *Middle American Research Series*, pub. 3. New Orleans.

Las Casas, B. de. 1958. *Apologetica historia* (1564). *B.A.E.*, vols. 105–106. Madrid.

Lincoln, J. S. 1942. The Maya calendar of the Ixil of Guatemala. *Carnegie Institution of Washington*, pub. 528, contr. 38. Washington, D.C.

Linton, R. 1926. The origin of the Skidi Pawnee sacrifice to the morning star. *American Anthropologist*, n.s. 28:457–466.

Lira, J. A. 1944. *Diccionario Kechuwa-Español*. Tucuman.

Lohman Villena, G. 1967. *See* Matienzo, J. de.

Lothrop, S. K. 1930. A modern survival of the ancient Maya calendar. In *Proceedings of the 23rd International Congress of Americanists*, pp. 652–655. New York.

Makemson, M. W. 1943. The astronomical tables of the Maya. *Carnegie Institution of Washington*, pub. 546, contr. 42. Washington, D.C.

Maler, T. 1911. Explorations in the department of Peten, Guatemala: Tikal. *Memoirs of the Peabody Museum, Harvard University* 5(1). Cambridge, Mass.

Malmstrom, V. H. 1973. Origin of the Mesoamerican 260-day calendar. *Science* 181:939–941.

Marcus, J. 1973. Territorial organization of the lowland classic Maya. *Science* 180:911–916.

Marquina, I. 1928. *Estudio arquitectonico comparativo de los monumentos arqueologicos de Mexico*. Mexico City: Sec. Educ. Pub.

Mathews, P., and L. Schele. 1974. Lords of Palenque—the glyphic evidence. In *Primera Mesa Redonda de Palenque*, part 1, pp. 63–76. Pebble Beach: Robert Louis Stevenson School.

Matienzo, J. de. 1967. *Gobierno de Peru* (1567). Edition et etude preliminaire par Guillermo Lohman Villena. Paris-Lima.

Maudslay, A. P. 1889–1902. *Archaeology, Biologia Centrali-Americana; or, contributions to the knowledge of the fauna and flora of Mexico and Central America*. 6 vols. London.

————. 1912. A note on the position and extent of the great temple enclosure of Tenochtitlan. In *Acts of 18th International Congress of Americanists*, pp. 173–175. London.

Mayer, D. 1975. Evidence for the depiction of star-patterns in Great Basin petroglyphs. In *Archaeoastronomy in pre-Columbian America*, edited by A. F. Aveni, pp. 109–130. Austin: University of Texas Press.

————. 1976. A possible astronomical petroglyph panel at Spanish Springs. In *Proceedings of the Symposium on Rock Art*, held by the Rock Art Research Association at El Paso, Texas, August 30–September 1.

Merrill, R. 1945. Maya sun calendar dictum disproved. *American Antiquity* 10:307–311.

Miller, A. G. 1974. West and east in Maya thought: Death and rebirth at Palenque and Tulum. In *Primera Mesa Redonda de Palenque*, part 2, pp. 45–49. Pebble Beach: Robert Louis Stevenson School.

Miller, W. 1955. Two prehistoric drawings of possible astronomical significance. *Astronomical Society of the Pacific Leaflet*, no. 314.

Millon, R. 1968. Urbanization at Teotihuacan: The Teotihuacan mapping project. In *Acts of 37th International Congress of Americanists* 1:105–120. Buenos Aires.

————, ed. 1973. *Urbanization at Teotihuacan*, vol. 1, parts 1 and 2. Austin: University of Texas Press.

Molina, A. 1974. Consideraciones sobre la restauracion arquitectonica en la arqueologia. M.A. Thesis, Escuela Nacional de Antropologia e Historia, Mexico City.

Molina, Cristobal de. 1943. *Relacion de las fabulas y ritos de los Incas* (1573). Lima.

Morissette, J., and L. Racine. 1973. La hierarchie des Wamani: Essai sur la pensee classificatoires Quechua. *Signes et langages des Ameriques: Recherches Amerindiennes au Quebec* 3(1,2):167–188.

Morley, S. G. 1910. The correlation of Maya and Christian chronology. *American Journal of Archaeology* 14:193–204.

————. 1914. An introduction to the study of Maya hieroglyphics. *Bureau of American Ethnology Bulletin*, no. 57. Washington, D.C.

————. 1920. The inscriptions at Copan. *Carnegie Institution of Washington*, pub. 219. Washington, D.C.

————. 1925. The Copan expedition. *Carnegie Institution of Washington Yearbook* 25:277. Washington, D.C.

————. 1937–38. The inscriptions of Peten. *Carnegie Institution of Washington*, pub. 437. 5 vols. Washington, D.C.

Müller, R. 1929. Intiwatana (Sonnenwarten) im alten Peru. *Baessler Arkiv* 13, parts 3–4, pp. 178–187. Berlin.

————. 1972. *Sonne, mond und sterne uber dem reich der Inka*. Berlin, Heidelberg, and New York: Springer Press.

Munich. Staatlichen Museums fur Volkerkunde Munchen. 1968. Ausstellung. Altamerikanische Kunst. Mexico-Peru. *Bearbeitung Text*. O. Zerries.

Murie, J. 1914. Pawnee Indian societies. *Anthropological Papers: American Mu-*

seum of Natural History 11, part 7, pp. 543–644.

Murua, M. de. 1962. *Historia general del Peru* (1613). Madrid.

Neihardt, J. G. 1932. *Black Elk speaks*. New York: Morrow.

Neugebauer, O. 1942. The origin of the Egyptian calendar. *Journal of Near Eastern Studies* 1 (January –October).

Nicholson, H. B. 1971. Religion in pre-hispanic central Mexico. In *Handbook of Middle American Indians*, edited by R. Wauchope, 10:395–446. Austin: University of Texas Press.

Nordenskiold, E. 1925. The secret of the Peruvian quipus: Calculations with years and months in the Peruvian quipus. *Comparative Ethnographical Studies* 6, parts 1 and 2. Goteborg.

Norton, A. P. 1973. *Norton's star atlas*. 16th ed. Cambridge, Mass.: Sky Publishing Corp.

Nunez del Prado, O. 1952. *La vida y la muerte en Chinchero*. Cusco.

Nuttall, Z. 1906. The astronomical methods of the ancient Mexicans. In *Boas Anniversary Volume*, edited by B. Laufer, pp. 290–298. New York: Stechert.

———. 1928. Nouvelles lumieres sur les civilisations americaines et le systeme du calendrier. In *Proceedings of the 22nd International Congress of Americanists*, pp. 119–148. Rome.

———. 1930. The cult of the sun at its zenith in ancient Mexico. *Revista de Turismo*, July.

Oberem, U. 1958. Diego de Ortegons Beschreibung der Gobernacion de los Quijos. Zumaco y la canela. Sin ethnographischer Bericht aus dem Jahre 1577. *Zeitschrift für Ethno*. 83:320–351.

Owen, N. 1975. The use of eclipse data to determine the Maya correlation number. In *Archaeoastronomy in pre-Columbian America*, edited by A. F. Aveni, pp. 237–246. Austin: University of Texas Press.

Pahl, G. W. 1970. History in glyphs at Copan. Unpublished manuscript.

———. 1974. A catalog of Maya hieroglyphics from Copan, Honduras. Unpublished manuscript.

———. 1976. A succession-relationship complex and associated signs. In *Segunda Mesa Redonda de Palenque*, edited by M. G. Robertson, pp. 35–44. Pebble Beach: Robert Louis Stevenson School.

Parsons, E. C. 1936. Taos Pueblo. *General Series in Anthropology*, no. 2. Menasha.

———. 1939a. *Pueblo Indian religion*. 2 vols. Chicago: University of Chicago Press.

———. 1939b. Picuris, New Mexico. *American Anthopologist*, n.s. 41(2): 206–222.

Peterson, F. 1959. *Ancient Mexico*. New York: Capricorn Books.

Pizarro, P. 1944. *Relacion del descubrimiento y conquista de los reinos del Peru* (1571). Buenos Aires: Ed. Futura.

Pogo, A. 1937. *Carnegie Institution of Washington Yearbook* 36:157–158. Washington, D.C.

Polo de Ondegardo, J. 1916. Los errores y supersticiones de los indios (1571).

Edited by Urteaga y Romero. *Col. Libr. Doc. Ref. Hist. Peru* 3:1–43. Lima.

Proskouriakoff, T. 1960. Historical implications of a pattern of dates at Piedras Negras, Guatemala. *American Antiquity* 25(4):454–475.

Ramos Gavilan. 1621. *Historia del celebre santuario de nuestra senora de Copacabana, y sus milagros invencion de la cruz de Carabuco*. Lima.

Rauh, J. H. 1972. Tentative reconstruction of the Peruvian calendar system. Unpublished manuscript.

Recinos, A., and D. Goetz. 1953. *The Annals of the Cakchiquels*. Norman: University of Oklahoma Press.

Reyman, J. E. 1971. *Mexican influence on southwestern ceremonialism*. Ann Arbor: University Microfilms.

———. 1973. Archaeo-astronomical fieldwork. Unpublished manuscript.

———. 1975*a*. The nature and nurture of archaeoastronomical studies. In *Archaeoastronomy in pre-Columbian America*, edited by A. F. Aveni, pp. 205–216. Austin: University of Texas Press.

———. 1975*b*. Sun Temple, Mesa Verde National Park: A re-evaluation. Paper presented at the 1975 Conference on Native American Astronomy, Colgate University.

Ricketson, O. G., Jr. 1928*a*. Astronomical observatories in the Maya area. *Geographical Review* 18:215–225.

———. 1928*b*. Notes on two Maya astronomic observatories. *American Anthropologist*, n.s. 30:434.

———. 1937. Uaxactun, Guatemala: Group E, 1926–1931. *Carnegie Institution of Washington*, pub. 477. Washington, D.C.

Rivard, J. 1970. A hierophany at Chichen Itza. *Katunob* 17(3):51–55.

Roberts, F. H. H. 1932. The Village of the Great Kivas on the Zuni Reservation, New Mexico. *Bureau of American Ethnology Bulletin*, no. 111. Washington, D.C.

Robicsek, F. 1972. *Copan, home of the Maya gods*. New York: Museum of the American Indian, Heyl Foundation.

Rostworowski de Diez Canseco, M. 1962. Nuevos datos sobre tenencia de tierras reales en el Incario. *Revista del Museo Nacional* 31. Lima.

———. 1969–70. Los ayarmaca. *Revista del Museo Nacional* 36:58–101. Lima.

———. 1970*a*. Mercaderes del valle de Chincha en la epoca prehispanica: Un documento y unos comentarios. *Revista Espana de Antropologia Americana* 5:135–178. Madrid.

———. 1970*b*. Etnohistoria de un valle costeno durante el Tahuantinsuyu. *Revista del Museo Nacional* 35. Lima.

Roys, R. L. 1967. *The book of Chilam Balam of Chumayel*. New ed. Norman: University of Oklahoma Press.

Ruppert, K. 1940. A special assemblage of Maya structures. In *The Maya and their neighbors*, pp. 222–231. London: D. Appleton-Century Co.

———, and J. H. Denison. 1943. Archaeological reconnaissance in Campeche, Quintana Roo, and Peten. *Carnegie Institution of Washington*, pub. 543. Washington, D.C.

Sahagun, B. de. 1938. *Historia general de las cosas de la Nueva Espana*. Edited by P. Robredo. 5 vols. Mexico City.

Sanford, A. L. 1974. Astro-geometric inter-structure alinements at Maya sites of Chichen Itza, Uaxactun, and Tikal. Unpublished manuscript.

Santacruz Pachacuti Yamqui, J. de. 1950. *Relacion de antiguedades desde reyno del Piru* (1613). Edited by Jimenez de la Espada. Asuncion, Paraguay.

Sarmiento de Gamboa, P. 1947. *Historia de los Incas* (1572). Buenos Aires: Biblioteca Emece.

Sartor, M. 1974. Algunas hipotesis acerca de la orientacion en el urbanismo pre-colombino. *Centro de Invest. Hist. y Est., Univ. Central* 19:28–42.

Satterthwaite, L. 1964. Long count positions of Maya dates in the Dresden Codex, with notes on lunar positions and the correlation problem. In *Proceedings of the 35th International Congress of Americanists*, part 2, pp. 47–67. Mexico City.

———. 1965. Calendrics of the Maya lowlands. In *Handbook of Middle American Indians*, edited by R. Wauchope, 3:603–631. Austin: University of Texas Press.

Schaafsma, P. 1972. *Rock art in New Mexico*. Santa Fe: State Planning Office.

Schele, L. 1976. The iconography of accession in the Group of the Cross at Palenque. In *Segunda Mesa Redonda de Palenque*, edited by M. G. Robertson, pp. 9–34. Pebble Beach: Robert Louis Stevenson School.

Schmitt, K., and I. O. Schmitt. 1952. *Wichita kinship, past and present*. Norman: University Book Exchange.

Scholes, F. V., and R. L. Roys. 1948. The Maya Chontal Indians of Acalan-Tixchel: A contribution to the history and ethnography of the Yucatan Peninsula. *Carnegie Institution of Washington*, pub. 560. Washington, D.C.

Schulman, A. 1950. Pre-Columbian towers in the Southwest. *American Antiquity* 4:288–297.

Smiley, C. H. 1975. The solar eclipse warning table in the Dresden Codex. In *Archaeoastronomy in pre-Columbian America*, edited by A. F. Aveni, pp. 247–256. Austin: University of Texas Press.

Smith, M. E. 1973. *Picture writing from ancient southern Mexico: Mixtec place signs and maps*. Norman: University of Oklahoma Press.

Spinden, H. J. 1913. A study of Maya art. *Memoirs of the Peabody Museum, Harvard University* 6:164. Cambridge, Mass.

———. 1924. The reduction of Mayan dates. *Papers of the Peabody Museum, Harvard University* 6(4). Cambridge, Mass.

———. 1928. Maya inscriptions dealing with Venus and the moon. *Bulletin of the Buffalo Society of Natural Sciences* 14(1):1–62.

———. 1930. Maya dates and what they reveal. *Brooklyn Institution of Arts and Sciences* 4(1). Brooklyn.

Spores, R. 1967. *The Mixtec kings and their people*. Norman: University of Oklahoma Press.

Stephen, A. M. 1936. In *Hopi Journal*, edited by E. C. Parsons. *Columbia Univer-*

sity Contributions to Anthropology, no. 23.

Stevenson, M. C. 1904. The Zuni Indians. *Bureau of American Ethnology Annual Report* 23:1–634. Washington, D.C.

Stubbs, S. A. 1950. *Bird's-eye view of the Pueblos*. Norman: University of Oklahoma Press.

Swanton, J. R. 1942. Source material on the history and ethnology of the Caddo Indians. *Bureau of American Ethnology Bulletin*, no. 132. Washington, D.C.

Teeple, J. E. 1925. Maya inscriptions: Glyphs C, D, and E of the supplementary series. *American Anthropologist*, n.s. 27:108–115.

———. 1926. Maya inscriptions: The Venus calendar and another correlation. *American Anthropologist*, n.s. 28:402–408.

———. 1930. Maya astronomy. *Carnegie Institution of Washington*, pub. 403, contr. 2. Washington, D.C.

Thom, A. 1967. *Megalithic sites in Britain*. Oxford: Clarendon Press.

———. 1971. *Megalithic lunar observatories*. Oxford: Clarendon Press.

Thompson, D. E., and J. V. Murra. 1966. *Puentes Incaicos en la region de Huanuco Pampa*. Cuadernos de Investigacion, no. 1. Antropologia. Huanuco, Peru: Universidad Emilio Valdizan.

Thompson, J. E. S. 1931*a*. Copan, an ancient Maya metropolis. *The Open Court* 45(907).

———. 1931*b*. On the origin of the 260-day almanac. *Anthropological Series of the Field Museum of Natural History* 7(3):349–353.

———. 1932. A Maya calendar from Alta Vera Paz, Guatemala. *American Anthropologist*, n.s. 34:449–454.

———. 1935. Maya chronology: The correlation question. *Carnegie Institution of Washington*, pub. 456, contr. 14. Washington, D.C.

———. 1950. Maya hieroglyphic writing: An introduction. *Carnegie Institution of Washington*, pub. 589. Washington, D.C.

———. 1960. *Maya hieroglyphic writing*. 2d ed. Norman: University of Oklahoma Press.

———. 1962. *A catalog of Maya hieroglyphs*. Norman: University of Oklahoma Press.

———. 1967. Creation myths (part 2). *Estudios de Cultura Maya*, vol. 5. Mexico City: UNAM.

———. 1970. *Maya history and religion*. Norman: University of Oklahoma Press.

———. 1971. *Maya hieroglyphic writing: An introduction*. 3rd ed. Norman: University of Oklahoma Press.

———. 1972. A commentary on the Dresden Codex: A Maya hieroglyphic book. *Memoirs of the American Philosophical Society* 93. Philadelphia.

———. 1974. Maya astronomy. *Philosophical Transactions of the Royal Society* 276:83–98. London.

Tichy, F. 1974. Deutung von orts- und flurnetzen im hochland von Mexiko als kultreligiose reliktformen altindianischer besiedlung. *Erdkunde* 28(3): 194–207.

Tozzer, A. M. 1911. Preliminary study of the ruins of Tikal, Guatemala. *Memoirs of* the Peabody Museum, Harvard University 5(2). Cambridge, Mass.

———. 1913. A preliminary study of the ruins of Nakum, Guatemala. *Memoirs of the Peabody Museum, Harvard University* 5(3). Cambridge, Mass.

———. 1941. Landa's relacion de las cosas de Yucatan. *Papers of the Peabody Museum, Harvard University*, no. 18. Cambridge, Mass.

Trik, A. 1939. Temple XXII at Copan. *Carnegie Institution of Washington*, pub. 509. Washington, D.C.

Trimborn, H., and A. Kelm. 1967. Francisco de Avila. In *Quellenwerke zur alten geschichte Amerikas*, vol. 8. Berlin.

Vallee, L. 1972. Cycle ecologique et cycle rituel: Le cas d'un village Andin. *Revues Canadienne de Sociologie et d'Anthropologie* 9(3):238–244.

van der Waerden, B. L. 1974. *Science awakening II*. New York: Oxford University Press.

Velasquez, P., trans. 1945. *Codex Chimpalpopoca*. Mexico City: Universidad Nacional Autonoma de Mexico, Instituto de Historia.

Villacorta, J. A., and C. A. Villacorta. 1930. *Codices Mayas: Reproducidos y desarrollados*. Guatemala City.

Vivian, G., and P. Reiter. 1960. The great kivas of Chaco Canyon and their relationships. *School of American Research and the Museum of New Mexico*, monograph 22. Santa Fe.

von Welhof, J. C. 1965. Rock art of Owens Valley, California. *Reports of the University of California Archaeological Survey*, no. 65. Berkeley.

Wassen, H. 1940. El antiguo abaco Peruano segun un manuscrito de Guaman Poma. *Ethnological Studies* 11:1–30.

Wedel, W. R. 1936. An introduction to Pawnee archeology. *Bureau of American Ethnology Bulletin* 112. Washington, D.C.

———. 1938. The direct-historical approach in Pawnee archeology. *Smithsonian Miscellaneous Collections* 97(7). Washington, D.C.

———. 1959. An introduction of Kansas archaeology. *Bureau of American Ethnology Bulletin* 172. Washington, D.C.

———. 1961. *Prehistoric man on the Great Plains*. Norman: University of Oklahoma Press.

———. 1967. The council circles of central Kansas: Were they solstice registers? *American Antiquity* 32:54–63.

———. 1968. After Coronado in Quivira. *Kansas Historical Quarterly* 34:369–385.

Wellmann, K. 1976. An astronomical petroglyph in Capitol Reef National Park, Utah. *Journal of Southwestern Lore* (in press).

Weltfish, G. 1965. *Lost Universe*. New York: Basic Books.

Whetten, N. L. 1961. *Guatemala: The land and the people*. New Haven: Yale University Press.

Williamson, R. A.; H. J. Fisher; A. F. Williamson; and C. Cochran. 1975. The astronomical record in Chaco Canyon, New Mexico. In *Archaeoastronomy in pre-Columbian America*, edited by A. F. Aveni, pp. 33–42. Austin: University of Texas Press.

Willson, R. W. 1924. Astronomical notes on the Maya codices. *Papers of the Peabody Museum, Harvard University* 6(3). Cambridge, Mass.

Wilson, M. 1975. New archaeological studies at the Big Horn Medicine Wheel.
        Paper presented at the 1975 Plains Conference, Lincoln.
Wissler, C. 1936. Star legends among the American Indians. *American Museum
        of Natural History Guide Leaflet Series*, no. 91. New York.
————, and H. J. Spinden. 1916. The Pawnee human sacrifice to the morning star.
        American Museum Journal 16:49–55.
Wittry, W. 1964. An American Woodhenge. *Cranbrook Institution of Science News
        Letter* 33(9):102–107.
Zuidema, R. T. 1964. *The ceque system of Cuzco: The social organization of the
        capital of the Inca*. Leiden: Ed. Brill.
————. 1966. El calendario Inca. In *Actas del XXXVI Congreso Internacional de
        Americanistas* 2:25–30. Seville.
————. 1973*a*. Kinship and ancestor cult in three Peruvian communities: Hernan-
        dez Principe's account in 1622. *Bulletin Institut Français des Etudes
        Andines* 2(1):16–33. Lima.
————. 1973*b*. La parente et le culte des ancetres dans trois communautes peru-
        viennes: Un compte-rendu de 1622 par Hernandez Principe. *Signes
        et Langages des Ameriques: Recherches Amerindiennes au Que-
        bec* 3(1,2):129–145.
————. 1973*c*. La quadrature du cercle dans l'ancien Peru. *Signes et Langages
        des Ameriques: Recherches Amerindiennes au Quebec* 3(1,2):
        147–165.
————. 1976. La imagen del sol y la huaca de Susurpuquio en el sistema astro-
        nomico de los Incas en el Cuzco. *Journal de la Societe des Ameri-
        canistas* (in press).

Index